A Guide to Prayer
for All God's People

A Guide to Prayer
for
All God's People

Rueben P. Job
Norman Shawchuck

UPPER
ROOM BOOKS
NASHVILLE

A Guide to Prayer
  for All God's People

The publisher gratefully acknowledges permission to reproduce the copyrighted material appearing in this book. Credit
lines for this material appear on page 391 and following.

Deluxe Edition First Printing: October 1990
Deluxe Edition Second Printing: August 1991
Library of Congress Catalog Card Number: 89-51767
ISBN 0-8358-0613-8

Printed in the United States of America

*For
all who pray*

Contents

MONTHLY RETREAT MODELS

Including Order of Retreat and Readings for Reflection

Preface

This book was prepared out of our own joy in finding the living God as a faithful, loving companion in our lives. It is sent forth in the hope that it will assist you in your own search for a deeper, more consistent walk with Christ.

Every scripture, prayer, and writing has been used for our own journey. We have pondered the scriptures and writings and have prayed the prayers. We have given ourselves to the daily discipline and monthly retreats. Through it all we have discovered God to be an extravagant giver, a loving parent, whose every desire is to delight us and beckon us toward an ever closer walk with Christ. The labor which has gone into this book is one way we wish to say, "Thank you, God, for life—constantly surprised by joy."

A few years ago we prepared *A Guide to Prayer for Ministers and Other Servants*. We thought the book would be used by persons in professional ministry—and so it was. But to our surprise and delight, the book has been used by persons from every walk of life. Soon we began hearing from people the world around suggesting another guide to prayer, one targeted to all God's people.

Here it is. We send it to you—whoever you are, wherever you are, and whatever your station in life. With it go our prayers that, in some small way, it may invite and entice you into a more consistent and fruitful Christian life. If this book does that for one other person we will be well rewarded.

Several years ago we entered into covenant with three of our friends, now become closer to us than brothers. We live our lives in the constant awareness that we are on the journey together. We come together regularly to search, dream, and pledge anew our commitment to the covenants we have made to give meaning and structure to our spiritual quests.

This book is for you as an individual and for covenant communities. Use it alone; use it with others.

We commend this book to you with the words of John Wesley (founder of the Methodist movement) to one of his lay preachers: "O begin! Fix some part of every day for private exercises. . . . Whether you like it or no, read and pray daily. It is for your life; there is no other way: else you will be a trifler all your days."

Rueben P. Job
Norman Shawchuck

How to Use This Book

This book contains materials for daily prayer and meditation and for monthly private retreats. The daily helps are clustered under weekly themes which basically follow the themes established by the Common Lectionary. We deviated from the ecumenical lectionary themes only when we felt other themes might be more helpful.

We have adopted a form to support your daily prayer and meditation. Those of you familiar with our earlier book, *A Guide to Prayer for Ministers and Other Servants,* will note the daily form has been altered slightly. The alterations are in response to numerous suggestions we have received regarding the earlier prayer form. The form for this book includes:

Invocation. A call to enter into the presence of the Lord in faith that the Lord is waiting to meet with us. We have included ancient and modern prayers, most written by ourselves in the form of a "collect." The collect form contains three parts: oblation, petition, and ascription. An oblation identifies the attribute of God which supports our petition. The collect ends with an ascription of the authority or name in which the prayer is offered. We encourage you to supplement all these prayers with the prayers you find most helpful to you, many of which you may write yourself.

Psalm. The Psalms were written as prayers. God's people have prayed these prayers for thousands of years as they have sought guidance and help in everyday experiences.

We, too, face struggles in the common pursuits of our daily existence. The journey into the wilderness by the children of Israel—there to confront enemies, terrors, hardships, and to discover the guardian care of God—is a true picture of our own journey. In our daily struggles the word of God is one of our greatest resources to find hope and direction.

We list one Psalm for each week, suggesting you live with that Psalm throughout the week. The best use of the Psalms is to pray them out loud.

Reading and Reflection. There is great value in immersing ourselves in another's experiences of God. As we listen to another person's story, we come to see more clearly the movement of God in our own lives. This has always been so. Whenever the Israelites became discouraged or frightened or forgetful, their leaders would get them together to tell them "the story" one more time. They would always find God hidden in the story. In finding God within another's experience they were able to interpret the movement of God within their own. It will be that way for you also.

The readings were selected to provide a variety of approaches to the theme for the week. All readings were chosen to speak to your life situation.

Because we hope that the readings will speak powerfully to all people, we have changed generic male language to more inclusive language wherever possible. In cases where copyright owners did not give us permission to make changes, we ask you to remember that these authors were writing without the benefit of recent discussions and new insights regarding gender restrictive language.

Daily Scripture Readings. The daily scripture readings are intended to support the theme for the week. The three-cycle Sunday scriptures follow the ecumenical Common Lectionary. If you wish to follow the ecumenical lectionary for the Sunday readings, please read the notations at the beginning of each week. We have also provided a list of Sunday dates for several years with appropriate week numbers on page 400.

We selected the weekday passages to be more specifically related to the spirituality and life experience of a person who is seeking a deeper walk in Christ. The Sunday scriptures are targeted more toward the life experience of the entire church.

You may want to read two passages each day—the one listed for that particular day and one selected from the Sunday passages. In addition, you may be led to a different passage which, for you, speaks powerfully to the theme in your own experience. When this happens, we urge you to record that scripture along with our selections in order that you may return to it in succeeding years of using these scriptures.

That which sets scripture apart from all other writing is its universal and its singular appeal. It speaks to persons of every tribe and generation as though it were written for each individual alone. In order to accomplish this it was written in symbolic language. A symbol is a representation of a greater reality. The symbol is not the reality but points to it. In order to grasp the truth of a symbol one must not look "at" it but "through" it to the greater reality which is waiting to be discovered by the one who has eyes to see and ears to hear (Matt. 11:15).

Jesus wanted his teaching to have universal and singular appeal, and for that reason he taught through parables (Mark 4:33-34). To the person who carefully searches each Bible story it will reveal hidden truth suited for that person's situation-in-life. For the person who does not dig deeply, the symbols will remain nontransparent.

To help you to see through the story, we suggest a two-step process for reading the scripture. First, read the passage with an open mind and heart letting words flow into your being. Then respond to the scripture. Be aware of the scripture in relation to your own history, actions, and desires. Enter into dialogue with the scripture with your heart, mind, and emotions. Read it not as a portion of a book written for everyone, but as a letter written just to you—the message of one thinking only of you when writing.

Through the analogies, metaphors, parables, and "plain talk," enter into a personal dialogue with God-as-author. Then, it will help to make the passage uniquely yours if you search for insight into certain questions: (1) What is this passage telling me about God? (2) What is this scripture telling me about myself? (3) What does this scripture have to say to me about my ministry or witness at this time?

It may be that you will want to read only one verse or a few verses and that you will want to stay with those few words for several days. You can do this knowing the Holy Spirit has still more to say to you out of the passage.

The point is to stay with each passage for a day or longer, until it builds for itself a nest in your heart from which it may speak to you all day long.

What we are suggesting is that you prayerfully ponder the passage—that you meditate upon it in such a way that it may flow into and through your life like oil through a sieve long after the last visible drop is gone. This is meditation.

Reflection: Silent and Written. At this point, we invite you to reflect on all the words, thoughts, and emotions you have experienced during the daily office and to record new insights, new commitments, a prayer. At other times, you will write about dullness, your struggle to pray at all, discouragement. For this you will need a prayer journal.

Be entirely honest in your writing. Write for yourself and God alone! Resist every temptation to quote from your journal or to allow anyone else to read any part of it. Your journal is to become a private log of your spiritual journey. The only exception to this may be when you share something in your journal with a spiritual guide.

Your journal is to become a personal record of your journey with God. It will enable you to reflect on the events and impulses of your life, to interpret their meanings, and to discover where God is leading you through those circumstances. Your journal will become a "travel log" and "road map" to help you recall and reflect on where you have been and to identify indicators of where you are going.

In order to do this, we suggest you use your journal daily, although you may find that writing weekly, or at those times when an emotion or insight prompts you to do so, is more suited to your needs. We also urge you to review your journal once a month, preferably at your monthly one-day private retreat. Over time, this will allow you to discern the movements and directions of God's leading in your life.

For your journal we recommend an inexpensive 8½″ × 11″ spiral bound notebook. Generally, write about one-half page a day, although at certain times you may find yourself writing much more. The point is to focus your writing. Do not ramble, be specific.

Prayers. All that increases our awareness of God is prayer; therefore, all that you do in your daily prayer time is prayer. You will pray the Psalm, pray the scripture, pray your personal and intercessory prayers. The hymn will become a time of poetic praying.

However, the daily office also includes a time for you to talk to God in your own way. There are various ways to pray, and each of us, while using several methods, generally will find one method which best fits our personality.

Two conditions are important to nurture a consistent prayer discipline, solitude and silence. Solitude is being by oneself. Silence is the quality of stillness within and around oneself. It will also help your praying to select one place to which you can go daily. You will soon find God is waiting for you in that place.

Our prayers can be strengthened by fasting. In Matthew 6, Jesus clearly taught an inexorable relationship between the two. Indeed, the "closet" in which effective praying is done must often be the "inner room" of fasting.

Fasting, perhaps as much as anything else, helps us to go into our "inner room," the space within ourselves. Fasting helps us shut the door of our inner selves to the outside attractions which crowd in and dissipate our prayer times and energies.

Fasting is the act of temporarily giving up something that is very important to us in order that we may use the time normally given to that thing for prayer and reflect upon the pain of the temporary "sacrifice" to better understand the mystery and meaning of Christ's passion and sacrifice for us.

Our prayers for others can be greatly strengthened by fasting. In our retreats, for example, we often meet persons who struggle with overweight, but who feel helpless against their desire to overeat. We collect their names and in our own periods of fasting (when we are feeling the pain of going without food), we pray for our friends who cannot yet bring themselves to eat less. And we pray for those who are hungry every day, for those who never know the privilege of a fast because they are forced to starve.

Hymn. One hymn related to the stated theme is recommended for each week. When you are unable to formulate your own prayer, you can let the hymn be your prayer. Pray the hymn. The words of the hymn are included as the final entry in the Readings for Reflection for each week.

A Special Word Regarding the Monthly One-Day Retreats. We recommend that you spend one day a month in private retreat. To assist you in this we have included in this book a schedule of themes, a design to follow, and supporting resources.

The retreat models are designed for individual use although they can be utilized by two or more persons. Each retreat is planned for a 24-hour period of time. Maximum benefit may be gained in a setting away from everyday routines. A retreat center, a camp, a motel room, a room in a church, or an unused room in the home can provide the necessary space. Only as a last resort use your office, study, or living room for your retreat.

Adjust the hours to fit your schedule, but try to give the necessary time to each segment of the retreat experience. Remember it is God who meets you and who provides for you. Have confidence that God's provision is adequate for your need. It is natural to wonder, what will I do? Have no fear. Countless numbers of persons have discovered that God is able to provide more than enough to sustain them in such a setting. Do not fear the solitude and silence of retreat. They can be the friends that reveal the presence of God. Many have discovered that the personal retreat setting is a good time to explore a spiritual formation book or resource in a more concentrated manner.

Some find that a day of fasting is an excellent preparation for a day of retreat. You may wish to try fasting during or following your retreat. Be sure to check with your health care specialist before embarking on a long fast for the first time.

Above all, feel at liberty to adjust the retreat to meet your needs. Remember, God is your leader and spiritual director.

Conclusion. In the journey of spirituality and faith, God will sometimes lead us into times when prayer is easy, spontaneous, and exciting; then after a while, we may be led into times when prayer is dull, thoughts become jumbled, words do not come, the heavens seem like barriers. God leads us into these times in order to keep us from spiritual pride—to remind us that even prayer is possible only through God's initiative. Prayer is a grace, a gift from God.

Nonetheless, we are to learn how to pray. What a dilemma! On the one hand, prayer is a gift. It is something we receive, and we are to wait in silent expectation for the gift. On the other hand, we can learn how to pray and we are to give ourselves to the discipline of learning how to pray.

We invite you to undertake this intentional journey for the next twelve months. You will discover God near as you journey. You will also discover that during the next twelve months your life will be transformed.

Weekly Devotional Themes

1: *Waiting and Watching*

I. Invocation

Gracious God, I put myself before you in this moment with waiting heart, expectant desire. Open my eyes that I may see your promise fulfilled; open my ears that I may hear your word whispered to my deepest being. Amen.

II. Psalm 97

III. Reading and Reflection

IV. Daily Scripture Readings

Monday	Luke 1:67-80
Tuesday	Colossians 1:9-23
Wednesday	Mark 1:1-8
Thursday	Isaiah 43:1-13
Friday	Hebrews 10:11-25
Saturday	Zephaniah 3:14-20
Sunday	A. Isaiah 2:1-5; Romans 13:11-14; Psalm 122; Matthew 24:36-44
	B. Isaiah 63:16–64:8; 1 Corinthians 1:3-9; Psalm 80:1-7; Mark 13:32-37
	C. Jeremiah 33:14-16; 1 Thessalonians 3:9–13; Psalm 25:1-10; Luke 21:25-36

V. Reflection: Silent and Written

VI. Prayers: For the Church, for Others, for Myself

VII. Hymn: "To a Maid Engaged to Joseph"

VIII. Benediction

My Lord, may all that I have seen of you and all that I have heard from your word now enflesh itself in me. Send me from this place as the incarnate promise of life to all whose life I will touch this day. Amen.

Readings for Reflection

   ~ Compassion is expressed in gentleness. When I think of the persons I know who model for me the depths of the spiritual life, I am struck by their gentleness. Their eyes communicate the residue of solitary battles with angels, the costs of caring for others, the deaths of ambition and ego, and the peace that comes from having very little left to lose in this life. They are gentle because they have honestly faced the struggles given to them and have learned the hard way that personal survival is not the point. Their caring is gentle because their self-aggrandizement is no longer at stake. There is nothing in it for them. Their vulnerability has been stretched to clear-eyed sensitivity to others and truly selfless love.

—From *Healing of Purpose* by John E. Biersdorf

   ~ The listening which can go on all day amid a variety of occupations is concentrated when we give up time to be alone with God in prayer. Prayer is an exposure to the reality of God. For those who pray regularly the time may come fairly soon when particular thoughts or words no longer seem to help. Prayer seems to have gone dead. The relationship is moving into a new phase, and you have to learn to change gear. At other times you may be able to find as much inspiration as ever in the Scriptures, in thinking about God and in the experiences that generally mediate his word to you, but when you try any of this in the time of prayer, you have the impression that this and real prayer are mutually exclusive. To be spending the time on that is somehow to dodge the issue. This can be a distressing and disconcerting experience, but it may be another "creative disintegration" and the way through to contemplative prayer.

     Provided that you are refusing God nothing, you can probably trust the inclination to let it ride a bit. Wait in silence, attentiveness, stillness, just aware of

God in some dim way and of your need of [God], but without particular efforts to formulate ideas or words, except perhaps just to bring yourself gently back when you stray. It is baffling and disconcerting, but in some way all-important to you to stay there like that in darkness and quiet.

—From *The Coming of God* by Maria Boulding

❧ O high and glorious God,
enlighten my heart.
Give me unwavering faith,
sure hope,
and perfect love.
Give me deep humility,
wisdom, and knowledge,
that I may keep your commandments. Amen.

—From *I, Francis* by Carlo Carretto

❧ At one point we were talking about the connection between contemplation and action, and I asked Metropolitan Bloom to define contemplation. He responded.

> Well I think this is where contemplation begins. Sit and listen—in religious terms it may be called waiting on God—but it's simply plain listening or looking in order to hear and to understand. If we did that with regard to the Word of God, with regard to the prayers of the saints, with regard to the situations in which we are, to everything people say to us or what they are in life, with regard to our own selves—we would be in that condition which one can call contemplation, which consists in pondering, thinking deeply, in waiting until one has understood in order to act. Then action would be much more efficient, less hasty, and filled, probably, with some amount of the Divine Wisdom.

That is a clear definition, but he made it even clearer by [this image]. . . . a nursery rhyme he learned in the United States.

A wise old owl
lived in an oak;
The more he saw
the less he spoke.
The less he spoke,
the more he heard.
Why can't we all be
like that bird?

—From *Alive in Christ* by Maxie Dunnam

ৡ When the door of the steambath is continually left open, the heat inside rapidly escapes through it; likewise the soul, in its desire to say many things, dissipates its remembrance of God through the door of speech, even though everything it says may be good. Thereafter the intellect, though lacking appropriate ideas, pours out a welter of confused thoughts to anyone it meets, as it no longer has the Holy Spirit to keep its understanding free from fantasy. Ideas of value always shun verbosity, being foreign to confusion and fantasy. Timely silence, then, is precious, for it is nothing less than the mother of the wisest thoughts.

—Diadachos of Photiki

ৡ Silence is the way to make solitude a reality. The Desert Fathers praise silence as the safest way to God. "I have often repented of having spoken," Arsenius said, "but never of having remained silent." One day Archbishop Theophilus came to the desert to visit Abba Pambo. But Abba Pambo did not speak to him. When the brethren finally said to Pambo, "Father, say something to the archbishop, so that he may be edified," he replied: "If he is not edified by my silence, he will not be edified by my speech."

—From *The Way of the Heart* by Henri J.M. Nouwen

ৡ Solitude in prayer is not privacy. The differences between privacy and solitude are profound. Privacy is our attempt to insulate the self from interference; solitude leaves the company of others for a time in order to listen to them more deeply, be aware of them, serve them. Privacy is getting away from others so that I don't have to be bothered with them; solitude is getting away from the crowd so that I can be instructed by the still, small voice of God, who is enthroned on the praises of the multitudes. Private prayers are selfish and thin; prayer in solitude enrolls in a multivoiced, century-layered community: with angels and archangels in all the company of heaven we sing, "Holy, Holy, Holy, Lord God Almighty."

We can no more have a private prayer than we can have a private language. A private language is impossible. Every word spoken carries with it a long history of development in complex communities of experience. All speech is relational, making a community of speakers and listeners. So too is prayer. Prayer is language used in the vast contextual awareness that God speaks and listens. We are involved, whether we will it or not, in a community of the Word—spoken or read, understood and obeyed (or misunderstood and disobeyed). We can do this in solitude, but we cannot do it in private. It involves an Other and others.

The self is only *it*self, healthy and whole, when it is in relationship, and that relationship is always dual, with God and with other human beings. Relationship implies mutuality, give and take, listening and responding.
—From *Earth and Altar* by Eugene H. Peterson

&. The gift of holiness—which, as has been suggested earlier, is in reality the gift of our full humanity—is received when we are able to see the world in a new way, when in faith we are able to discern and respond to God's vision of the world through the eyes of Christ. This kind of seeing is the fruit of a contemplative vision—a vision that can only be nourished in solitude and in prayer. Prayer for the Christian therefore is not something added to our lives, something extra we do, but rather it is as fundamental to our lives as the act of breathing. It is through prayer that we are caught up in the rhythm and the energy of the Kingdom that is amongst us and learn to see in a new way.

—From *Invitation to Holiness* by James C. Fenhagen

&❧ The holiness and utter transcendence of God over all of creation has always been an absolutely central affirmation of the Judeo-Christian tradition. God as God— source, redeemer, and goal of all—is illimitable mystery who, while immanently present, cannot be measured or controlled. The doctrine of divine incomprehensibility is a corollary of this divine transcendence. In essence, God's unlikeness to the corporal and spiritual finite world is total; hence we simply cannot understand God. No human concept, word, or image, all of which originate in experience of created reality, can circumscribe the divine reality, nor can any human construct express with any measure of adequacy the mystery of God, who is ineffable. This situation is due not to some reluctance on the part of God to self-reveal in a full way, nor to the sinful condition of the human race making reception of such a revelation impossible, nor even to our contemporary mentality of skepticism in religious matters. Rather, it is proper to God as God to transcend all direct similarity to creatures, and thus never to be known comprehensively or essentially as God.

—From Elizabeth A. Johnson in *Women's Spirituality* edited by Joann Wolski Conn

Hymn: To a Maid Engaged to Joseph

To a maid engaged to Joseph,
The angel Gabriel came.
"Fear not," the angel told her,
"I come to bring good news,
Good news I come to tell you,
Good news, I say, good news.

"For you are highly favored
By God the Lord of all,

Who even now is with you.
You are on earth most blest,
You are most blest, most blessed,
God chose you, you are blest!"

But Mary was most troubled
To hear the angel's word.
What was the angel saying?
It troubled her to hear,
To hear the angel's message,
It troubled her to hear.

"Fear not, for God is with you,
And you shall bear a child.
His name shall be called Jesus,
God's offspring from on high.
And he shall reign forever,
Forever reign on high."

"How shall this be?" said Mary,
"I am not yet a wife."
The angel answered quickly,
"The power of the Most High
Will come upon you shortly,
Your child will be God's child."

As Mary heard the angel,
She wondered at his words.
"Behold, I am your handmaid,"
She said unto her God.
"So be it; I am ready
According to your Word."
—Gracia Grindal

Second Sunday in Advent
2: Getting Ready

I. Invocation
Gracious God, who sent your own Son to prepare the way for our salvation, give us the grace
to heed his word and accept his forgiveness of
our many sins. In the name of Jesus Christ who
lives with you and with us, now and forever.
Amen.

II. Psalm 62

III. Reading and Reflection

IV. Daily Scripture Readings
Monday   Luke 1:5-25
Tuesday   Luke 1:57-80
Wednesday   Matthew 3:1-12
Thursday   Isaiah 62:1-12
Friday   Luke 12:35-48
Saturday   Isaiah 51:1-8
Sunday   A. Isaiah 11:1-10; Romans 15:4-13;
               Psalm 72:1-8; Matthew 3:1-12
            B. Isaiah 40:1-11; 2 Peter 3:8-15a;
               Psalm 85:8-13; Mark 1:1-8
            C. Malachi 3:1-4; Philippians 1:3-
               11; Psalm 126; Luke 3:1-6

V. Reflection: Silent and Written

VI. Prayers: For the Church, for Others, for Myself

VII. Hymn: "My Soul Gives Glory to My God"

VIII. Benediction
And now, my God, send me to prepare the way
for others, that they, too, may gladly accept the
coming of Jesus Christ into their life situations.
Amen.

Readings for Reflection

&. "The only strength for me is to be found in the sense of a personal presence everywhere. It scarcely matters whether it be called human or divine; a presence which only makes itself felt at first in this or that particular form and picture. . . . Into this presence we come, not by leaving behind what are usually called earthly things; or by loving them less, but by living more intensely in them, and loving more what is really lovable in them; for it is literally true that this world is everything to us, if only we choose to make it so, if only we 'live in the present' because it is eternity." Thus wrote Henry Nettleship toward the end of the nineteenth century.

In a very real sense we are earthbound creatures, caught always in the rigid context by which our experiences are defined. The particular fact or experience which we are facing at the moment, or the memory of other particular facts or experiences from other moments—these are our openings, these are the doors through which we enter into wider meanings, into wider contexts. When our little world of particular experiences seems to be illumined by more, much more, than itself, and we seem to be caught up into something bigger than our little lives, we give to such moments special names. They become watershed times. We mark the times in special ways, with special symbols. If it is the love of man and woman, it is the ring, the ceremonial, or the deep stillness of intimate disclosure; if it is the peak of joy, the emptying of the soul in suffering, or the fragmented activities of the daily round, there is the sense of Altar, the searching phrase from the holy book, or the gathered tear and the quickening pulse. At such times, and myriad others perhaps, we know that we live our way deeply in the present, only to discover that we are invaded by the Eternal.

> Sensitize our spirits, our Father, that we may tread reverently in the common way, mindful that the glory of the Eternal is our companion. May we

shrink not from the present intensity of our experiences lest we turn away from the redeeming power of Thy Perfect Love. Amen.

—From *The Inward Journey* by Howard Thurman

❧ I keep wishing that Jesus had kept notebooks during his 40 days in the wilderness and afterward—then maybe we would have more to go on as to what he thought or meant. We tend to think he saw things through our eyes and minds, and it is hard to try to see things through his eyes and mind. He said, "All I have done you shall do and more," and I am beginning to wonder if maybe we are supposed to start with 40 days in the wilderness, as he did, and go on from there, in our own way, thinking things through. I am trying to do my "40 days" now in my own way, and it may take me 40 years! It is certainly taking me a lot longer to think things through than it took Jesus, but then, it might have taken him longer if he had done it in the 20th century, for there are so many more things to think through now than there were in the first century—2000 years worth of more stuff, near-abouts.

—From *The Gospel According to Abbie Jane Wells* by Abbie Jane Wells

❧ Paul as well as Clinton Marsh and just about everybody else tends to forget that it took a "yes" from Mary before God could "sent forth his Son"—and if there is any truth to that "when the time had fully come," it is that *Mary's* time had come when she went into labor at the end of her pregnancy: *that's* when the time had fully come—*that* is when Jesus's time to be born had fully come!

As for "Had Jesus come to a different people in a different place at a different time . . ." I don't think you can juggle his place in history—or Mary's—that way; and since Jesus *was* born of Mary, you'd have to get her as well as Jesus into "a different people in a different place at a different time"—which isn't humanly, or Godly, possible.

Of course, it is possible for God to have a Son of a woman "in a different people in a different place at a different time"—but *that* son wouldn't be Jesus, for Jesus was Mary's son as well as God's—which lottsa people tend to forget at times.

For all I know—for all anybody knows—God may have "proposed" (or propositioned?) . . . through the ages but, *as far as we know,* Mary was the first one to say an unqualified "yes." . . .

"When the time had fully come," . . . and the "Time had fully come" only because the woman Mary said "yes."

—From *The Gospel According to Abbie Jane Wells* by Abbie Jane Wells

ᔢ The call to ministry is a basic idea in the life of the church. The Greek word from the New Testament is *diakonia*. Its meaning is service. To be a member of the community of those who follow Jesus is to be part of a community committed to service. Jesus called disciples to lives of obedience and service; and he commissioned them to gather others who would commit themselves to his idea and vision. Jesus proposed an inversion of the usual way in which women and men think about greatness and service. Greatness in the eyes of the world involves power, rights and privileges. According to Jesus, greatness has to do with the relinquishing of such human values and the commitment to service and sacrifice. Trying to explain this to his disciples, Jesus said, "You know that those who are supposed to rule over the Gentiles lord it over them, and their great men exercise authority over them. But it shall not be so among you; but whoever would be great among you must be your servant, and whoever would be first among you must be slave of all. For the Son of man also came not to be served but to serve, and to give his life as a ransom for many" (Mark 10:42-45). Jesus himself is thus the great exemplar of service. He gave his life that others might live. As the body of Jesus Christ in the world, the entirety of the church exists for service.

Entry into the church is therefore entry into ministry. Baptism, the sacrament by which persons are initiated into the Christian community, may be thought of as an admission to the general ministry of the church. The vows of Baptism, reaffirmed in Confirmation or other services of baptismal renewal, commit the Christian to a life of love and service in the world as a member of the body of Christ.

—From *The Yoke of Obedience* by Dennis M. Campbell

❧ At the heart of all fidelity, says Gabriel Marcel, lies the ability to be faithful to oneself. "To thine own self be true": this has often been said, but does it mean more than the preservation of an inner integrity, the refusal to abandon convictions one has made one's own? Yes, says Marcel, because to be faithful to myself means to remain alive, which is not nearly as easy as it sounds. It means above all "not to be hypnotized by what I have achieved but on the contrary to get clear of it", that is, to go on living and find renewal.

—From *The Original Vision* by Edward Robinson

❧ Lord, the calendar calls for Christmas. We have traveled this way before. During this Advent season we would see what we have never seen before, accept what we have refused to think, and hear what we need to understand. Be with us in our goings that we may meet you in your coming. Astonish us until we sing "Glory!" and then enable us to live it out with love and peace. In the name of your Incarnate Word, even Jesus Christ. *Amen.*

—From *The Unsettling Season* by Donald J. Shelby

Hymn: My Soul Gives Glory to My God

My soul gives glory to my God.
My heart pours out its praise.
God lifted up my lowliness
In many marvelous ways.

My God has done great things for me:
Yes, holy is this name.
All people will declare me blessed,
And blessings they shall claim.

From age to age, to all who fear,
Such mercy love imparts,
Dispensing justice far and near,
Dismissing selfish hearts.

Love casts the mighty from their thrones,
Promotes the insecure,
Leaves hungry spirits satisfied,
The rich seem suddenly poor.

Praise God, whose loving covenant
Supports those in distress,
Remembering past promises
With present faithfulness.
—Miriam Therese Winter

3: *Good News*

I. Invocation
Thank you, my God, for the Good News which awaits my coming to you today, and always. Thank you for the grace and mercy which promise to set me free of all the sins and disappointments of life which yet hinder me on my journey toward your kingdom. Amen.

II. Psalm 80

III. Reading and Reflection

IV. Daily Scripture Readings
Monday	Mark 13:1-13
Tuesday	Luke 21:25-36
Wednesday	Revelation 1:1-8
Thursday	John 1:14-18
Friday	Ezekiel 34:11-16
Saturday	Acts 1:1-11
Sunday	A. Isaiah 35:1-10; James 5:7-10; Psalm 146:5-10; Matthew 11:2-11
	B. Isaiah 61:1-4, 8-11; Luke 1:46b-55; 1 Thessalonians 5:16-24; John 1:6-8, 19-28
	C. Zephaniah 3:14-20; Isaiah 12:2-6; Philippians 4:4-9; Luke 3:7-18

V. Reflection: Silent and Written

VI. Prayers: For the Church, for Others, for Myself

VII. Hymn: "Blessed Be the God of Israel"

VIII. Benediction
And now, my Lord, send me from this quiet place to be a living oracle of Good News for all persons I will meet who are yet lost in darkness and who cry in despair. Amen.

Readings for Reflection

❧ The heart of the prayer of discernment is intercession. For prayer is ultimately living out the realization that we are meant to be the community of co-creators with God, bringing the creation to the fulfillment of its promise. To act without the prayerful discernment of God's action would be foolish. To pray and then not to act in co-creation would be empty. Intercession is God's desiring through our desiring the specific healing and redemptive work to which we are called. In discernment we listen for the concrete acts of mission that are given to us. In intercession our passion, our desire is linked to God's desire for that healing and redemption. Sometimes we do not understand why we are prompted to pray for a specific person and cause. Sometimes we do not understand why we are *not* called to pray in a specific situation. Often there is no visible effect of our prayer; sometimes there is a dramatic one. It makes no difference—intercession is the way we live our vocation to manifest God's love, living our faith.

—From *Healing of Purpose* by John E. Biersdorf

❧ We were all pulled in two opposite directions— especially I, who bore the common responsibility.

We were drawn to silence, solitude, and prolonged prayer, of course.

We loved solitary places—abandoned churches, like Saint Damian, Saint Peter, Saint Mary of the Angels.

We would never have abandoned our hermitages so full of silence and peace, where just being with God became almost palpable.

We prayed a great deal.

But then too we were drawn to the proclamation of the Word to the poor, the missionary endeavor, the invitation of the Gospel to call human beings to penance and conversion.

What were we to do?

How were we to choose?

We held a great many discussions.

Then something happened.

I remember it as if it were yesterday. It was the twenty-fourth of February, 1208, the Feast of Saint Matthias.

As I was listening to the Gospel at Mass that day I was struck by the words Jesus addressed to the apostles as he sent them into the world.

—From *I, Francis* by Carlo Carretto

&ambar; Our Father, give us the faith to believe that it is possible for us to live victoriously even in the midst of dangerous opportunity that we call crisis.

Help us see that there is something better than patient endurance or keeping a stiff upper lip, and that whistling in the dark is not really bravery.

Bless us with the greatness of humility, that we may feel no shame in expressing our need of a living God. Forgive the pride that causes us to strut about like knights in shining armour when we know full well that we are but beggars in tattered rags.

Plant a seed of faith in us today and nurture it that it may grow. Then, trusting in thee may we have the faith that goes singing in the rain, knowing that all things work together for good to them that love Thee. Through Jesus Christ, our Lord. Amen.

—From *Letters from the Desert* by Carlo Carretto

&ambar; My mother reminds me in many ways of the woman the mother of Jesus must have been. Mary could not have been a "holy" person who makes other people uncomfortable and speechless. I am beginning to think of Mary as she advanced in age to what her cousin Elizabeth was when she carried John. Imagine Mary with wrinkles, but still with the smoldering fire of the Holy Spirit deep within her. She must have been the light and joy of the entire neighborhood, drawing so many to herself to experience a hint and hope of what lay ahead for them.

Mary must have lived each day so full of grace, joy, peace and contentment that nothing more could be added, poured into this moment, this day.

We might offer this litany to Mary our mother:

Woman
Mom
Mary of rattling tea cups and homemade cookies
Mary of open door, open hearth, open heart
Queen of warmth and hospitality
Mary of varicose veins and chapped hands
Strong, fragile woman
Vulnerable, unshakable woman
Believer in love, reality, people, God
Back stooped and ear bent in listening to life's
    stories and to the giver of life
Stubborn fidelity to life in the face of death
Unflinching spirit that stares light into the dark-
    ness of the tomb
Heart that breaks and pours love over the thirsty
    earth
Missing her son when he is gone to another home
Looking up in the sudden expectancy of hearing
    his voice
Smiling wryly to herself and waiting
Waiting, gestating the kingdom once more
Growing in expectancy of second birth—this time
    her own
The moment of reunion rushes to meet her with
    open arms
And their laughter rocks the universe
Sending happy shock waves to echo in our dreams
Tugging our reluctant mouths into smiles of hope
    and anticipation.
Amen, it will be so, Amen.
—From *Gathering the Fragments* by Edward J. Farrell

❦ At the heart of *Christian faith* lies the deep conviction that we can know and love God because God first loved and knew us. The one truly existent God, we believe, has been so poured out, so made known to us in Christ and the Spirit, that we can respond with mutal personal knowledge, and in the intimacy and awe of love.

In terms of the universe, we see Jesus Christ as the personal and eternal Word of God, as creator and redeemer. In terms of his earthly life, we see the cross and the resurrection as the sacrificial climax and achievement, and as the axis of every Christian's understanding of history, from death to life. In terms of application, we see justification by faith and forgiveness as the pattern of God's grace coming as a gift to the undeserving.
—From *The Lord of the Journey* edited by Roger Pooley and Philip Seddon

❧ When I am grasped by the image of the kingdom of God, I know that genuine interdependence and community within the human family is possible. What we experience now is but a taste of what will be. It is through the image of the kingdom that I experience what it means to say that "Christ is Lord." The destructiveness of human sin—the greed and the injustice and the arrogance—that so plagues the human community is not the last word. Christ is risen and the kingdom of God is here.
—From *Mutual Ministry* by James C. Fenhagen

❧ What I am suggesting here is that everything in your life is a stepping-stone to holiness if only you recognize that you do have within you the grace to be present to each moment. Your presence is an energy that you can choose to give or not give. Every experience, every thought, every word, every person in your life is a part of a larger picture of your growth. That's why I call them crumbs. They are not the whole loaf, but they can be nourishing if you give them your real presence. Let everything energize you. Let everything bless you. Even your limping can bless you.
—From *A Tree Full of Angels* by Macrina Wiederkehr

❧ When the perfect and ultimate message, the joy which is *The Great Joy,* explodes silently upon the world, there is no longer any room for sadness. Therefore no circumstance in the Christmas Gospel, however trivial it may seem, is to be left out of The Great Joy. In the special and heavenly light which shines around the coming of the Word into the world, all ordinary things are transfigured. In the mystery of Peace which is proclaimed to a world that cannot live in peace, a world of suspicion, hatred and distrust, even the rejection of the Prince of Peace takes on something of the color and atmosphere of peace.

—From *Raids on the Unspeakable* by Thomas Merton

Hymn: Blessed Be the God of Israel

Blessed be the God of Israel,
Who comes to set us free,
Who visits and redeems us
And grants us liberty.
The prophets spoke of mercy,
Of freedom and release;
God shall fulfill the promise
To bring our people peace.

Now from the house of David
A child of grace is given;
A Savior comes among us
To raise us up to heaven.
Before him goes the herald,
Forerunner in the way,
The prophet of salvation,
The harbinger of day.

On prisoners of darkness
The sun begins to rise,
The dawning of forgiveness
Upon the sinner's eyes,
To guide the feet of pilgrims
Along the paths of peace;
O bless our God and Savior,
With songs that never cease!
—Michael Perry

Fourth Sunday in Advent
4: *When God Comes*

I. Invocation
My God, what joy it is when you come to us in daily visitation; what peace is ours when by your coming we find life anew. Come, O come to live with us and reign within, now and forever. Amen.

II. Psalm 65

III. Reading and Reflection

IV. Daily Scripture Readings
Monday   James 5:7-18
Tuesday   Matthew 1:18-25
Wednesday   Isaiah 40:1-11
Thursday   Ezekiel 34:17-31
Friday   Isaiah 9:1-7
Saturday   Philippians 4:4-9
Sunday   A. Isaiah 7:10-16; Romans 1:1-7; Psalm 24; Matthew 1:18-25
         B. 2 Samuel 7:8-16; Romans 16:25-27; Psalm 89:1-4, 19-24; Luke 1:26-38
         C. Micah 5:2-5a, (5:1-4a); Hebrews 10:5-10; Psalm 80:1-7; Luke 1:39-55

V. Reflection: Silent and Written

VI. Prayers: For the Church, for Others, for Myself

VII. Hymn: "Tell Out, My Soul"

VIII. Benediction
My Lord, let me go to my appointed place—there to live and work in the unity of your Holy Spirit, now and forever. Amen.

Readings for Reflection

❧ If you want God, and long for union with him, yet sometimes wonder what that means or whether it can mean anything at all, you are already walking with the God who comes. If you are at times so weary and involved with the struggle of living that you have no strength even to want [God], yet are still dissatisfied that you don't, you are already keeping Advent in your life. If you have ever had an obscure intuition that the truth of things is somehow better, greater, more wonderful than you deserve or desire, that the touch of God in your life stills you by its gentleness, that there is a mercy beyond anything you could ever suspect, you are already drawn into the central mystery of salvation.
—From *The Coming of God* by Maria Boulding

❧ Late have I loved thee, beauty so ancient and so new!
Late have I loved thee!
Thou wast within me, and I stood without.
I sought thee here, hurling my ugly self on the
    beauty of thy creatures.
Thou wast with me, but I was not with thee.
Thou hast called me, thy cry has vanquished my
    deafness.
Thou hast shone, and thy light has vanquished my
    blindness.
Thou hast broadcast thy perfume, and I have breathed
    it: now I sigh for thee.
I have tasted thee, and now I hunger for thee.
Thou hast touched me, and now I burn with desire
    for thy peace.
—St. Augustine

❧ Once a priest friend said something about John the Baptist's first recognition of Jesus—how he knew who Jesus was the minute he saw him in the desert, like he had had a vision or was told by God—and I said, "Of course he knew who Jesus was! He had always known.

His mom, Elizabeth, had told him how he leapt in her womb when she saw Mary." In fact, he had probably heard that story many, many times—we all have a habit of talking forever after about our unusual and breathtaking experiences. Perhaps the first thing Elizabeth told her son John as soon as he was able to understand, and maybe even before that, was about the son of Mary and what had happened the moment she saw Mary.

—From *The Gospel According to Abbie Jane Wells* by Abbie Jane Wells

❧ The hearer par excellence is the virgin, who becomes pregnant with the Word and bears it as her Son and the Father's. As for herself, even as Mother she remains a handmaid; the Father alone is Lord, together with the Son who is her life and who fashions it. She is the product of him who is the fruit of her womb. She still carries him within herself, even after she has given birth to him; to find him, all she has to do is to look into her heart, which is full of him.

—From *Prayer* by Hans Urs von Balthasar

❧ The world is the place where we meet God because it is the place where God meets us in the person of Jesus Christ. Christ did not merely inhabit human flesh; he became flesh. He made himself, as God, to be one with humanity in the concrete, historical realities of human life. Truly, God has entered into the world and it is in the world that Christians must turn to find God.

—From *Merton's Palace of Nowhere* by James Finley

❧ Christ has identified himself with the human family, especially the poor and the forgotten. In loving them we love him in them. And they, in turn, encounter him in us in the love we give them. And in this the bonds of charity are formed, building up one Christ unto the eternal glory of the Father.

—From *Merton's Palace of Nowhere* by James Finley

⁊ Prayer is a daring venture into speech that juxtaposes our words with the sharply alive words that pierce and divide souls and spirit, joints and marrow, pitilessly exposing every thought and intention of the heart (Heb. 4:12-13; Rev. 1:16). If we had kept our mouths shut we would not have involved ourselves in such a relentlessly fearsome exposure. If we had been content to speak to the women and men and children in the neighborhood we could have gotten by with using words in ways that would have them thinking well of us while concealing what we preferred to keep to ourselves. But when we venture into prayer every word may, at any moment, come to mean just what it *means* and involve us with a holy God who wills our holiness. All we had counted on was some religious small talk, a little numinous gossip, and we are suddenly involved, without intending it and without having calculated the consequences, in something *eternal*.

—From *Working the Angles* by Eugene H. Peterson

⁊ Where there is love, there is pain. But whatever our walk in life, this kind of pain is God's way of teaching us how to pray. Everything that happens to us spiritually, everything that causes us to grow, will bring us closer to God if we say yes. This is what spiritual growth means. It doesn't come from what we do, necessarily, from all our actions and good works. Sometimes it comes from simply sitting and seeing the shambles of what we tried to accomplish, from watching what was seemingly God's work go to pot. You can't do anything about it, but watch. This happened to me. I knew dimly then what I see more clearly today, that this was the moment when God really picked me up and said, "Now I am offering you the union you seek. The other side of my cross is empty. Come, be nailed upon it. This is our marriage bed."

All we can answer in response to that invitation is, "Help me, God! I don't have the courage to climb on this cross."

—From *Soul of My Soul* by Catherine de Hueck Doherty

❧ Now with the special gift of imagination, picture yourself approaching the crowd around Jesus. You long to get through to him about someone you love. Now see the crowd part and the open corridor directly to the Lord made for you. He is there for you. Now stand before him face to face, heart to heart. He is waiting for you to ask for what he is ready to give. Tell him about a person or persons on your heart. Then wait for his answer. At this very moment you prayed, says Jesus, my power has been released in the person for whom you interceded. My will shall be done, in my timing, according to my plan, and for the now and forever blessing of your loved one. You and I are of one heart now. We both love and care. Now go your way in faithfulness.

—From *Radiance of the Inner Splendor* by Lloyd John
  Ogilvie

Hymn: Tell Out, My Soul

Tell out, my soul, the greatness of the Lord!
Unnumbered blessings give my spirit voice;
Tender to me the promise of God's word;
In God my Savior shall my heart rejoice.

Tell out, my soul, the greatness of God's name!
Make known God's might, who wondrous deeds has
    done;
God's mercy sure, from age to age the same;
God's holy name, the Lord, the mighty One.

Tell out, my soul, the greatness of God's might!
Powers and dominions lay their glory by;
Proud hearts and stubborn wills are put to flight,
The hungry fed, the humble lifted high.

Tell out, my soul, the glories of God's word!
Firm is the promise and God's mercy sure.
Tell out, my soul, the greatness of the Lord
To children's children and forevermore!
—Timothy Dudley-Smith

Christmas Day or First Sunday after Christmas
5: God's Greatest Gift

I. Invocation
Ever-loving God, who came into the world clothed in our garment of flesh and who willingly gave yourself to the cross, clothe us in your own Spirit, that persons will recognize you in us and receive your great gift of love. In the name of Jesus, your greatest gift. Amen.

II. Psalm 96

III. Reading and Reflection

IV. Daily Scripture Readings
Monday	Exodus 20:18-26
Tuesday	Galatians 3:23–4:7
Wednesday	2 Corinthians 5:16-21
Thursday	John 3:1-8
Friday	Ephesians 1:3-14
Saturday	Colossians 1:15-23
Sunday	A. Isaiah 63:7-9; Hebrews 2:10-18; Psalm 111; Matthew 2:13-15, 19-23
	B. Isaiah 61:10–62:3; Galatians 4:47; Psalm 111; Luke 2:22-40
	C. 1 Samuel 2:18-20, 26; Colossians 3:12-17; Psalm 111; Luke 2:41-52

V. Reflection: Silent and Written

VI. Prayers: For the Church, for Others, for Myself

VII. Hymn: "In the Bleak Midwinter"

VIII. Benediction
Now clothe yourself with my flesh, Lord Jesus, and do your good work in me and through me today. Amen.

Readings for Reflection

ᶻᵃ Lord Jesus Christ, Thou Son of the Most High, Prince of Peace, be born again into our world. Wherever there is war in this world, wherever there is pain, wherever there is loneliness, wherever there is no hope, come, thou long-expected one, with healing in thy wings.

Holy Child, whom the shepherds and the kings and the dumb beasts adored, be born again. Wherever there is boredom, wherever there is fear of failure, wherever there is temptation too strong to resist, wherever there is bitterness of heart, come, thou blessed one, with healing in thy wings.

—From *The Hungering Dark* by Frederick Buechner

ᶻᵃ He who has told us, "Love your enemies, do good to those who hate you" (Luke 6:27), is scarcely likely to behave by another standard himself!

Love, real love, can only help, re-create, wait, and even say on the cross to the criminal who turns to him, "today you will be with me in paradise."

What hope, what sweetness there is in this terrible scene on Calvary! And the Church itself, the Church of Jesus, is born at this moment in an encounter between God and [humanity] when love achieves the miracle of eternal reconciliation.

"Today you will be with me in paradise."

This is God's today.

This is the Church's today.

This is completely new.

This is the price of blood. Human beings are vanquished by the blood of a God.

—From *Why, O Lord?* by Carlo Carretto

ᶻᵃ The fact of the matter is that loving is difficult. And so is forgiving, truly forgiving.

It is difficult for us and hard for the Church.

Since forgiving an adulteress or an ex-priest irks the sensibilities of the "body religious" it is easier to put that body's interests before the plain word of God. To avoid causing scandal, to set a good example, it is wiser not to accept the scandal of the cross which in any case offends our sense of justice! To defend morals it is more sensible to excommunicate someone, to deprive someone of the Eucharist.

By so doing we avoid offending a community that wants to see justice done, that feels the need to see a sinner punished.

We have not succeeded in grasping that we have been bought at the price of blood and that, as Jesus said, "A man can have no greater love than to lay down his life for his friends" (John 15:13).

And God himself has given us the example.

—From *Why, O Lord?* by Carlo Carretto

❧ Dear Jesus,
    Help us to spread your fragrance everywhere we go.
    Flood our souls with your spirit and life.
    Penetrate and possess our whole being so utterly
        that our lives may only be a radiance of yours.
    Shine through us
    and be so in us
    that every soul we come in contact with
        may feel your presence in our soul.
    Let them look up and see no longer us
    but only Jesus.
    Stay with us
    and then we shall begin to shine as you shine,
    so to shine as to be light to others.
    The light, O Jesus, will be all from you.
    None of it will be ours.
    It will be you shining on others through us.
    Let us thus praise you in the way you love best
        by shining on those around us. . . . Amen.
    —From *Words to Love By* by Mother Teresa

❧ God, we are as confounded as Joseph and Mary, as busy as the innkeepers, as lonely as the shepherds, as frightened as Herod, as wayfaring as the Magi. Turn us

again to the place where, with quietness, you wrap up your truth and promise, your love and salvation in the Child born in a rude stable. We would ponder these things as the noise and clamor of the world is stilled for a time and there is a peace that settles deep within us. Bring us to Bethlehem, to the place where he was homeless but where we are truly at home. *Amen.*
—From *The Unsettling Season* by Donald J. Shelby

   ❧ Human beings are worth the price of blood.

Love is superior to law.

Forgiveness is the first law of the community willed by Jesus.

Let us not forget this.

Though we are convinced that justice and enlightened behaviour require us to uphold the law, punish the erring, refuse to overlook a person's transgression when the innocent have suffered, we must also remember there is a contrary law which systematizes things much better than we can and, as far as the thirst for restoring the balance of justice is concerned, is much more demanding and harsher than we are.

Having discovered this by personal experience I then realized that God does not renounce justice, . . . human beings punish themselves by their own malice.

People who sin enter their own hell of their own volition and are constrained by the very mechanism they have themselves set in motion to drink to the dregs the bitter cup of their mistakes, their arrogance, their selfishness, their disobedience to the law of God.

No, brothers and sisters, there is no joy for the sinner, there is no future for the fugitive from love.

If you leave the Father's house where on earth can you run to? Where can you find peace, serenity, contemplation, or joy once you have rejected love?

Such audacity will be crushed under the hammer of vice. For such, anguish will haunt their nights, fear make them slaves, idolatry lead them to mortal weariness. No one can live without God: who flees [God] is already in hell.
—From *Why, O Lord?* by Carlo Carretto

Hymn: In the Bleak Midwinter

In the bleak midwinter, frosty wind made moan,
Earth stood hard as iron, water like a stone;
Snow had fallen, snow on snow, snow on snow,
In the bleak midwinter, long ago.

Our God, heaven cannot hold him, nor earth sustain;
Heaven and earth shall flee away when he comes to
    reign.
In the bleak midwinter a stable place sufficed
The Lord God Almighty, Jesus Christ.

Angels and archangels may have gathered there,
Cherubim and seraphim thronged the air;
But his mother only, in her maiden bliss,
Worshiped the beloved with a kiss.

What can I give him, poor as I am?
If I were a shepherd, I would bring a lamb;
If I were a Wise Man, I would do my part;
Yet what I can I give him: give my heart.
—Christina G. Rossetti

6: *Chosen by God*

I. Invocation
In this moment of prayer let me hear again, O Lord, that it was not I who first chose you, but you who chose me. Save me from all false pride which might dare lead me to believe that you chose me because of merit. Amen.

II. Psalm 89:1-18

III. Reading and Reflection

IV. Daily Scripture Readings
Monday	John 15:12-17
Tuesday	1 Thessalonians 1:2-10
Wednesday	Isaiah 42:1-9
Thursday	Luke 10:1-12
Friday	1 Peter 2:1-10
Saturday	Colossians 3:12-17

Sunday A. Isaiah 60:1-6; Psalm 72:1-14; Ephesians 3:1-12; Matthew 2:1-12

B. Isaiah 60:1-6; Psalm 72:1-14; Ephesians 3:1-12; Matthew 2:1-12

C. Isaiah 60:1-6; Psalm 72:1-14; Ephesians 3:1-12; Matthew 2:1-12

V. Reflection: Silent and Written

VI. Prayers: For the Church, for Others, for Myself

VII. Hymn: "Infant Holy, Infant Lowly"

VIII. Benediction
And now, my Lord, send me to my duty with confidence in your grace to transform this day's labor into that which is pleasing to you. Amen.

**If this is first Sunday after Epiphany, use Week 7.*

Readings for Reflection

❧ Every time I say no to the birthing and dying that is set before me at the table of daily life, I seem to hear the echo of Jesus' words to the woman at the well, "If you but knew the gift of God . . ." Whether God weeps at the beauty and potential of our lives at birth or the lost potential of graced moments along the way, I hear that voice urging us to claim our splendor and our glory. "If you but knew the gift of God . . ."

The gift of God is the Divine Indwelling. It comes quietly into your frailty at baptism. You become a tabernacle for the Source of Life. When you come to understand this old yet often forgotten truth, you will know what is meant by the words *heaven on earth*. This is it! You are beginning to live heaven on earth in the Divine Indwelling. You, frail earth-creature, having given your frailty over to God, have created a place of splendor within the depths of your being, a holy and eternal space where you meet God face to face. Cherish this truth. It is costly grace.

—From *A Tree Full of Angels* by Macrina Wiederkehr

❧ What if one were to envision God as friend, even as a feminist friend, rather than father or mother? What if God is friend to humanity as a whole, and even more intimately, friend to the individual, to me? A friend whose presence is joy, ever-deepening relationship and love, ever available in direct address, in communion and presence? A friend whose person is fundamentally a mystery, inexhaustible, never fully known, always surprising? Yet a friend, familiar, comforting, at home with us: a friend who urges our freedom and autonomy in decision, yet who is present in the community of interdependence and in fact creates it? A friend who widens our perspectives daily and who deepens our passion for freedom—our own and that of others? What if? Jesus' relationship to his disciples was that of friendship, chosen friends; he was rather critical of familial ties. His friendship transformed their lives—both women and men—expanded their horizons; his Spirit pressed them forward. Can we pray to the God of Jesus, through the Spirit, as friends?

—From Ann Carr in *Women's Spirituality* edited by Joann Wolski Conn

  Nearly all wisdom we possess, that is to say, true and sound wisdom, consists of two parts: the knowledge of God and of ourselves. But, while joined by many bonds, which one precedes and bring forth the other is not easy to discern. In the first place, no one can look upon [oneself] without immediately turning . . . thoughts to the contemplation of God, in whom [one] "lives and moves" (Acts 17:28). For, quite clearly, the mighty gifts with which we are endowed are hardly from ourselves; indeed, our very being is nothing but subsistence in the one God.

—John Calvin

  O my Lord and my God, I scarcely know how to bear the greatness of Your glory, now that Romans 6:8 has been disclosed to me. O God, how great You are! I can only stand in worship before You and rejoice that I am Yours, that my old self has been crucified and buried with You and that it is no longer my ego that lives, usurping Your rightful place, but rather You in me! Teach me to reckon with You at all times, and with Your power by which You created the heavens, the earth and the waters, and subdue them. O Lord Jesus, let me show my gratitude for such a wonderful Lord, by spending myself completely for You. Let me only strive to attain the goal that lies ahead. To be a pillar for You—let this be my sole aim.

—From *I Found the Key to the Heart of God* by Basilea Schlink

With all my ways,
Thou art acquainted:
 The silent coming together of all the streams
 Nourished by springs of Being
 Fountained in ancient sires
 Since Life began:
  The quiet shaping of patterns,
  That gave meaning and substance
  To all I know as mine:
   The nurture of mother,
   The molding of climate,
   The rending of heritage
   That stamped their mark in tender mind
    and growing limb:
   The tutoring by playmates
    and those who instruct;
   The sure hand of Spirit
    that held in keeping
     sensitive meanings of right and wrong...

With all my ways
Thou art acquainted:
 The making of plans far below the level
  of the daily mind
  that find their way to guide
  the movement of the deed—
 Habits that monitor the freshness
  in all spontaneity
  and tame the glory of the creative act;
 The unrestrained joy of impulse
  sweeping all before it in riotous rejoicing;
 The great tenderness called to life
  by that which invades the heart
  and circles all desires;
 The little malices;
 The big hostilities;
 The subtle envies;
 The robust greeds;
 The whimpering contrition;

The great confession;
The single resolve;
The fearful commitment;
The tryst with Death
 that broods over the zest for life
 like intermittent shadows
 from sunrise to sunset—

Thou art acquainted—
Thou art acquainted—
With all my ways.
—From *The Inward Journey* by Howard Thurman

❦ All too often we bemoan our imperfections rather than embrace them as part of the process in which we are brought to God. Cherished emptiness gives God space in which to work. We are pure capacity for God. Let us not, then, take our littleness lightly. It is a wonderful grace. It is a gift to receive. At the same time, let us not get trapped in the confines of our littleness, but keep pushing on to claim our greatness. Remind yourself often, "I am pure capacity for God; I can be *more*."
—From *A Tree Full of Angels* by Macrina Wiederkehr

Hymn: Infant Holy, Infant Lowly

Infant holy,
Infant lowly
For his bed a cattle stall;
Oxen lowing,
Little knowing,
Christ the babe is Lord of all.
Swift are winging
Angels singing,
Noels ringing,
Tidings bringing,
Christ the babe is Lord of all.

Flocks were sleeping
Shepherds keeping
Vigil till the morning new
Saw the glory,
Heard the story,
Tidings of a gospel true.
Thus rejoicing,
Free from sorrow,
Praises voicing,
Greet the morrow,
Christ the babe was born for you.
—Translated by Edith M. G. Reed

First Sunday after Epiphany
(between January 7 and 13)

7: God's Eternal Purpose

I. Invocation
    O God, sovereign Lord over all creation, without whom all purposes are futile, grant me today the assistance of your Spirit. In all the surprises and changes of life, may I fix my heart upon you, so that your eternal purposes may be fixed in me. In the name of Jesus, who came to make your eternal purpose clear. Amen.

II. Psalm 45

III. Reading and Reflection

IV. Daily Scripture Readings
    Monday   Isaiah 46:5-11
    Tuesday   Hebrews 6:9-20
    Wednesday   Matthew 19:16-30
    Thursday   Matthew 6:25-34
    Friday   1 Corinthians 3:10-17
    Saturday   2 Timothy 1:1-14
    Sunday   A. Isaiah 42:1-9; Acts 10:34-43; Psalm 29; Matthew 3:13-17
                 B. Genesis 1:1-5; Acts 19:1-7; Psalm 29; Mark 4:1-11
                 C. Isaiah 61:1-4; Acts 8:14-17; Psalm 29; Luke 3:15-17; 21-22

V. Reflection: Silent and Written

VI. Prayers: For the Church, for Others, for Myself

VII. Hymn: "Lord, You Give the Great Commission"

VIII. Benediction
    And now, my Lord, as I return to the duties of life, let me go in the confidence of your protection that I may come to the end of this day in peace and happiness. Amen.

Readings for Reflection

❧ In very simple terms, the view of reality emerging from subatomic physics and modern astronomy looks like this: Physical reality is not composed of fundamental building blocks of matter, but of fields of energy which comprise the universe. Subatomic physics, in its search for fundamental building blocks or particles, has found them to disappear and change into mutating patterns of energy best understood through field theory. Matter becomes, then, a temporary condensation or density of a field of energy.
—From *Healing of Purpose* by John E. Biersdorf

❧ For the power Thou hast given me to lay hold of
   things unseen:
   For the strong sense I have that this is not my home:
   For my restless heart which nothing finite can satisfy:
               I give Thee thanks, O God.
   For the invasion of my soul by Thy Holy Spirit:
   For all human love and goodness that speak to me
   of thee:
   For the fullness of Thy glory outpoured in Jesus
   Christ:
               I give Thee thanks, O God.
   —From *A Diary of Private Prayer* by John Baillie

❧ The story in Luke 24 of the disciples going to Emmaus is a work of genius. The two travellers are not just two people who happened to be there that night; they are the Church, they are you and I, because this is Luke's inspired picture of how things are in the Easter Church, the Church of Word and Sacrament; the long journey, the distress and bewilderment, the knowing yet not knowing, the patient tenderness of Christ as he tries to open their minds to understand the Scriptures, their burning hearts, their eventual recognition that they have indeed known the Lord in the breaking of the bread of the Word and the bread of Eucharist. The word is not always clarifying; it is mysterious, because it is the presence and self-communication of God. It is not always informative; it is performative, creative: changing and converting and renewing us. And there is something about the journey, the long experience of the road, that makes us able to hear it.

"We had hoped," say the travellers to the Lord. "We had hoped that things would go like this. . . ." We had our plans, but now. . . . Easter is utterly disconcerting, because it is the power and mystery of God taking hold of our frail mortality, our limited hopes. "Don't you see," their unrecognized fellow-pilgrim asks them. Don't you see that it had to be like that? Was it not written? Isn't it what all the Scripures are about, from end to end? Don't you understand that the Christ had to suffer and so enter into his glory? Don't you understand that it can't be otherwise for you? You have to jettison your small plans, because the Father's plans for you are unthinkably greater and more wonderful. You have to leap into [God's] hands, say an unconditional "Yes" and be born anew. [God's] love exceeds all that you deserve or even desire.
—From *The Coming of God* by Maria Boulding

❧ Do you believe that everything is part of a plan, a design, an intervention of God in our affairs? I do. And I am convinced that God's love can transform the darkness of a disaster or the irrationality of an earthquake into an event that can influence, or even completely change, our lives. . . . I came upon this passage in Augustine: "God can permit evil only in so far as he is capable of transforming it into a good."
—From *I Sought and I Found* by Carlo Carretto

❧ Now the Fathers of the Church well understood the importance of a certain "holy leisure"—*otium sanctum*. We cannot give ourselves to spiritual things if we are always swept off our feet by a multitude of external activities. Business is not the supreme virtue, and sanctity is not measured by the amount of work we accom-

plish. Perfection is found in the purity of our love for
God, and this pure love is a delicate plant that grows
best where there is plenty of time for it to mature.
—From *Spiritual Direction and Meditation* by Thomas
   Merton

 ⥆ God's love is such a powerful companion for us that
no matter how searing or how intense the hurt of a loss
is we know that our spirit need not be destroyed by it;
we know that God will help us to recover our hope, our
courage and our direction in life.
—From *Praying Our Goodbyes* by Joyce Rupp

 ⥆ Thou Hast Beset Me Behind and Before
   (*selected lines*)

> Thou hast beset me behind and before
> And laid Thine hand upon me!

>> The upward push of life awakes the egg,
>>> an inner stirring sends it forth
>>> to be in all its parts according to its law.
>> The blossom opens wide its heart
>>> to wind and bee,
>>> then closes.
>>> Deep within its pulsing core
>>> the dream of fruit takes shape
>>> and life decrees what it must be!
>> The little chick mingles sound with
>>> baby duck and goose,
>>> sharing each the common food,
>>> drinking from the single trough;
>> Day after day breezes blow—
>> Rains bring to one and all the glad
>>> refreshment from the summer's sun—
>> Yet, each follows his appointed way,
>>> without an awkward turn;
>> Each fulfills the pattern of his own design.
>> From tiny cell or ripened fruit,
>> From baby chick or mammoth oak
>>> the same refrain goes forth:

Thou hast beset me behind and before
And laid Thine hand upon me!
—From *The Inward Journey* by Howard Thurman

 ❧ We contemplate Christ, his world, his truth, in order to encounter God and "see" him. We do this with the eyes of faith, but they are genuine, objective eyes; and they are the eyes of our mind and senses, but they have been enlightened interiorly by the Holy Spirit dwelling in us. We have already spoken of this illumination. Now we are concerned with the object of our contemplation: God. Everything else, creation, humanity, salvation history, is considered within the context of God in order that we may find him there. But this finding is to be a spiritual and personal encounter in which, by faith, we become aware of that "life" which God gives to the believer objectively in the form of grace, i.e., in the form of a participation in the divine nature, with its triune exchange of life and love.
—From *Prayer* by Hans Urs von Balthasar

 ❧ The wise Rabbi Bunam once said in old age, when he had already grown blind: "I should not like to change places with our father Abraham! What good would it do God if Abraham became like a blind Bunam, and blind Bunam became like Abraham? Rather than have this happen, I think I shall try to become a little more like myself."

The same idea was expressed with even greater pregnancy by Rabbi Zusya when he said, a short while before his death: "In the world to come I shall not be asked: 'Why were you not Moses?' I shall be asked: 'Why were you not Zusya?'"
—From *Modern Spirituality* edited by John Garvey

 ❧ What about the will of God? Does God will our suffering? God does not send our suffering or want us to have it, but God does allow it to be there. Jesus himself struggled with the "will of the Father" when he was in his moment of agony (Lk 22:39-46). Jesus was fully human. He did not want the pain. He begged his Father to enter into his goodbye moment and to take away the pain: "Father," he said, "if you are willing, take this cup away from me." When Jesus continued with "Nevertheless, let your will be done, not mine," he was accepting his painful situation. The Father did not enter in, did not perform a miracle and keep him from the cross . . . did not save Jesus from being human. [God] allowed Jesus to have full participation in the human condition just as all of us have to enter fully into it. God's will for us is that of our happiness, our peace of mind and heart. God does not will us or want us to suffer life's hurts, but God does allow the suffering to happen because, as Rabbi Kushner says so clearly, for God to do otherwise would be to block our human nature and our human condition. Accidents do happen, death does come to us all, disease is prevalent in our world, but God is not doing those things to us. We are full and finite human beings living on an earth where natural disasters occur, where genetic conditions exist, where we sometimes make poor or sinful choices, where life does not always work as we had planned and hoped it would. We are blessed and burdened with our humanity, with the mystery of growing into a wholeness of personhood which involves continual goodbyes. We are frail and unfinished, subject always to the possibility of pain. We live in a world where we know we cannot escape our own mortality, our final goodbye before the eternal hello.

—From *Praying Our Goodbyes* by Joyce Rupp

Hymn: Lord, You Give the Great Commission

Lord, you give the great commission:
"Heal the sick and preach the word."
Lest the church neglect its mission,
And the gospel go unheard,
Help us witness to your purpose
With renewed integrity.

With the Spirit's gifts empower us
For the work of ministry.

Lord, you call us to your service:
"In my name baptize and teach."
That the world may trust your promise,
Life abundant meant for each,
Give us all new fervor, draw us
Closer in community.

With the Spirit's gifts empower us
For the work of ministry.

Lord, you make the common holy;
"This my body, this my blood."
Let us all, for earth's true glory,
Daily lift life heavenward,
Asking that the world around us
Share your children's liberty.

With the Spirit's gifts empower us
For the work of ministry.

Lord, you show us love's true measure:
"Father, what they do, forgive."
Yet we hoard as private treasure
All that you so freely give.
May your care and mercy lead us
To a just society.

With the Spirit's gifts empower us
For the work of ministry.

Lord, you bless with words assuring:
"I am with you to the end."
Faith and hope and love restoring,
May we serve as you intend
And, amid the cares that claim us,
Hold in mind eternity.

With the Spirit's gifts empower us
For the work of ministry.
—Jeffery Rowthorn

8: Following Jesus

I.   Invocation
     O Lord Jesus, in this hour let me hear again your call, "Follow me." My steps are prone to wander. Come therefore, I pray, and make your way clear before me. Amen.

II. Psalm 148

III. Reading and Reflection

IV. Daily Scripture Readings
Monday	John 1:35-51
Tuesday	Matthew 9:9-13
Wednesday	Luke 9:23-27
Thursday	Matthew 10:34-42
Friday	John 10:22-30
Saturday	Matthew 11:25-30
Sunday	A. Isaiah 49:1-7; 1 Corinthians 1:1-9; Psalm 40:1-11; John 1:29-34
	B. 1 Samuel 3:1-10, (11-20); 1 Corinthians 6:12-20; Psalm 63:1-8; John 1:35-42
	C. Isaiah 62:1-5; 1 Corinthians 12:1-11; Psalm 36:5-10; John 2:1-11

V.   Reflection: Silent and Written

VI. Prayers: For the Church, for Others, for Myself

VII. Hymn: "We Would See Jesus"

VIII. Benediction
     Dear Jesus, assist me to follow God's will, even as you followed your own destiny. Shed light upon my path, and keep close to me that I may follow close to you. Amen.

Readings for Reflection

❧ Jesus was poor and a workman. Astonishing! The Son of God—who, more than anyone else, was free to choose what he would—chose not only a mother and a people, but also a social position. And he wanted to be a wage earner.

That Jesus had *voluntarily* lost himself in an obscure Middle Eastern village; annihilated himself in the daily monotony of thirty years' rough, miserable work; separated himself from the society that "counts"; and died in total anonymity.

—From *Letters from the Desert* by Carlo Carretto

❧ Today, a woman must hear the words of Jesus as a man hears them; and if Jesus says, "Go and make disciples of all nations," it must no longer be that a man hears this in one way and a woman in another.

—From *I, Francis* by Carlo Carretto

❧ What Christ Said

> I said, "Let me walk in the fields."
>   He said, "No; walk in the town."
> I said, "There are no flowers there."
>   He said, "No flowers, but a crown."
>
> I said, "But the skies are black,
>   There is nothing but noise and din";
> And he wept as he sent me back;
>   "There is more," he said, "there is sin."
>
> I said, "But the air is thick,
>   And fogs are veiling the sun."
> He answered, "Yet souls are sick,
>   And souls in the dark undone."

I said, "I shall miss the light,
  And friends will miss me, they say."
He answered, "Choose tonight
  If I am to miss you, or they."

I pleaded for time to be given.
  He said, "Is it hard to decide?
It will not seem hard in Heaven
  To have followed the steps of your Guide."

I cast one look at the fields,
  Then set my face to the town;
He said, "My child, do you yield?
  Will you leave the flowers for the crown?"

Then into his hand went mine;
  And into my heart came he;
And I walk in a light divine,
  The path I had feared to see.
—George MacDonald

❧ Lord, You know what is most profitable to me; do this or that according to Your will. Give me what You will, as much as You will, and when You will. Do with me as You know what is best to be done, as it shall please You, and as it shall be most to Your honor. Put me where You will. I am Your creature, and in Your hands; lead me and turn me where You will. Lo, I am Your servant, ready to do all things that You command, for I do not desire to live to myself, but to You. Would to God that I might live worthily and profitably, and to Your honor.
—From *The Imitation of Christ* by Thomas à Kempis

❧ O Lord Jesus, your words to your Father were born out of your silence. Lead me into this silence, so that my words may be spoken in your name and thus be fruitful. It is so hard to be silent, silent with my mouth, but even more, silent with my heart. There is so much talking going on within me. It seems that I am always involved in inner debates with myself, my friends, my enemies, my supporters, my opponents, my colleagues, and my rivals. But this inner debate reveals how far my heart is from you. If I were simply to rest at your feet and realize that I belong to you and you alone, I would easily stop arguing with all the real and imagined people around me. These arguments show my insecurity, my fear, my apprehensions, and my need for being recognized and receiving attention. You, O Lord, will give me all the attention I need if I would simply stop talking and start listening to you. I know that in the silence of my heart you will speak to me and show me your love. Give me, O Lord, that silence. Let me be patient and grow slowly into this silence in which I can be with you. Amen.

—From *A Cry for Mercy* by Henri J. M. Nouwen

ᐓ Dear Lord Jesus Christ, You know my soul and know that I cannot sufficiently express my ardent love for You. Your goodness and greatness are infinite. No one could ever praise You enough. Lord Jesus Christ, if only I could demonstrate my overflowing gratitude to You! Oh, let me suffer, let me be despised, if it should please You, and if I might be cleansed and able to glorify You all the more. Lord Jesus, use me as Your instrument so that I may bring You glory. Let me proclaim Your almighty love and power, and bring souls to You and make them happy... I do not know whether I can bear it yet, but I long to suffer for Your sake. Let Your love flow deep into my heart and abide there so that it stands the test in suffering. Oh, if only I have You, I will gladly endure everything.

—From *I Found the Key to the Heart of God* by Basilea Schlink

ᐓ The Christian faith for most people is not communicated by doctrinal pronouncements or the solemn assembly of ecclesiastical dignitaries, but by what goes on in the church in its most local setting. It is here, in the

church down the street, that people are caught up in the Gospel promise—or are turned away.
—From *Mutual Ministry* by James C. Fenhagen

ᕈ This sense of connection between inner growth and outer change permeates the Christian understanding of reality. St. Paul was an activist of the first order. Every time he entered a new place he created major disruptions, but his activism was the fruit of the relationship he enjoyed with the living Christ. The great hymns of praise that seem to burst out in epistle after epistle are a testimony to the reality of this relationship. The ministries of Mother Teresa in the slums of Calcutta or of Martin Luther King in the streets of Montgomery, or of the countless people whose faith has touched your life and mine and indeed has affected the life of the world are expressions of lived prayer. These people went deep enough in prayer to embrace life with some degree of abandon. These inner experiences literally drove them in ministry to others.
—From *Invitation to Holiness* by James C. Fenhagen

ᕈ A conversion is the starting point of every spiritual journey. It involves a break with the life lived up to that point; it is a prerequisite for entering the kingdom: "The time is fulfilled, and the kingdom of God is at hand; repent, and believe in the gospel" (Mark 1:15). It presupposes also, and above all, that one decides to set out on a new path: "Sell all that you have . . . and come, follow me" (Luke 18:22). Without this second aspect the break would lack the focus that a fixed horizon provides and would ultimately be deprived of meaning.

Because of this second aspect a conversion is not something that is done once and for all. It entails a development, even a painful one, that is not without uncertainties, doubts, and temptations to turn back on the road that has been traveled. The experience of the Jewish people after its departure from Egypt is still prototypical here. Fidelity to the word of God implies a permanent conversion. This is a central theme in the teaching of the prophets.

On the other hand, the path of conversion is not one marked only by stumbling blocks; there is a growth in maturity. Throughout the gospels we are repeatedly told that after some word or deed of Jesus "his disciples believed in him." The point of this statement is not that up to that point they had no faith, but rather that their faith deepened with the passage of time. To believe in God is more than simply to profess God's existence; it is to enter into communion with God and—the two being inseparable—with our fellow human beings as well. And all this adds up to a process.

—From *We Drink from Our Own Wells* by Gustavo Gutiérrez

❧ We take a giant step forward in Christian devotion when we see it more as a life to be lived than as a time to be observed. Consequently, it is more appropriate to speak of a "devotional life" than a "devotional time." When we study Wesley's spirituality, we see this coming through loud and clear. He never divided his life into compartments. For him, the essence of life was spiritual. All of it could properly be called devotional.

—From *Devotional Life in the Wesleyan Tradition* by Steve Harper

❧ All Christian believers are called to ministry. Sometimes this idea is not understood because of the tendency to use the term "ministry" to refer popularly to those who are engaged in full-time professional service in the church, usually ordained ministers. Thus we speak of one entering "the ministry" and we mean the occupation of the clergy, full-time ministry for pay, sociologically not unlike other classic professions of medicine and law, or other occupations by which men and women earn livings in our society. This narrow usage of the term ministry is unfortunate, however, because it seriously truncates the wider and richer understanding of Christian ministry in the Bible and church teaching.

—From *The Yoke of Obedience* by Dennis M. Campbell

❧ A reading of the New Testament, especially the Gospels that tell what Jesus looked for in people, produces a picture of a quality church member as one who has been touched and changed by the Holy Spirit. He or she is committed to doing the will of God even though sin will test the commitment. Over the years the church has required that a part of a person's commitment to God is expressed by attendance at worship and regular observance of certain disciplines of a holy life such as prayer, sacrifice, and care for others. To specify how these must be done or carried out is not only inappropriate but is arrogant. God's relationship to people determines how they should pray, sacrifice, and care for others.

—From *Facts and Possibilities* by Douglas W. Johnson
  and Alan K. Waltz

Hymn: We Would See Jesus

We would see Jesus; lo! his star is shining
Above the stable while the angels sing;
There in a manger on the hay reclining;
Haste, let us lay our gifts before the King.

We would see Jesus, on the mountain teaching,
With all the listening people gathered round;
While birds and flowers and sky above are preaching
The blessedness which simple trust has found.

We would see Jesus, in his working of healing,
At eventide before the sun was set;
Divine and human, in his deep revealing
Of God made flesh, in loving service met.

We would see Jesus, in the early morning,
Still as of old, he calleth, "Follow me!"
Let us arise, all meaner service scorning;
Lord, we are thine, we give ourselves to thee.
—J. Edgar Park

Third Sunday after Epiphany
(between January 21 and 27)

9: The Call of God

I.   Invocation
     Almighty God, father of our Lord Jesus Christ, I
     commit all my ways unto you. I pledge my life
     to your service. Speak to me of duty and
     faithfulness. Show me my noble task, and
     strengthen me to walk in it. Amen.

II. Psalm 131

III. Reading and Reflection

IV. Daily Scripture Readings
     Monday   Luke 5:1-11
     Tuesday   Jeremiah 1:1-10
     Wednesday   Romans 1:1-7
     Thursday   1 Peter 1:13-25
     Friday   1 Peter 3:8-12
     Saturday   John 21:15-23
     Sunday   A. Isaiah 9:1-4; 1 Corinthians 1:10-17;
                    Psalm 27:1-6; Matthew 4:12-23
                B. Jonah 3:1-5, 10; 1 Corinthians
                    7:29-31, (32-35); Psalm 62:5-12;
                    Mark 1:14-20
                C. Nehemiah 8:1-4a, 5-6, 8-10;
                    1 Corinthians 12:12-30; Psalm
                    19:7-14; Luke 4:14-21

V.   Reflection: Silent and Written

VI. Prayers: For the Church, for Others, for Myself

VII. Hymn: "Lord God, Your Love Has Called Us
           Here"

VIII. Benediction
      My God, I give myself to you as a gift of love. I
      place my life in your hands to do with as you
      will. Only use me, my Lord, that my life be not
      wasted. Amen.

Readings for Reflection

❧ Whether you are on the sand worshipping, or at the teacher's desk in a classroom, what does it matter as long as you are doing the will of God?

And if the will of God urges you to seek out the poor, to give up all you possess, or to leave for distant lands, what does the rest matter? Or if it calls you to found a family, or take on a job in a city, why should you have any doubts?

"His will is our peace," says Dante. And perhaps that is the expression which best brings into focus our deep dependence on God.

—From *Letters from the Desert* by Carlo Carretto

❧ The first thing that you are to do when you are upon your knees is to shut your eyes. Then with a short silence let your soul place itself in the presence of God. That is, you are to use this or some other better method to separate yourself from all common thoughts, and make your heart as sensible as you can of the divine presence.

—From *A Serious Call to a Devout and Holy Life* by William Law

❧ I carry within me an image of a covenant between God and humankind that reaches back into the origins of time. It is a covenant both of accountability and forgiveness, calling us to a life of faithfulness in relation to the holiness of God and the needs of the human family. We are indeed "our brother's keeper," and we will be held accountable for the way in which we live out this responsibility. The biblical image of the covenant is an image of human and divine solidarity, of relatedness and moral responsibility. It is in relation to this deep sense of belonging that my sense of identity comes—the sense that who I am and who I will become is tied up with my capacity to live with integrity and compassion in relation to the human family of which I am a part. It is a sense that who I am is intimately connected with my capacity for relationships of depth which, at the deepest level, I both yearn for and resist. When grasped by this image of the covenant, I am aware that the freedom and possibility I experience in life is somehow bound up in the figure of the man Jesus, who in some incredible life-giving way makes himself present in the deep places of my life. I have a sense—sometimes fleeting, sometimes very real—of what St. Paul meant when he said, "It is no longer I who live, but Christ who lives in me." It is this awareness that calls me into covenant with the mystery of life whom we call God.

—From *Mutual Ministry* by James C. Fenhagen

ɞ A speaker was once introduced by the perfect chairman who said simply, "Mr. Weaver, we are ready. Are you ready?" When I gather myself for prayer it is almost as if God were so addressing me: "Douglas Steere, I am ready. Are you ready?" And my answer is, "O Lord, you are always ready, but am I ever ready? O Lord, make me ready, or at least make me more ready to be made ready."

—From *Together in Solitude* by Douglas V. Steere

ɞ *Every Christian has a vocation*. We are called to share in the ministry of Jesus Christ *in* and *through* the world. In the Sacrament of Baptism this call is incarnated, giving us both a clear *identity* in the world and a sense of purpose about what our lives are ultimately for. Sharing in the ministry of Jesus Christ involves living in the world as an expression of the holiness we see in him—a holiness expressed through his compassion, his concern for justice (righteousness), and through his healing and reconciling presence in the world. The relationship he offers to us—when entered into with seriousness—results in those qualities we see in him being expressed through us, sometimes even despite ourselves. We cannot, therefore, limit this expression to a particular profession or a particular role or a particular job.

—From *Invitation to Holiness* by James C. Fenhagen

❧ The pathway to holiness leads us to link ourselves in a serious way to a Kingdom value toward whose realization we are willing to commit our energy. Mahatma Gandhi and Martin Luther King were touched by holiness in their pursuit of justice through non-violence, clear Kingdom values. The holiness of Mother Teresa and Desmond Tutu is the holiness that emerges out of their compassion for the poor and oppressed. And there is holiness present in those who struggle for peace and the abolition of the threat of nuclear war. We can't do everything, but each of us can do something. What we do—what we pay attention to—depends, of course, on the tune we hear.

—From *Invitation to Holiness* by James C. Fenhagen

❧ Spirituality as life-experience and as a field of study is no longer identified simply with asceticism and mysticism, or with the practice of virtue and methods of prayer. From the perspective of the actualization of the human capacity to be spiritual, to be self-transcending— that is, relational and freely committed spirituality encompasses all of life. In general, religious spirituality is a matter of the experience and/or study of the actualization of human self-transcendence by the Holy, by Ultimate Concern—that is, by what is acknowledged as "religious." Specifically, Christian spirituality involves the actualization of this human capacity through the experience of God, in Jesus the Christ, through the gift of the Spirit. Because this God, Jesus, and the Spirit are experienced through body-community-history-influenced human life and symbols, Christian spirituality includes *every* dimension of human life. Thus, Christian spiritual development cannot legitimately be identified as soul development, nor be exclusively associated with development in prayer and virtue. To be adequately experienced and studied, it should be viewed as total human development.

—From Joann Wolski Conn in *Women's Spirituality* edited by Joann Wolski Conn

❧ Prayer is contact with God such as lovers have, such as friends have. It doesn't need solitude to exist. Occasionally it is nice to have it but let's not make the mistake of thinking that we can only pray to God if we can get away from the mob and escape to the solitude of a Russian–style poustinia. We have to be realistic about prayer. Prayer is, first and foremost, standing still before God. Before you even begin to ask questions about prayer, you must stand still.

—From *Soul of My Soul* by Catherine de Hueck Doherty

❧ The complementarity of all Christian ministries is an important theological concept. To assert that all Christians are ministers is not to "put down" the clergy. It is to remind us of the complex interaction between laity and clergy. To assert the importance and integrity of the clergy is not to "put down" the laity; rather it is to recognize distinctions of functions in the community. This chapter has described the reasons for the distinction between laity and clergy and has shown the development of ministry in the history of the church. I have told this history in the context of the theological concept of wholeness to remind us that lay persons have honorable and vital ministries and that ordination is seriously misunderstood if it is thought that clergy are more important or central to the church. Similarly, it is wrong not to appreciate the legitimate contributions of the ordained. Perhaps the most important thing to be learned from this chapter is that, at its best, the church has dealt with ministry not in terms of power, rights or privileges, but in terms of service and giving. Through the grace of the Lord Jesus Christ, and the gift of the Holy Spirit, ministry is given to the church for the sake of the world. Though we are not all the same, we are all one, and we are all dependent upon God and called to make our wills conform to God's will. Our equality in ministry is in our subjectivity to God. We do not share "rights," we share common subjection to God. We all are equally needful; and, like Christ, we do not exalt ourselves, but we seek humble obedience to God's will.

—From *The Yoke of Obedience* by Dennis M. Campbell

Hymn: Lord God, Your Love Has Called Us Here

Lord God, your love has called us here,
As we, by love, for love were made;
Your living likeness still we bear,
Though marred, dishonored, disobeyed;
We come, with all our heart and mind,
Your call to hear, your love to find.

We come with self-inflicted pains
Of broken trust and chosen wrong,
Half-free, half-bound by inner chains,
By social forces swept along,
By powers and systems close confined,
Yet seeking hope for humankind.

Lord God, in Christ you call our name,
And then receive us as your own;
Not through some merit, right, or claim,
But by your gracious love alone;
We strain to glimpse your mercy seat,
And find you kneeling at our feet.

Then take the towel, and break the bread,
And humble us, and call us friends;
Suffer and serve till all are fed,
And show how grandly love intends
To work till all creation sings,
To fill all worlds, to crown all things.

Lord God, in Christ you set us free
Your life to live, your joy to share;
Give us your Spirit's liberty
To turn from guilt and dull despair,
And offer all that faith can do,
While love is making all things new.
—Brian Wren

Fourth Sunday after Epiphany*
(between January 28 and February 3)

10: The Power of God's Word

I. Invocation
At your word, O Lord, the worlds were created,
and by your word new life is given. Open now
my ears that I may hear your special word
spoken to me today. Amen.

II. Psalm 29

III. Reading and Reflection

IV. Daily Scripture Readings

Monday	John 1:1-13
Tuesday	Genesis 1:1-19
Wednesday	Genesis 1:20-31
Thursday	Matthew 9:1-8
Friday	2 Corinthians 12:1-10
Saturday	1 Peter 1:3-9
Sunday	A. Micah 6:1-8; 1 Corinthians 1:18-31; Psalm 37:1-11; Matthew 5:1-12
	B. Deuteronomy 18:15-20; 1 Corinthians 8:1-13; Psalm 111; Mark 1:21-28
	C. Jeremiah 1:4-10; 1 Corinthians 13:1-13; Psalm 71:1-6; Luke 4:21-30

V. Reflection: Silent and Written

VI. Prayers: For the Church, for Others, for Myself

VII. Hymn: "Send Your Word"

VIII. Benediction
And now Jesus, God's Word enfleshed, I hear
you knocking and I open the door. Come into
my heart and mind, and speak to me from that
interior place—all the day long. Amen.

*If this is the Last Sunday after Epiphany, use Week 15.

Readings for Reflection

❧ We gladly acknowledge that we must be saved only and alone through faith and that our works or godly life contribute neither much nor little to our salvation, for as a fruit of our faith our works are connected with the gratitude which we owe to God, who has already given us who believe the gift of righteousness and salvation. Far be it from us to depart even a finger's breadth from this teaching, for we would rather give up our life and the whole world than yield the smallest part of it.

We also gladly acknowledge the power of the Word of God when it is preached, since it is the power of God for salvation to everyone who has faith (Rom. 1:16). We are bound diligently to hear the Word of God not only because we are commanded to do so but also because it is the divine hand which offers and presents grace to the believer, whom the Word itself awakens through the Holy Spirit.

—From *Pia Desideria* by Philipp Jakob Spener

❧ John Wesley knew that an objective standard was necessary for genuine spirituality. For him, that standard was the Bible. He was committed to the centrality and authority of scripture. Although Wesley read hundreds of books on a wide range of subjects, he continually referred to himself as *homo unis libri*—a man of one book. Even though he published approximately six hundred works on various themes, he resolutely maintained that he allowed no rule, whether of faith or practice, other than the Holy Scriptures. In the preface to his *Standard Sermons* Wesley exclaims, "O give me that book! At any price, give me the book of God! . . . Here is knowledge enough for me."

—From *Devotional Life in the Wesleyan Tradition* by Steve Harper

We do not always realize what a radical suggestion it is for us to read to be formed and transformed rather than to gather information. We are information seekers. We love to cover territory. It is not easy for us to stop reading when the heart is touched; we are a people who like to get finished. Lectio offers us a new way to read. Read with a vulnerable heart. Expect to be blessed in the reading. Read as one awake, one waiting for the beloved. Read with reverence.

We are naturally reverent beings, but much of our natural reverence has been torn away from us because we have been born into a world that hurries. There is no time to be reverent with the earth or with each other. We are all hurrying into progress. And for all our hurrying we lose sight of our true nature a little more each day. This is precisely why we need to believe in the eye of God hovering over us. We are not alone. There is One with us who wants to give back our reverence. There is One with us who wants to give us back the gift of time.

Read the Scriptures, then, with reverence, giving up the lie that you don't have time. Read under the eye of God. Read as one who has nothing but time.

Before you read, you may wish to pray:

All-Seeing One,
above me, around me, within me.
Be my seeing as I read these sacred words.
Look down upon me
Look out from within me
Look all around me
See through my eyes
Hear through my ears
Feel through my heart
Touch me where I need to be touched;
    and when my heart is touched,
      give me the grace to lay down this Holy Book
      and ask significant questions:
Why has my heart been touched?
How am I to be changed through this touch?
All-Seeing One,

I need to change
I need to look a little more like You
May these sacred words change and transform me.
Then I can meet You face to face
    without dying
    because I've finally died enough.
To die is to be healed a little more each death,
    until that final death
    when I'll be healed forever.
It will be a healing that will last.
Your Words are healing
    although they bring about my death.

O Eye of God, look not away.
—From *A Tree Full of Angels* by Macrina Wiederkehr

❦ As Divine Reading becomes a way of life for us, it is easy to see that it is more of a process than a technique. For example, it is not necessary in this process to start with reading. I do not look at reading as the beginning, but rather as part of the process. Being a frequent guest at the table of Scripture, I have enough of the Word of God stored in my heart that I can, at any moment, bring forth food for my prayer. I can begin with meditation or some other aspect of prayer. I can begin by adoring. The secret of Divine Reading is to live my life around the Word of God to such an extent that I am constantly aware of God praying in me. The Word of God becomes at home in me. I am like a portable sanctuary filled with the real presence of God. Being a temple of God, how can I but see God everywhere I look? Within your temple, Lord, I sing about your glory. I am that temple, but you are the glory.
—From *A Tree Full of Angels* by Macrina Wiederkehr

❦ Just as old or bleary-eyed [people] and those with weak vision, if you thrust before them a most beautiful volume, even if they recognize it to be some sort of writing, yet can scarcely construe two words, but with the aid of spectacles will begin to read distinctly; so

Scripture, gathering up the otherwise confused knowledge of God in our minds, having dispersed our dullness, clearly shows us the true God. This, therefore, is a special gift, where God, to instruct the church, not merely uses mute teachers but also opens his own most hallowed lips. Not only does [God] teach the elect to look upon a god, but also shows himself as the God upon whom they are to look.
—John Calvin

* Before I go any farther, it is worthwhile to say something about the authority of Scripture, not only to prepare our hearts to reverence it, but to banish all doubt. When that which is set forth is acknowledged to be the Word of God, there is no one so deplorably insolent—unless devoid also both of common sense and of humanity itself—as to dare impugn the credibility of [the One] who speaks. Now daily oracles are not sent from heaven, for it pleased the Lord to hallow ... truth to everlasting remembrance in the Scriptures alone (cf. John 5:39). Hence the Scriptures obtain full authority among believers only when [people] regard them as having sprung from heaven, as if there the living words of God were heard.
—John Calvin

* The world of invitation and decision concretizes the stories of hope and justice, trust and freedom; and the stories of hope and justice, trust and freedom support the world of invitation and decision. The first two sets of stories create convictions and values but do not investigate how these are carried out in actual life. Hope, justice, trust, and freedom are not static ideals but a redemptive process enacted in a world of invitation and decision. In a way, the stories of hope and justice, trust and freedom are the content of God and the story of invitation and decision is the form. On the other hand, the world of invitation and decision can appear unyielding. There is a purging aspect to the redemptive process which the parables do not shy away from. The halting, never-ending movement from sin to redemption would paralyze and debilitate us if we did not tell the other stories. From these stories we know that the Mystery is love and that the conversion process, no matter how painful, is the way of our well-being. All three of these tales, therefore, merge into a single story of God, and, of course, God's story is ours.

—From *Stories of God* by John Shea

🍃 There is, in a word, nothing comfortable about the Bible—until we manage to get so used to it that we make it comfortable for ourselves. But then we are perhaps too used to it and too at home in it. Let us not be too sure we know the Bible . . . just because we have learned not to have problems with it. Have we perhaps learned . . . not to really pay attention to it? Have we ceased to question the book and be questioned by it?

—From *Opening the Bible* by Thomas Merton

🍃 One of the most important features of the liturgical renewal is insistence on *listening* to the Word of God . . . and then participating in a corporate reply. For this listening to be effective, a certain interior silence is required. This in turn implies the ability to let go of one's congested, habitual thoughts and preoccupations so that one can freely open the heart to the message of the sacred text.

—From *Cistercian Life* by Thomas Merton

Hymn: Send Your Word

Send your Word, O Lord, like the rain,
Falling down upon the earth.
Send your Word.
We seek your endless grace,
With souls that hunger and thirst,
Sorrow and agonize.
We would all be lost in dark
Without your guiding light.

Send your Word, O Lord, like the wind,
Blowing down upon the earth.
Send your Word.
We seek your wondrous power,
Pureness that rejects all sins,
Though they persist and cling.
Bring us to complete victory;
Set us all free indeed.

Send your Word, O Lord, like the dew,
Coming gently upon the hills.
Send your Word.
We seek your endless love.
For life that suffers in strife
With adversities and hurts,
Send your healing power of love;
We long for your new world.
—Yasushige Imakoma, trans. by Nobuaki Hanaoka

11: The Meaning of Discipleship

I. Invocation
Almighty God, creator and keeper of the world
and all that is in it, help us, we pray, to know
the duty you have assigned us and to so live our
lives that the world may be a better place for all
your creatures. In the name of Jesus. Amen.

II. Psalm 32

III. Reading and Reflection

IV. Daily Scripture Readings
Monday   Luke 14:7-14
Tuesday   Luke 9:57-62
Wednesday   Luke 14:25-34
Thursday   John 6:60-71
Friday   Acts 4:32-37
Saturday   Romans 15:1-13
Sunday   A. Isaiah 58:3-9a; 1 Corinthians 2:1-
               11; Psalm 112:4-9; Matthew 5:
               13-16
            B. Job 7:1-7; 1 Corinthians 9:16-23;
               Psalm 147:1-11; Mark 1:29-39
            C. Isaiah 6:1-8, (9-13); 1 Corinthians
               15:1-11; Psalm 138; Luke 5:1-11

V. Reflection: Silent and Written

VI. Prayers: For the Church, for Others, for Myself

VII. Hymn: "Lord, Whose Love Through Humble
Service"

VIII. Benediction
And now as I leave this place of quiet to return
to the duties which await me, go with me, my
God; and keep me all the day long. Amen.

*If this is the Last Sunday after Epiphany, use Week 15.

Readings for Reflection

❧ In one of the parables Jesus tells the story of a certain nobleman who went abroad to obtain power for himself and then return. Before he left he called his ten servants, giving them each a twenty-dollar bill, and telling them, "Trade with this until I come back." When he returned he ordered his servants to be brought before him for their report.

The first man said, "Sir your twenty dollars have made one hundred."

"Fine," said the nobleman.

The second man said, "Sir, your twenty dollars have made fifty dollars."

"Excellent," said the nobleman.

The third man was the only one who made a speech. He said, "Sir, here is your twenty dollars. I kept it safe in a napkin, for I was afraid of you. Perhaps you do not know this, but you have a reputation of being a very hard man. You pick up what you have never put down. You reap where you have not sown, you gather into barns what you have not planted!"

The nobleman was incensed. He ordered the servant cast off his place into "outer darkness."

Here, I make an end of the story. The unfortunate servant was not "cast off" because he did not realize any profit for the nobleman. No. He was cast off because he did not "work at it."

We are never under obligation to achieve results. Of course, results are important and it may be that that is the reason effort is put forth. But results are not mandatory. Much of the energy and effort and many anxious hours are spent over the probable failure or success of our ventures. No man likes to fail. But it is important to remember that under certain circumstances, failure is its own success.

To keep one's eye on results is to detract markedly from the business at hand. This is to be diverted from the task itself. It is to be only partially available to demands at hand. Very often it causes one to betray one's own inner sense of values because to hold fast to the integrity of the act may create the kind of displeasure which in the end will affect the results. However, if the results are left free to form themselves in terms of the quality and character of the act, then all of one's resources can be put at the disposal of the act itself.

There are many forces over which the individual can exercise no control whatsoever. A man plants a seed in the ground and the seed sprouts and grows. The weather, the winds, the elements, cannot be controlled by the farmer. The result is never a sure thing. So what does the farmer do? He plants. Always he plants. Again and again he works at it—the ultimate confidence and assurance that even though his seed does not grow to fruition, seeds do grow and they do come to fruition.

The task of men who work for the Kingdom of God, is to *Work* for the Kingdom of God. The result beyond this demand is not in their hands. He who keeps his eyes on results cannot give himself wholeheartedly to his task, however simple or complex that task may be.

—From *The Inward Journey* by Howard Thurman

❧ The changes being demanded of us are almost beyond comprehension. For vast numbers of people living in the West—the world of the "haves"—it will mean a total reorientation of life-styles. It will mean learning how to resist the urge to buy and the urge to eat, where submitting to those urges is our custom. It will mean discovering the simplicity which comes from an intentional life lived from inside out rather than from outside in. In the riches of the Christian tradition there are patterns for this kind of pursuit, easily adapted to present needs. To adopt them, however, will require not only assistance, but ongoing support.

—From *Mutual Ministry* by James C. Fenhagen

❧ Ministries of caring, ministries on behalf of justice and reconciliation, ministries of witness, ministries of

dialogue, ministries that bring Christian values to bear on the decision–making process of politics and business, ministries of support—all potentially stem from the local congregation, and when carried out with wisdom and compassion are signs of life. The congregation *is* mission. The congregation is also evangelistic. Both are essential to its very nature. In looking for signs of life I find myself immediately looking for how this sense of mission is being expressed, and by whom. Mission, be it explicit or implicit, is the primary task of the laity. It is a task that requires training and support, a task that is essential as we confront the chaos of a world faced with cataclysmic change.
—From *Mutual Ministry* by James C. Fenhagen

&. The point is that ministry is more than simply doing good. Ministry is an act performed *in [God's] name*. Therefore, it is not something we do solely on our own, but something Christ does in us, through us, and with us. Ministry has been given to us. Our task is to uncover what is already present so that the ministry of the church might be carried out in all of its fullness. The ministry of the church is exercised by every man, woman, and child who bears the mark of baptism.
—From *Mutual Ministry* by James C. Fenhagen

&. Values are more than the ideals or moral absolutes to which we aspire. A value is an inner construct blending together religious beliefs, ethical principles, societal norms, and life experiences in a way that empowers us to act. Everything we do, be it the decisions we make or the actions we take during the course of a day, is based on some consciously or unconsciously held value. Values are freely held and important enough to cause us to want to act on their behalf. One of the things that makes me unique is the particular value structure that empowers my life. There are elements of this structure that I might hold in common with others, but the particular combination is mine. This means, of course, that Christians can agree on certain ethical

principles and yet live their lives differently. It is our values that create and sustain our life-style.
—From *Mutual Ministry* by James C. Fenhagen

ও To become a disciple means to see for oneself the values that energized the life of Jesus of Nazareth, to struggle with them, until there comes that moment when by the grace of God they become our own. Commitment to an ongoing and disciplined enrichment of our relationship to God, the affirmation of human need and worth in the face of the demonic pretensions of those principalities and powers that control our lives, the desire to serve life out of love rather than power or reward, and a deep identification with the poor and the hungry and the oppressed; these are values that we can see in the life of Jesus. They are values which when affirmed and lived will make a profound difference in the quality of life of the world that is emerging. It is through psychic and spiritual intercourse with values such as these that we are called to be value bearers in the name of Christ.
—From *Mutual Ministry* by James C. Fenhagen

Hymn: Lord, Whose Love through Humble Service

Lord, whose love through humble service
Bore the weight of human need,
Who upon the cross, forsaken,
Offered mercy's perfect deed:
We, your servants, bring the worship
Not of voice alone, but heart,
Consecrating to your purpose
Every gift that you impart.

Still your children wander homeless;
Still the hungry cry for bread;
Still the captives long for freedom;
Still in grief we mourn our dead.
As, O Lord, your deep compassion
Healed the sick and freed the soul,

Use the love your spirit kindles
Still to save and make us whole.

As we worship, grant us vision,
Till your love's revealing light
In its height and depth and greatness
Dawns upon our quickened sight,
Making known the needs and burdens
Your compassion bids us bear,
Stirring us to tireless striving
Your abundant life to share.

Called by worship to your service,
Forth in your dear name we go
To the child, the youth, the aged,
Love in living deeds to show;
Hope and health, good will and comfort,
Counsel, aid, and peace we give,
That your servants, Lord, in freedom
May your mercy know, and live.
—Albert Frederick Bayly

12: Choose Life

I. Invocation
Today, my God, let me hear again your word,
"Choose this day whom you will serve" and
assist me to choose the way of life eternal.
Speak my Lord; your servant is listening. Amen.

II. Psalm 51

III. Reading and Reflection

IV. Daily Scripture Readings
Monday   Philippians 3:8-16
Tuesday   1 Timothy 6:3-19
Wednesday   Matthew 7:1-14
Thursday   Ephesians 4:1-8
Friday   Luke 12:22-32
Saturday   1 Thessalonians 4:1-18
Sunday   A. Deuteronomy 30:15-20; 1 Corin-
               thians 3:1-9; Psalm 119:1-8; Mat-
               thew 5:17-26
            B. 2 Kings 5:1-14; 1 Corinthians 9:
               24-27; Psalm 32; Mark 1:40-45
            C. Jeremiah 17:5-10; 1 Corinthians
               15:12-20; Psalm 1; Luke 6:17-26

V. Reflection: Silent and Written

VI. Prayers: For the Church, for Others, for Myself

VII. Hymn: "Still, for Thy Loving-kindness, Lord"

VIII. Benediction
My God, in all the great and small choices I will
make this day, be in my heart and in my choosing that I may come to day's end knowing I
have chosen wisely—for you. Amen.

*If this is the Last Sunday after Epiphany, use Week 15.

Readings for Reflection

❧ Is this going to be a period of purification, Lord? Is this going to be the time when you give me insight into the chains that bind me and the courage to throw them off? Is this going to be my chance to see my prison and escape it?

John Eudes said: "This is a time of purification. A time to identify your ambiguous relationships and your ambivalent attitudes, and to make some decisions and choose some directions." Lord, it is you who said this to me. If I believe in your church and the voice of those who speak in her name, in your name, then it was you who pointed out to me the meaning of my stay here: "Identify and choose."

And you also said, "Pray even when you do not feel attracted to it." Yes, Lord, I will try to pray, even when I am afraid to face you and myself, even when I keep falling asleep or feel as though I am going around in circles, even when it seems that nothing is happening. Yes, Lord, I will pray—not only with others, not only supported by the rhythms of the choir, but also alone with you. I will try not to be afraid. Lord, give me courage and strength. Let me see myself in the light of your mercy and choose you. Amen.

—From *A Cry for Mercy* by Henri J.M. Nouwen

❧ Curiously enough, each of us has a philosopher, a contemplator if you like, within us. It is a gift that is not optional but that is built-in equipment. This inward companion of ours is able to carry on quite as ruthless a querying of our actions as Cineas managed for the King of Epire. As a matter of fact, this kind of inner dialogue may be going on in us all the time if we are only aware of it. It keeps on asking us, "What, in this world, are you doing?" "Who are you?" "Where did you come from?" "Where are you going?" "Is this foreground of your life, in which you live such an agitated existence, all that there is?" "Have you taken your companions, your wife, your children for granted?"

"Does each of them have a destiny of their own and do you know how you are really related to them?"
—From *Centuries of Meditations* by Thomas Traherne

❧ My aim in these pages has been to reflect on the experience of "walking" that is going on today in Latin America, the experience of the road to holiness—to use a term not often mentioned in discussion of such difficult and controversial contexts as ours. I am convinced, nonetheless, of the universality and urgency of the call of Jesus: "You, therefore, must be perfect, as your heavenly Father is perfect" (Matt. 5:48). In addition, I think that in the final analysis only holiness can certify, and render binding on the entire church, the testimony of those who are trying to express their faith and hope through solidarity with, and love for, the poor and oppressed of Latin America—those who thus express their option for life.

Spirituality is a community enterprise. It is the passage of a people through the solitude and dangers of the desert, as it carves out its own way in the following of Jesus Christ. This spiritual experience is the well from which we must drink. From it we draw the promise of resurrection.
—From *We Drink from Our Own Wells* by Gustavo Gutiérrez

❧ Conversion is what happens between birth and death. By putting emphasis on conversion as a process, I do not mean to disclaim the many accounts of people being suddenly and mysteriously touched by God and changed tremendously. There are too many stories of radical change in people's lives to take them lightly. However, even people who have had a dramatic encounter with the Divine, still must go through that daily purifying process of continued conversion. A deep and lasting conversion is a process, an unfolding, a slow turning and turning again.

We are saved every day. We are saved from our self-righteousness, our narrow minds, our own wills, our obstinate clinging. We are saved from our blindness. Salvation stands before us at every moment. It meets us face to face. It asks us to make a choice. Do we have the courage to accept it? It is costly, yet it brings life. The cross is always costly. It costs us our lives. The dust of our Lenten ashes turns before our very eyes into Easter glory. Our frailty fades into splendor. Our life given becomes life received and renewed.

Transformation! This is a wondrous, glorious truth. It is the Paschal Mystery. Life meets death. Death meets resurrection. This is our hope. We are frail and glorious creatures. Our frailty need not cripple us; our glory need not be denied. Embraced and cherished as part of the process that we are, these qualities become God's greatest advantage in our lives.

—From *A Tree Full of Angels* by Macrina Wiederkehr

❧ Imagine a man sound asleep. His wife, who has been away for a very long time, returns unexpectedly in the middle of the night, approaches his bed, bends down and awakens him. The awakening is exquisite, not just because it is tender and caring, a gift beyond compare, but because it awakens in him a desire that meets the desire of the one that has awakened him. With the leash of love's longing this desire unites and binds together in a union that gives way to bliss.

God the eternal lover comes to us in the incomprehensible sense of creating us in [God's] image and likeness for himself alone.... The eternal love of God could not bear to see us living in ignorance, walking about in the sleep of unawareness, and so [God] awakened us to his eternal love for us in Christ. [God] awakened a desire for him which [God] has placed within us. Indeed, this desire for God is an expression of our inmost Self, our God-given identity, considered as a capacity to receive, return and enter into the fulfillment of the divine rapture of God's personal creation.

Our personal awakening to this capacity for divine union is our conversion, which has all the excitement of unexpectedly finding a pearl of great price. Our

decision to live in fidelity to the discovered gift is our discipleship, which involves all the risk and daring of selling everything we own in order to make the gift our own. Surrendering to the divine gift is our prayer.
—From *The Awakening Call* by James Finley

Hymn: Still, for Thy Loving-kindness, Lord

Still, for thy loving-kindness, Lord,
I in thy temple wait:
I look to find thee in thy word,
Or at thy table meet.

Here, in thine own appointed ways,
I wait to learn thy will:
Silent I stand before thy face,
And hear thee say, —Be still!

Be still! and know that I am God;
'Tis all I live to know;
To feel the virtue of thy blood,
And spread its praise below.

I wait my vigor to renew,
Thine image to retrieve;
The veil of outward things pass through,
And gasp in thee to live.
—Charles Wesley

13: The Abundance of God's Mercy

I. Invocation
    Merciful God, were it not for your mercy, I would remain lost in sin and confusion. Thank you for your extravagant grace and your mercy without limit. In this hour hold me in love, even as a mother cradles her child. Amen.

II. Psalm 116

III. Reading and Reflection

IV. Daily Scripture Readings
Monday	1 Peter 2:1-10
Tuesday	Jeremiah 3:1-14
Wednesday	Luke 1:47-56
Thursday	Isaiah 63:7-14
Friday	James 2:1-13
Saturday	Luke 6:27-36

    Sunday A. Isaiah 49:8-13; 1 Corinthians 3:10-11, 16-23; Psalm 62:5-12; Matthew 5:27-37
    B. Isaiah 43:18-25; 2 Corinthians 1:18-22; Psalm 41; Mark 2:1-12
    C. Genesis 45:3-11, 15; 1 Corinthians 15:35-38, 42-50; Psalm 37:1-11; Luke 6:27-38

V. Reflection: Silent and Written

VI. Prayers: For the Church, for Others, for Myself

VII. Hymn: "Jesus, Lover of My Soul"

VIII. Benediction
    Now, my Lord, as I leave this place, may your mercy be in me a flowing river reaching out to all whose paths shall touch my own. Amen.

If this is the Last Sunday after Epiphany, use Week 15.

Readings for Reflection

❧ I believe that, as a general rule, the weight of my prayer when I turn to God to acknowledge my failure should rest neither on self-blame nor on petition for forgiveness but on my overarching need for divine help, for wisdom to see and strength to do what is right. An old but familiar prayer perfectly expresses this need; "O God, forasmuch as without thee we are not able to please thee, mercifully grant that thy Holy Spirit may in all things direct and rule our hearts."
—From *The Heart in Pilgrimage* by Christopher Bryant

❧ None can believe how powerful prayer is, and what it is able to effect, but those who have learned it by experience. It is a great matter when in extreme need to take hold on prayer. I know, whenever I have prayed earnestly, that I have been amply heard, and have obtained more than I prayed for. God indeed sometimes delayed, but at last [God] came.
—Martin Luther

❧ It is not enough to begin to pray, nor to pray aright; nor is it enough to continue *for a time* to pray; but we must patiently, believingly, continue in prayer until we obtain an answer; and further we have not only to *continue* in prayer unto the end, but we have also *to believe* that God does hear us, and will answer our prayers. Most frequently we fail *in not continuing* in prayer until the blessing is obtained, and *in not expecting* the blessing.
—From *Autobiography* by George Müeller

❧ My Lord Jesus, I really long to thank You once more with all my heart for Your amazing grace in granting me the privilege of being Your child. My joy at this overwhelming act of grace and this glorious privilege, and my love for You are sometimes so great that I feel as though I shall burst. All I can do is praise You. Yet I have often been so cold towards You for long periods of time. Forgive me, Lord. But now let my life be aflame with love for You alone. And when I do not abide fully in You, lead me along paths of lowliness until I am free of all worldly, human interests and belong to You alone. Grant me the grace to glorify Your name wherever You place me. Oh, that I may reflect Your countenance one day so that even non-Christians would know that it was only Your doing, Lord Jesus. Take my life, Lord. I long to live for You. Use me. I surrender myself to You with all that I am and have. . . . Grant that I may be clothed with Your love and humility.

—From *I Found the Key to the Heart of God* by Basilea Schlink

❧ I know a Norwegian pastor who was arrested for his share in the underground, and after a trial in Germany was sentenced to death and who, by a series of extraordinary events, was still among the living when the war ground to a close in 1945. I once asked him what happens inside a [person] when a sentence of death is passed upon him [or her]. He could only speak for himself, he replied, but for him, it was an occasion when a great flood of heavenly mercy poured into his heart: for his judges, for his captors, for the Norwegian Quislings, for his countrymen, for all [people] everywhere. It was a mercy so clean that he regretted his own death only because he would no longer be about to try to change the hearts of [people] at the war's close to help them to make their decisions in this all-encompassing climate of compassion.

—From *Together in Solitude* by Douglas V. Steere

❧ Holiness, I believe, involves rediscovering the moral vision Jesus embodies in a way that invokes in us a sense of thirst rather than demand. "Happy are they who have not walked in the counsel of the wicked, nor lingered in the way of sinners, nor sat in the seat of the scornful! Their *delight* is in the law of the Lord, and they meditate on his law day and night" (Ps. 1:1-2). "O

Lord I *love* your Law; all the day long it is on my mind"
(Ps. 119:97). The commandments of God have too often
been presented in our tradition only as moral precepts
by which we can judge our neighbors, rather than as a
vision in which the call to holiness is rooted. Our
concern is not to have presented to us a blueprint for
life that will allow us to avoid risk, but rather a vision
of integrity from which decisions are made and life is
lived. Similarly, our concern for the Law and the prophetic insight into the power of evil as it operates in the
world is not to win God's acceptance by so-called right
behavior, but to know within ourselves the desperate
need we have for the Grace offered to us in Jesus
Christ.
—From *Invitation to Holiness* by James C. Fenhagen

&ewline; John Wesley sought for ways to express his spiritual
life throughout the day. He found the way in what he
called the "means of grace." These were spiritual disciplines which people used to express their faith and
receive God's grace. They were divided into two cate-
gories: the instituted means of grace and the prudential
means of grace. The instituted means were those disciplines evident in the life and teaching of Jesus. The
prudential means were those which had been developed
by the church to give further order and expression to
the Christian life. Taken together, they enabled a person to live a devotional life.
—From *Devotional Life in the Wesleyan Tradition* by Steve
Harper

&ewline; We stand in the midst of nourishment and we
starve. We dwell in the land of plenty, yet we persist in
going hungry. Not only do we dwell in the land of
plenty; we have the capacity to be filled with the utter
fullness of God (Eph. 3:16-19). In the light of such
possibility, what happens? Why do we drag our hearts?
Lock up our souls? Why do we limp? Why do we
straddle the issues? Why do we live so feebly, so dimly?
Why aren't we saints?

Each of us could come up with individual answers to all these questions, but I want to suggest here a common cause. The reason we live life so dimly and with such divided hearts is that we have never really learned how to be present with quality to God, to self, to others, to experiences and events, to all created things. We have never learned to gather up the crumbs of whatever appears in our path at every moment. We meet all of these lovely gifts only half there. Presence is what we are all starving for. Real presence! We are too busy to be present, too blind to see the nourishment and salvation in the crumbs of life, the experiences of each moment. Yet the secret of daily life is this: *There are no leftovers!*

There is nothing—no thing, no person, no experience, no thought, no joy or pain—that cannot be harvested and used for nourishment on our journey to God.

—From *A Tree Full of Angels* by Macrina Wiederkehr

Hymn: Jesus, Lover of My Soul

Jesus, lover of my soul,
Let me to thy bosom fly,
While the nearer waters roll,
While the tempest still is high.
Hide me, O my Savior, hide,
Till the storm of life is past;
Safe into the haven guide,
O receive my soul at last.

Other refuge have I none
Hangs my helpless soul on thee;
Leave, ah! leave me not alone,
Still support and comfort me.
All my trust on thee is stayed,
All my help from thee I bring;
Cover my defenseless head
With the shadow of thy wing.

Thou, O Christ, art all I want,
More than all in thee I find;
Raise the fallen, cheer the faint,
Heal the sick, and lead the blind.
Just and holy is thy name,
I am all unrighteousness;
False and full of sin I am;
Thou art full of truth and grace.

Plenteous grace with thee is found,
Grace to cover all my sin;
Let the healing streams abound,
Make and keep me pure within.
Thou of life the fountain art,
Freely let me take of thee;
Spring thou up within my heart;
Rise to all eternity.
—Charles Wesley

*Eighth Sunday after Epiphany**
(between February 25 and 29)

14: Good People—Good Actions

I. Invocation
    Almighty God, who created us and whose we are, help us to number our days and to live them wisely. Give us your Holy Spirit to guide and strengthen us—to the end that the world may be a better place because we have passed through it. In the name of Jesus. Amen.

II. Psalm 37:1-11

III. Reading and Reflection

IV. Daily Scripture Readings
Monday	Hosea 14:1-9
Tuesday	Micah 6:1-8
Wednesday	Matthew 12:22-37
Thursday	Luke 19:11-27
Friday	Hebrews 13:1-16
Saturday	Ephesians 2:1-10

Sunday   A. Leviticus 19:1-2, 9-18; 1 Corinthians 4:1-5; Psalm 119:33-40; Matthew 5:38-48
          B. Hosea 2:14-20; 2 Corinthians 3:1-6; Psalm 103:1-13; Mark 2:18-22
          C. Isaiah 55:10-13; 1 Corinthians 15:51-58; Psalm 92:1-4, 12-15; Luke 6:39-49

V. Reflection: Silent and Written

VI. Prayers: For the Church, for Others, for Myself

VII. Hymn: "Forth in Thy Name, O Lord"

VIII. Benediction
    My Lord, go with me into this day that I may show faith by my good deeds. Amen.

If this is the Last Sunday after Epiphany, use Week 15.

Readings for Reflection

🌿 Buckminster Fuller put forth the idea that the purpose of people on earth is to counteract the tide of entropy described in the Second Law of Thermodynamics. Physical things are falling apart at a terrific rate; people, on the other hand, put things together. People build bridges and cities and roads; they write music and novels and constitutions; they have ideas. That is why people are here. The universe *needs* somebody or something to keep it from falling apart. Fuller didn't include prayer in his work list, so I will supplement him: prayer remakes undoing.

—From *Earth and Altar* by Eugene H. Peterson

🌿 "Prayer is the language of Christian community," writes Henri Nouwen. "In prayer the nature of the community becomes visible because in prayer we direct ourselves to the one who forms the community. We do not pray to each other, but together we pray to God, who calls us and makes us a new people." It is in the act of worship that we experience the gift of community at its deepest level. In the eucharistic offering of bread and wine, our brokenness and separation are offered in symbolic union with the broken body of Christ, and then given back transformed and made whole as a sign of that new community brought into being by his resurrection. If we are to understand what it means to be community-builders, we must do so from this perspective. Ministry is given to us by God. It remains authentic only as it is empowered at its source, supported and guided by the community of faith, and then shared with others. "Make me an instrument of your peace," prayed St. Francis. "Where there is hatred, let me sow love; where there is injury, pardon; where there is discord, union." This is what it means to exercise a community-building ministry, to be in the fullest sense, an ambassador of reconciliation.

—From *Mutual Ministry* by James C. Fenhagen

❧ Poverty keeps people in moral equilibrium, keeps hard-working families virtuous, sets limits to their desire for possessions, preserves humility in personal relationships, encourages them to be industrious, nourishes hope.

I say "poverty," not misery.

Poverty is the happy medium between two curses.

The one is wealth, which is nearly always the fruit of exploitation, injustice or extortion; the other, misery, is evidence of an evil deed committed by you or by others against you.

—From *Why, O Lord?* by Carlo Carretto

❧ Goodness is something so simple: always to live for others, never to seek one's own advantage.

—From *Markings* by Dag Hammarskjöld

❧ Almighty God, Heavenly Father,
Loving-Healing-Caring, hear my prayer.
As I thank you for all your love
 your presence
 your holy presence
 your loving acceptance,
  it comforts me
  to know you
  care for me.

All around me are loving-affirming people,
 people who love you
 care for you
 serve you.

Thank you, Lord, for those here who
 strengthen my faith—who share the
 ministry of your word.

I pray, Lord, for a renewal of spirit,
a healing of my body
 and I praise you, Lord,
 for the victories that have been
 won by your power.

Lord, be with those who call upon you for
help in the deep times of their lives.
Help me—and those I minister to—
to fix their eyes—their minds
on Jesus Christ
And to remember that
you are the Lord of our life
and the Lord of our death.

Living we serve you.
Dying we are with you.
Dispel our fears
And fill us with a confidence
that you are the God
always, now and *forever,*
even where we do not understand the forever.
Hear my prayer.
Thank you Lord.
In Jesus' name
I pray. Amen.
—From the journal of Richard Allen Ward

ঌ However, prayer is no panacea, no substitute for
action. It is, rather, like a beam thrown from a flashlight
before us into the darkness. It is in this light that we
who grope, stumble and climb, discover where we
stand, what surrounds us, and the course which we
should choose. Prayer makes visible the right, and
reveals what is hampering and false. In its radiance, we
behold the worth of our efforts, the range of our hopes,
and the meaning of our deeds. Envy and fear, despair
and resentment, anguish and grief, which lie heavily
upon the heart, are dispelled like shadows by its light.
—From *Quest for God* by Abraham Joshua Heschel

ঌ So the hunger that many of us exhibit, our thirst for
living water unadulterated by passion or selfishness, is
in faith's view a desire to partake in God's own life.
The God who has left witness everywhere is trying to
show us the greater fullness of life we could find if we

would leave our worldly passions and open ourselves to the divine Mysteries.

From this perspective (of the theology of grace), the struggles of conscience that we go through are more than just exercises in character building or good citizenship. What is at issue in our choices for honesty or cheating, selfishness or generosity, fidelity or adultery is opening or closing to the Mystery of God, the offer of divine life. It certainly helps to have this offer clarified by the revelation of Jesus and to place oneself in the midst of the Christian church. But there are people outside the church who are responding generously to God's grace and people inside the church who have closed themselves. Indeed, the sinfulness and closure of many churchgoers is a prime stumbling block to those weighing the claims of the gospel, just as the goodness and openness of many churchgoers is a prime attraction. Wholeness requires a willingness to keep going, keep putting off selfishness and sloth. Many more people wish they were whole than are willing to work hard to become whole.

—From *Maturing a Christian Conscience* by John Carmody

❧ Most people's notion of goodness is related to agreeable behavior or flawless morality. God's idea of goodness is concerned with something much more than that. . . . [God] created the world and all of the aspects of it, . . . [God] reviewed his work and concluded, "It is good." At the end of the sixth day of creation . . . [God] formed a human being, and then . . . said, "It is very good."

In the Hebrew text there is nothing uncomplicated about the use of the word *good* in this passage. It means that all of the aspects of creation are ready and able to fulfill their purpose. The plant life, the seas, the fish that swim in the seas, the animals that roam the plains, and the supreme and sublime level of his creation, human beings, are all able to function as they were intended. All are good.

Now all of creation is to be a glory to God and a manifestation of [God's] power. Our essential purpose

in creation is to glorify God and enjoy [God] forever. Insofar as "all creatures great and small" keep a life consistent with the basic reason for which they exist, goodness is maintained.
—From *Radiance of the Inner Splendor* by Lloyd John Ogilvie

꙳ Make us, O Lord, to flourish like pure lilies in the courts of Thine house, and to show forth to the faithful the fragrance of good words, and the example of a Godly life, through Thy mercy and grace. Amen.
—Mozarabic Sacramentary

Hymn: Forth in Thy Name, O Lord

Forth in thy name, O Lord, I go,
My daily labor to pursue;
Thee, only thee, resolved to know
In all I think or speak or do.

The task thy wisdom hath assigned,
O let me cheerfully fulfill;
In all my works thy presence find,
And prove thy good and perfect will.

Thee may I set at my right hand,
Whose eyes mine inmost substance see,
And labor on at thy command,
And offer all my works to thee.

For thee delightfully employ
Whate'er thy bounteous grace hath given;
And run my course with even joy,
And closely walk with thee to heaven.
—Charles Wesley

15: *God's Transforming Power*

I.   Invocation
Almighty God, who is able to make all things new and to restore life anew every morning, help me never to be conformed to the world but to be transformed by the constant renewing of my mind. Through the Spirit of Christ. Amen.

II.   Psalm 66

III.   Reading and Reflection

IV.   Daily Scripture Readings

Monday	2 Corinthians 3:4-18
Tuesday	1 Peter 1:13-25
Wednesday	Hebrews 1:1-4
Thursday	Jeremiah 32:16-27
Friday	Luke 9:1-6
Saturday	Luke 24:36-53
Sunday	A. Exodus 24:12-18; 2 Peter 1:16-21; Psalm 2:6-11; Matthew 17:1-9
	B. 2 Kings 2:1-12a; 2 Corinthians 4:3-6; Psalm 50:1-6; Mark 9:2-9
	C. Exodus 34:29-35; 2 Corinthians 3:12–4:2; Psalm 99; Luke 9:28-36

V.   Reflection: Silent and Written

VI.   Prayers: For the Church, for Others, for Myself

VII.   Hymn: "Creating God, Your Fingers Trace"

VIII.   Benediction
Help me today, my Lord, to discover your good, perfect, and acceptable will and to focus all of my desire and energy upon doing it. Amen.

Readings for Reflection

❧ As I have said before, there are only two ways of losing our sense of dependence, of subservience to the opinion of others: pride or humility. There is that form of humility which consists in accepting neither [people's] censure nor their praise, but in remaining simply before the judgement of God and one's own conscience, as in the story of a brother who wanted to know how he should respond to praise and to criticism. "Go to the graveyard," said his spiritual father, "and abuse the dead." He did so and when he came back his father asked him what the dead had done. "Nothing," said the young monk, "they remained silent." "Go back and praise them," said the elder. And when his disciple had reported that the cemetery stayed as silent as before, he said: "Do the same as the dead; human judgement no longer affects them for they stand always in the sight of God."

—From *Meditations on a Theme* by Anthony of Sourozh

❧ Perhaps you remember the touching and heart-rending phrase of young St. Vincent de Paul: "O God, I am too ugly for human beings, perhaps you have a use for me?" We are all ugly but we are all dear to God who has faith in us. Would [God] otherwise have taken the risk of calling into existence for all eternity—not for a passing moment—each one of us? . . . Instead of asking ceaselessly the question "what is wrong with me?" why not ask ourselves the question "in what way am I already akin to God? in harmony with [God]? How far am I on the way of reaching the full measure of the stature of Christ?" Would not that be more inspiring in our striving for perfection?

—From *Meditations on a Theme* by Anthony of Sourozh

❧ May there fall upon me now, O God, a great sense of Thy power and Thy glory, so that I may see all earthly things in their true measure.

Let me not be ignorant of this great thing, that one day is with Thee as a thousand years and a thousand years as one day.

Give me now such understanding of Thy perfect holiness as will make an end of all pride in my own attainment.

Grant unto me now such a vision of Thine uncreated beauty as will make me dissatisfied with all lesser beauties

> *Though earth and [all] were gone,*
> *And suns and universes cease to be,*
> *And Thou wert left alone,*
> *Every existence would exist in Thee.*

I am content, O Father, to leave my life in Thy hands, believing that the very hairs upon my head are numbered by Thee. I am content to give over my will to Thy control, believing that I can find in Thee a righteousness that I could never have won for myself. I am content to leave all my dear ones to Thy care, believing that Thy love for them is greater than my own. I am content to leave in Thy hands the causes of truth and of justice, and the coming of Thy Kingdom in the hearts of [people], believing that my ardour for them is but a feeble shadow of Thy purpose. To Thee, O God, be glory for ever. Amen.

—From *A Diary of Private Prayer* by John Baillie

ی۔ The will of God. That's what rules the world and moves the stars, what converts the nations, what starts all life and brings triumph out of death.

The will of God raised up Abraham, our father in faith; it called Moses, inspired David, prepared Mary, sustained Joseph, made Christ incarnate and demanded his sacrifice; this it was that founded the Church. And it is God's will still to continue the work of redemption until the end of time.

—From *Letters from the Desert* by Carlo Carretto

❧ Everything disappears in comparison with the eternal God, and the greatest things become as nothing.
—From *Love Is for Living* by Carlo Carretto

❧ Later the soul will bring forth fruit exactly in the measure in which the inner life is developed in it. If there is no inner life, however great may be the zeal, the high intention, the hard work, no fruit will come forth; it is like a spring that would give out sanctity to others but cannot, having none to give; one can only give that which one has. It is in solitude, in that lonely life alone with God, in profound recollection of soul, in forgetfulness of all created things, that God gives himself to the soul that thus gives itself whole and entire to [God].
—From *Meditations of a Hermit* by Charles de Foucauld

❧ There is much wisdom in the old joke about the man who falls off a cliff and is on his way down a two-hundred-foot drop. At about one hundred feet he grasps a single, unsturdy branch. As he hangs there he cries for help. A voice comes over the side of the hill, saying, "Yes, my son." The man cries up, "Who are you?" The voice answers, "I am God." The man says "Help me." The voice says, "Certainly." The man questions: "What do I have to do?" The voice says, "Let go of the branch." The man looks down, looks up, and pleads: "Is there anyone else up there?"
—From *Inviting the Mystic, Supporting the Prophet* by Katherine Marie Dyckman and L. Patrick Carroll

❧ There is a power that destroys. There is also a power that creates. The power that creates gives life and joy and peace. It is freedom and not bondage, life and not death, transformation and not coercion. The power that creates restores relationship and gives the gift of wholeness to all. The power that creates is spiritual power, the power that proceeds from God.
—From *Money, Sex and Power* by Richard J. Foster

ᐅ Merton often bemoaned the widespread mistrust of mysticism by monks, as well as by those in other walks of life. Too many no longer even believe in the possibility of genuine mystical union with God, much less see it as a vital dimension of the holiness of the Church. Merton would say that we dare not place any limitation on what is possible in prayer. We dare not waver from the childlike faith that knows without reserve that all things are possible in prayer.

—From *Merton's Palace of Nowhere* by James Finley

ᐅ Prayer, as the distilled awareness of our whole life before God, is meant to lead us to a radical transformation of consciousness in which all of life becomes a symbol. All of life is seen as God sees it. All of life is seen simply as it is.

Prayer is the fertile soil in which the insight into our true self in God takes root and grows. As our true awareness grows, as we see through the eyes of the Person we are, we see with a new vision. We see the Presence of God in all that is. Each thing becomes a symbol of communion with God just by being the thing it is.

—From *Merton's Palace of Nowhere* by James Finley

ᐅ If the emphasis on prayer were an escape from direct engagement with the many needs and pains of our world, then it would not be a real discipline of the compassionate life. Prayer challenges us to be fully aware of the world in which we live and to present it with all its needs and pains to God. It is this compassionate prayer that calls for compassionate action. The disciple is called to follow the Lord not only into the desert and onto the mountain to pray but also into the valley of tears, where help is needed, and onto the cross, where humanity is in agony. Prayer and action, therefore, can never be seen as contradictory or mutually exclusive. Prayer without action grows into powerless pietism, and action without prayer degenerates into questionable manipulation. If prayer leads us into a deeper unity with the compassionate Christ, it will always give rise to concrete acts of service. And if concrete acts of service do indeed lead us into a deeper solidarity with the poor, the hungry, the sick, the dying, and the oppressed, they will always give rise to prayer. In prayer we meet Christ, and in him all human suffering. In service we meet people, and in them the suffering Christ.

—From *Compassion: A Reflection on the Christian Life* by Donald P. McNeill, Douglas A. Morrison and Henri J.M. Nouwen

❧ Now let this *perfection* appear in its native form, and who can speak one word against it? Will any dare to speak against loving the Lord our God with all our heart, and our neighbor as ourselves? Against a renewal of heart, not only in part, but in the whole image of God? Who...will open his [or her] mouth against being cleansed from all pollution both of flesh and spirit? Or against having all the mind that was in Christ, and walking in all things as Christ walked? ... What serious [person] would oppose the giving God all our heart and the having one design ruling all our tempers?

—John Wesley (*Classics of Western Spirituality* Series)

Hymn: Creating God, Your Fingers Trace

Creating God, your fingers trace
The bold designs of farthest space;
Let sun and moon and stars and light
And what lies hidden praise your might.

Redeeming God, your arms embrace
All now despised for creed or race;
Let peace, descending like a dove,
Make known on earth your healing love.

Indwelling God, your gospel claims
One family with a billion names;
Let every life be touched by grace
Until we praise you face to face.

—Jeffery Rowthorn

16: Getting Ready to Serve

I. Invocation
Ever-vigilant God, who calls and equips me to serve your creation, help me to live in constant readiness, so that upon your return I may be numbered among those wise maidens who carried sufficient oil to keep their lamps burning. Through the power of Christ. Amen.

II. Psalm 19

III. Reading and Reflection

IV. Daily Scripture Readings

Monday	Luke 16:1-13
Tuesday	Matthew 20:20-28
Wednesday	Philippians 2:1-11
Thursday	Hebrews 12:12-17
Friday	1 Peter 4:1-11
Saturday	John 12:20-36
Sunday	A. Genesis 2:4b-9, 15-17, 25–3:7; Romans 5:12-19; Psalm 130; Matthew 4:1-11
	B. Genesis 9:8-17; 1 Peter 3:18-22; Psalm 25:1-10; Mark 1:9-15
	C. Deuteronomy 26:1-11; Romans 10:8b-13; Psalm 91:9-16; Luke 4:1-13

V. Reflection: Silent and Written

VI. Prayers: For the Church, for Others, for Myself

VII. Hymn: "Dear Lord, Whose Loving Eyes Can See"

VIII. Benediction
Lord, help me remember the wise maidens and those foolish ones who were unprepared for your coming—that I may choose the better way. Amen.

Readings for Reflection

❧ The Desert Fathers renounced speech in order to learn compassion. A charming story is told of Abbot Macarius, who said to the brethren in the Church of Scete, "Brethren, flee." Perplexed, one of the brothers asked, "How can we fly further than this, seeing we are here in the desert?" Macarius placed his finger to his mouth and said, "Flee from this." When Arsenius, the Roman educator who gave up his status and wealth for the solitude of the desert, prayed, "Lord, lead me into the way of salvation," he heard a voice saying, "Be silent."

Silence frees us from the need to control others. One reason we can hardly bear to remain silent is that it makes us feel so helpless. We are accustomed to relying upon words to manage and control others. A frantic stream of words flows from us in an attempt to straighten others out. We want so desperately for them to agree with us, to see things our way. We evaluate people, judge people, condemn people. We devour people with our words. Silence is one of the deepest Disciplines of the Spirit simply because it puts the stopper on that.

—From *Freedom of Simplicity* by Richard J. Foster

❧ There is one thing still remaining which cannot be neglected without great injury to your devotions: to begin all your prayers with a psalm.

There is nothing that so clears a way for your prayers, nothing that so disperses dullness of heart, nothing that so purifies the soul from poor and little passions, nothing that so opens heaven or carries your heart so near it as these songs of praise. They create a sense of delight in God; they awaken holy desires; they teach how to ask; and they prevail with God to give. They kindle a holy flame; they turn your heart into an altar; they turn your prayers into incense and carry them as sweet-smelling savor to the throne of grace.

—From *A Serious Call to a Devout and Holy Life* by William Law

❧ Listen, O Lord, to my prayers. Listen to my desire to be with you, to dwell in your house, and to let my whole being be filled with your presence. But none of this is possible without you. When you are not the one who fills me, I am soon filled with endless thoughts and concerns that divide me and tear me away from you. Even thoughts about you, good spiritual thoughts, can be little more than distractions when you are not their author.

O Lord, thinking about you, being fascinated with theological ideas and discussions, being excited about histories of Christian spirituality and stimulated by thoughts and ideas about prayer and meditation, all of this can be as much an expression of greed as the unruly desire for food, possessions, or power.

Every day I see again that only you can teach me to pray, only you can set my heart at rest, only you can let me dwell in your presence. No book, no idea, no concept or theory will ever bring me close to you unless you yourself are the one who lets these instruments become the way to you.

But, Lord, let me at least remain open to your initiative; let me wait patiently and attentively for that hour when you will come and break through all the walls I have erected. Teach me, O Lord, to pray. Amen.
—From *A Cry for Mercy* by Henri J. M. Nouwen

❧ The more aware we become of the range of human need that surrounds us, the more overwhelmed we can become to the point that we end up doing nothing. The secret of the compassionate life is to focus our care on a few things that we can do something about, including in our intercessions those concerns that are beyond our reach. I know of one person who chose to focus all of his energy on dealing with the problem of Vietnamese refugees. He stayed with this until he felt he had made some genuine contribution, resisting the sometimes angry entreaties of friends to take on things which, to them, were more urgent. The ability to bring into focus the energy we expend is of critical importance to the

Christian journey. It allows us to give to others without losing touch with ourselves. It reminds us that we are finite, with the freedom to say no as well as yes in the recognition that our particular gifts can be used in some ways better than others.

—From *Mutual Ministry* by James C. Fenhagen

❧ I have long known that if I want to be happy on earth I must fall madly in love with God and the things of God.

Then, all things being equal, in time of suffering the easiest way to allay the suffering, especially if it is really sharp, is to get out of myself—yes, get out of myself; visit someone who is suffering worse than I am, do something to remind me of the sufferings of the world, set my heart in order if I feel a residual dislike of someone, write a cheque for the world's poorest mission, answer a tiresome letter from someone who wants me to tell him whether hell exists, or what he should not do to leave his nasty possessive wife.

In other words, perform an act of love that requires patience and honesty.

—From *Why, O Lord?* by Carlo Carretto

❧ No, it is not easy to grasp that the only way to suffer less is to love more, especially in politics. At the risk of seeming weaker. Yes, at the risk of seeming weaker I shall not build an atomic bomb, I shall not give my enemy a whack in the eye to show that I am stronger, I shall not make war, I shall not squash my tomatoes and apples with a tractor to keep the price up, I shall not destroy forests to build factories, I shall not poison the sea.

If love is the rule of my politics and the thrust of my action, yes, I really shall suffer less and I shall cause less suffering in others, some I shall be loving more.

—From *Why, O Lord?* by Carlo Carretto

❧ When you pray, you profess that you are not God and that you wouldn't want to be, that you haven't

reached your goal yet, and that you never will reach it in this life, that you must constantly stretch out your hands and wait again for the gift which gives new life. This attitude is difficult because it makes you vulnerable.
—From *With Open Hands* by Henri J. M. Nouwen

❧ The grace of giving is often a tremendous stimulant to the life of faith. This is why the offering is correctly placed as part of the worship experience.

In Isaiah 58 we read of a very religious people whose pious devotion counted for nothing because it was not matched with active caring for the poor and the oppressed. "Is not this the fast that I choose," proclaims God, "to loose the bonds of wickedness, to undo the thongs of the yoke, to let the oppressed go free, and to break every yoke?" (Isa. 58:6). Religious piety is bankrupt without justice. If you want your fasting to have true spiritual content, then you are to "share your bread with the hungry, and bring the homeless poor into your house" (Isa. 58:7).
—From *Money, Sex and Power* by Richard J. Foster

❧ It is to these alone who, knowing they have not yet attained, neither are already perfect, mind this one thing, and, pressing toward the mark, despise no assistance which is offered them, that the following advices are proposed, concerning the manner of reading this (or any other religious) treatise.

First: Assign some stated time every day for this employment; and observe it, so far as you possibly can, inviolably. But if necessary business, which you could not foresee or defer, should sometimes rob you of your hour of retirement, take the next to it; or, if you cannot have that, at least the nearest you can.

Secondly: Prepare yourself for reading, by purity of intention singly aiming at the good of your soul, and by fervent prayer [that you be enabled] to see [God's] will, and give you a firm resolution to perform it. An excellent form of prayer for this very purpose you have in the second or third book of this treatise.

Thirdly: Be sure to read, not cursorily or hastily, but leisurely, seriously, and with great attention; with proper pauses and intervals, and that you may allow time for the enlightenings of the divine grace. To this end, recollect, every now and then, what you have read, and consider how to reduce it to practice.

—John Wesley (*Classics of Western Spirituality* Series)

Hymn: Dear Lord, Whose Loving Eyes Can See

Dear Lord, whose loving eyes can see
Each troubled mind without, within,
We bring our week of life to thee,
All soiled and worn and marred with sin.

We bring our bitterness of heart,
Our hate and want of charity.
Help us to choose the better part,
And learn to love, dear Lord, like thee.

We bring our care for daily bread,
The fear that turns the heart to stone.
We cry to thee; lift up our head
And show us we are not alone.

We bring the faith that over all,
Though faint and feeble, flickers still.
Increase it, Lord, that at thy call
We may our daily task fulfill.

Lord, make us pure; enrich our life
With heavenly love for evermore.
Give us thy strength to face the strife,
And serve thee better than before.

—Edwin Gilbert

17: What God Has Promised

I. Invocation
    O God, whose promises are true, help me never to stagger in disbelief at your promises but to claim them as my own. In the name of Christ. Amen.

II. Psalm 119:33-48

III. Reading and Reflection

IV. Daily Scripture Readings
     Monday   1 Kings 8:22-30
     Tuesday   Nehemiah 9:6-25
     Wednesday   Romans 4:16-25
     Thursday   James 1:1-15
     Friday   2 Corinthians 1:12-22
     Saturday   2 Peter 3:5-13
     Sunday   A. Genesis 12:1-4a, (46-8); Romans 4:1-5, (6-12), 13-17; Psalm 33: 18-22; John 3:1-17
                B. Genesis 17:1-10, 15-19; Romans 4:16-25; Psalm 105:1-11; Mark 8: 31-38
                C. Genesis 15:1-12, 17-18; Philippians 3:17–4:1; Psalm 127; Luke 13:31-35

V. Reflection: Silent and Written

VI. Prayers: For the Church, for Others, for Myself

VII. Hymn: "O God of Every Nation"

VIII. Benediction
       How good it is to know you, my Lord, as the one who ever lives to make your promise good. In this confidence I go now in your name. Amen.

Readings for Reflection

❧ Even at the physical level we are not autonomous. We depend entirely on a distant sun. If the sun should fail for a single week we would be plunged into icy chaotic destruction.

As the earth depends on the sun, so human beings depend on their sun. What this sun is is something I have got to find out; but I certainly depend on a sun. And it is from this sun that life comes, since my own is not sufficient in itself and I long for a life that will be eternal.

It is unthinkable that the inventor of [humankind] would have destined us to futile extinction.
—From *Why, O Lord?* by Carlo Carretto

❧ Get these three Principles fixed in your hearts: that Things eternal are much more considerable than Things temporal; that Things not seen are as certain as the Things that are seen; that upon your present choice depends your eternal lot. Choose Christ and his ways, and you are blessed forever; refuse, and you are undone forever.
—John Wesley (*Classics of Western Spirituality* Series)

❧ Contemplative prayer is the world in which God can do anything. To move into that realm is the greatest adventure. It is to be open to the Infinite and hence to infinite possibilities. Our private, self-made worlds come to an end; a new world appears within and around us and the impossible becomes an everyday experience. Yet the world that prayer reveals is barely noticeable in the ordinary course of events.

Christian life and growth are founded on faith in our own basic goodness, in the being that God has given us with its transcendent potential. This gift of being is our true Self. Through our consent by faith, Christ is born in us and He and our true Self become one. Our awakening to the presence and action of the Spirit is the unfolding of Christ's resurrection in us.

All true prayer is based on the conviction of the presence of the Spirit in us and of [the Spirit's] unfailing and continual inspiration. Every prayer in this sense is prayer in the Spirit. Still, it seems more accurate to reserve the term *prayer in the Spirit*, for that prayer in which the inspiration of the Spirit is given directly to our spirit without the intermediary of our own reflections or acts of will. In other words, the Spirit prays in us and we consent. The traditional term for this kind of prayer is contemplation.

—*Open Mind, Open Heart* by Thomas Keating

ᦰ We reach the conclusion that faith alone justifies us and fulfils the law; and this because faith brings us the spirit gained by the merits of Christ. The spirit, in turn, gives us the happiness and freedom at which the law aims; and this shows that good works really proceed from faith. That is Paul's meaning in chapter 3 (:31) when, after having condemned the works of the law, he sounds as if he had meant to abrogate the law by faith; but says that, on the contrary, we confirm the law through faith, i.e., we fulfil it by faith.

—Martin Luther

ᦰ Permit me to add a few plain words to you likewise who overvalue reason. Why should you roam from one extreme to the other? Is not the middle way best? Let reason do all that reason can; employ it as far as it will go. But, at the same time, acknowledge it is utterly incapable of giving either faith, hope or love, and, consequently of producing either real virtue or substantial happiness. Expect these from a higher source, even from the Father of the spirits of all flesh. Seek and receive them, not as your own acquisition, but as the gift of God.

—John Wesley

ᦰ O Lord, Thou knowest what is the better way; let this or that be done as Thou shalt please. Give what Thou wilt, and how much Thou wilt, and when Thou wilt. Deal with me as Thou knowest, and best pleaseth Thee, and is most for Thy honor. Set me where Thou wilt and deal with me in all things as Thou wilt. I am in Thy hand; turn me round and turn me back again, even as a wheel. Behold I am Thy servant, prepared for all things; for I desire not to live unto myself, but unto Thee; and Oh that I could do it worthy and perfectly!

—Thomas à Kempis

  ❧ O eternal Father! O fiery abyss of charity! O eternal beauty, O eternal wisdom, O eternal goodness, O eternal mercy! O hope and refuge of sinners! O immeasurable generosity! O eternal, infinite Good! O mad lover! And you have need of your creature? It seems so to me, for you act as if you could not live without her, in spite of the fact that you are Life itself, and everything has life from you and nothing can have life without you. Why then are you so mad? Because you have fallen in love with what you have made! You are pleased and delighted over her within yourself, as if you were drunk (with desire) for her salvation. She runs away from you and you go looking for her. She strays and you draw closer to her. You clothed yourself in our humanity, and nearer than that you could not have come.

And what shall I say? I will stutter, "A-a," because there is nothing else I know how to say. Finite language cannot express the emotion of the soul who longs for you infinitely. I think I could echo Paul's words: The tongue cannot speak nor the ear hear nor the eye see nor the heart imagine what I have seen! What have you seen? "I have seen the hidden things of God!" And I—what do I say? I have nothing to add from these clumsy emotions (of mine). I say only, my soul, that you have tasted and seen the abyss of supreme eternal providence.

—From *The Dialogue* by Catherine of Siena (*Classics of Western Spirituality* Series)

Hymn: O God of Every Nation

O God of every nation,
Of every race and land,
Redeem your whole creation
With your almighty hand;
Where hate and fear divide us,
And bitter threats are hurled,
In love and mercy guide us,
And heal our strife-torn world.

From search for wealth and power
And scorn of truth and right,
From trust in bombs that shower
Destruction through the night,
From pride of race and station
And blindness to your way,
Deliver every nation,
Eternal God, we pray.

Lord, strengthen all who labor
That all may find release
From fear of rattling saber,
From dread of war's increase;
When hope and courage falter,
Lord, let your voice be heard;
With faith that none can alter,
Your servants undergird.

Keep bright in us the vision
Of days when war shall cease,
When hatred and division
Give way to love and peace,
Till dawns the morning glorious
When truth and justice reign,
And Christ shall rule victorious
O'er all the world's domain.
—William W. Reid, Jr.

Third Sunday in Lent
18: Meeting God Face to Face

I. Invocation
I come before you, my God, in all of my weakness seeking your strength. Though I am far from the model you set before my eyes, one day I will see you—and upon that seeing, I will become like you. O glorious anticipation! Amen.

II. Psalm 27

III. Reading and Reflection

IV. Daily Scripture Readings
Monday   Genesis 32:22-32
Tuesday   Exodus 3:1-12
Wednesday   Isaiah 55
Thursday   2 Corinthians 4:1-6
Friday   1 Corinthians 13:1-13
Saturday   Romans 8:1-17
Sunday   A. Exodus 17:3-7; Romans 5:1-11; Psalm 95; John 4:5-26, (27-42)
          B. Exodus 20:1-17; 1 Corinthians 1:22-25; Psalm 19:7-14; John 2:13-22
          C. Exodus 3:1-15; 1 Corinthians 10:1-13; Psalm 103:1-13; Luke 13:1-9

V. Reflection: Silent and Written

VI. Prayers: For the Church, for Others, for Myself

VII. Hymn: "Christ, upon the Mountain Peak"

VIII. Benediction
I go now from this place as one who sees through a glass dimly. Give me clear vision that I may not stumble but walk a straight path in your glorious light. Amen.

Readings for Reflection

&. As each one of us enters into the deeper places through contemplation, we come to see ourselves in our truest being, at the Source of our being in God. We come to see ourselves each moment coming forth from our Source, and not only ourselves but all others with us. By the intuition of the Spirit we come to know our solidarity with all being. This cannot but lead to compassion—compassion for our fellow humans who are one with us in our Source, in our call, and in our fate. We will know that in their completeness lies our completeness, and vice versa. We will continue to seek our own fullness, that we might be a source of fullness. And we will suffer our fellows' lack and rejoice in their fullness as our own lack and fullness. Moreover, we will know that oneness and compassion with the rest of creation that is the source of good stewardship and a true ecology.

—From M. Basil Pennington in *Living with Apocalypse* edited by Tilden H. Edwards

&. That God exists is no secret. It is clear to see!

That the human being is eternal is no secret. It's in the logic of things!

That God is good is no secret. It is the experience of every ready heart...

That God is immense is no secret. All you have to do is look at the universe.

That God is the memory of the world is no secret. All you have to do is glance at the computer.

That God is near is no secret. You only need to look at a couple on their honeymoon, or a hen with her chicks, or two friends talking, or an expectant mother.

But then, where is the secret?

Here it is: God is a crucified God.

God is the God who allows himself to be defeated, God is the God who has revealed himself in the poor.

God is the God who has washed my feet, God is Jesus of Nazareth.

We were not accustomed to a God like this.

—From *Why, O Lord?* by Carlo Caretto

᠈᠊ There is a story in the Talmud of a man who had a little daughter. She was his only child and when she became sick and died the father was filled with grief. His friends tried to comfort him, but he would not be comforted. Then one night he had a dream. He seemed to be in heaven and many little girls were there, acting their parts in a pageant. Each one carried a lighted candle, except for one whose candle was not lit. Looking more closely, he saw that the child with the unlit candle was his daughter. He took her in his arms and caressed her, then asked her why her candle was not burning like the others. "Often it does light," she answered him, "but your tears keep making it go out."

Mystery and miracle once meant the same thing. Now, as we orient ourselves to a new way of living, those two words may have again the same meaning. There are many things that cannot be explained. To try to force an explanation in pursuit of the mystery may, in this case, lessen the miracle. Don't try to grapple with the event of death with logic, but meet it with faith.

—From *Up the Golden Stair* by Elizabeth Yates

᠈᠊ God is actively present in each tiny human event persuading us by loving visions to transform ourselves continually. God is one of our constant relationships. God is in the midst of our deepest processes. Like one unique voice in a choir, one special instrument in an orchestra that blends with the many others, God is present persuading the many to become one in beauteous harmony.

—From *Where in the World Is God?* by Robert Brizee

᠈᠊ The day I stopped by to visit one of our church members, I discovered that she was having a very

difficult time. Her life was filled with one tragedy after another. She told me that sometimes she woke up in the morning not knowing how she was going to face the day as she wondered what sort of tragedy would come next. But then the tension in the muscles of her face seemed to relax, her mouth began to form a smile, her eyes began to brighten, and she said, "You know what I do? Every night I sit down with my Bible; I start to read and pray, and during those times it is as if Jesus is so close I could reach out and touch him. That is what gets me through." That is exactly what Jesus promised. He gives us himself; we are never left alone.
—From *Jesus Makes the Difference!* by James A. Harnish

❧ This is one part of the mystery of suffering:
God permits it.
God wounds me.
God destroys my harvests.
God rages in the storm.
God leads me to my death.
But precisely in wounding me [God] draws out the best in me.
If I were not wounded—how unbearable I should be in my fiendish security! How sure of myself!
Wounded, I remain calm and learn to weep. Weeping I learn to understand others, I learn the blessedness of poverty.
This is a fact.
If human beings had no pain, were never pushed to the limits of endurance, how hard it would be for them to enter the road to salvation!
If the Israelites had enjoyed freedom in Egypt, Moses could never have persuaded them to attempt the march of liberation.
If the desert had been full of beguiling oases instead of snakes, hunger and thirst, they would never have reached the Promised Land.
No spur can move us towards tomorrow more effectively than suffering.
That's why God struck Jacob on the hip.
—From *Why, O Lord?* by Carlo Carretto

જ Conversion to God, therefore, means a simultaneous conversion to the other persons who live with you on this earth. The farmer, the worker, the student, the prisoner, the sick, the black [person], the white [person], the weak, the strong, the oppressed and the oppressor, the patient and the one who heals, the tortured and the torturer, the boss and the flunky, not only are they people like you, but they are also called to make themselves heard and to give God a chance to be the God of all.

Thus compassion removes all pretensions, just as it removes false modesty. It invites you to understand everything, to see yourself in the light of God and to joyfully tell everyone you meet that there is no reason to fear; the land is free to be cultivated and to yield a rich harvest.

—From *With Open Hands* by Henri J. M. Nouwen

જ Have I been zealous to do, and active in doing, good? That is, have I embraced every probable opportunity of doing good, and preventing, removing, or lessening evil? Have I pursued it with my might? Have I thought anything too dear to part with, to serve my neighbor?

—John Wesley (*Classics of Western Spirituality* Series)

જ At this season we usually distribute coals and bread among the poor of the Society; but I now considered they wanted clothes as well as food. So on this and the four following days I walked through the town and begged two hundred pounds, in order to clothe them that wanted it most. But it was hard work, as most of the streets were filled with melting snow, which often lay ankle-deep, so that my feet were steeped in snow-water from morning till evening. I held it out pretty well till Saturday evening, when I was laid up with a violent flux.

—John Wesley

Hymn: Christ, upon the Mountain Peak

Christ, upon the mountain peak,
Stands alone in glory blazing;
Let us, if we dare to speak,
With the saints and angels praise him:
Alleluia!

Trembling at his feet we saw
Moses and Elijah speaking.
All the prophets and the law
Shout thru them their joyful greeting:
Alleluia!

Swift the cloud of glory came,
God proclaiming in its thunder
Jesus as the Son by name!
Nations, cry aloud in wonder:
Alleluia!

This is God's beloved Son!
Law and prophets fade before him;
First and last and only one,
Let creation now adore him:
Alleluia!
—Brian Wren

Fourth Sunday in Lent
19: The God Who Seeks

I.   Invocation
      O God, whose love is forever seeking communion with us, help us not to hide from you in this appointed encounter but to present ourselves open-faced before you. Through Jesus Christ. Amen.

II.   Psalm 107

III. Reading and Reflection

IV.   Daily Scripture Readings
      Monday   Luke 19:1-10
      Tuesday   Matthew 18:10-14
      Wednesday   Ezekiel 36:22-30
      Thursday   Jeremiah 30:1-10
      Friday   Hebrews 2:1-18
      Saturday   Romans 5:1-11
      Sunday   A. 1 Samuel 16:1-13; Ephesians 5:8-14; Psalm 23; John 9:1-41
                  B. 2 Chronicles 36:14-23; Ephesians 2:4-10; Psalm 137:1-6; John 3:14-21
                  C. Joshua 5:9-12; 2 Corinthians 5:16-21; Psalm 34:1-8; Luke 15:1-3, 11-32

V.   Reflection: Silent and Written

VI.   Prayers: For the Church, for Others, for Myself

VII. Hymn: "Lord, Save Thy World"

VIII. Benediction
      In this moment, my Lord, I have struggled to be honestly present to you. Thank you for staying with me. Go with me, stay with me the whole day through. Amen.

Readings for Reflection

❧ Contemplation does not lead to inactivity. It is in itself the highest actuality of our being. In its compassion it leads to the deepest concern and the fullest activity, according to our particular vocations, for the well-being of the entire human family and its global environment. One cannot steadily see the created reality in the face of the loving and compassionate Father and not be transformed and transforming.

—From Basil Pennington in *Living with Apocalypse* edited by Tilden H. Edwards

❧ When we are brought face to face with the theological task, we see that this whole issue of picturing God begins from a new departure point. It rearranges the task, gets at it from the other side, so to speak, not the self's side, but the other's. For we come up against a hard fact that is right at the center of our faith—that we really do not get to God from our side, that we do not get to God by strictly human effort. We may think we have long grown beyond the idea of God as a sort of scoutmaster from whom we earn merit badges, a Santa Claus to whom we submit our lists of needs and wants. But old habits die hard. Our ideas of God may just be more refined versions of the old ones. We may be working strenuously to remake our pictures of God in order to reach God, or believe that through our well-intentioned social causes, we are coming closer to God. But we always must come up against the hard fact at the center of the Gospel: we do not get to God by our own efforts. God comes to us.

God's word is not separable from God's being. God's action is not separable from God's being. So where God's word and action are, there God is, invading us as an event, invading human will and human imagination, rearranging all the ways we see and picture who we are, who others are, who God is. This invasion is no mere proffering of possibilities, among which we will then decide. It is not a well-mannered offering of choices. No, this invasion of power alters the entire force field in which we live, making a new creation for us, not a small change in direction.

—From *Picturing God* by Ann Belford Ulanov

🙠 God's life and our lives are bound together, as a vine with branches, as a body with members. *So corporate* are we that no one can give a cup of cold water to the least person in the world without giving it to [God]!

—From *The Double Search* by Rufus M. Jones

🙠 We are in danger of drowning on the open sea, and God's word is the rope ladder thrown down to us so that we can climb up into the rescuing vessel. It is the carpet, rolled out toward us so that we can walk along it to the Father's throne. It is the lantern which shines in the darkness of the world (a world which keeps silence and refuses to reveal its own nature); it casts a softer light on the riddles which torment us and encourages us to keep going.

—From *Prayer* by Hans Urs von Balthasar

🙠 One author speaks of an "existential loneliness" that permeates every human spirit, a kind of unnamed pain inside, deep within us, a restlessness, an anxiety, a sense of "all aloneness" that calls out to us. I prefer to name it an "existential ache." It is a persistent longing in us and it happens because we are human. It is as strongly present in us as autumn is present in the cycle of the seasons. I believe that this ache is within us because we are composed of both physical and spiritual dimensions. Our body belongs to the earth but our spirit does not. Our final home is not here, although "here" is where we are meant to be transformed by treasuring, reverencing and growing through our human journey. No matter how good the "good earth" is, there is always a part of us that is yearning, longing, quietly crying out for the true homeland where life is no longer difficult or unfair.

—From *Praying Our Goodbyes* by Joyce Rupp

❧ Thou Hast Searched Me and Known Me

In all places
> Where I have dallied in joyous abandon,
> Where I have responded to ancient desires and yielded to impulses old as life, blinded like things that move without sight;
> Where chores have remained chores, unfulfilled by laziness of spirit and sluggishness of mind;
> Where work has been stripped of joy by the ruthless pruning of vagrant ambition;
> Where the task has been betrayed by slovenly effort;
> Where the response to human need has been half-hearted and weak;
> Where the surge of strength has spent itself in great concentration and I have been left a shaking reed in the wind;
> Where hope has mounted until from its quivering height I have seen the glory and wonder of the new dawn of great awakening;
> Where the quiet hush of utter surrender envelopes me in the great silence of intimate commitment;

Thou has known me!

> When I have lost my way, and thick fog has shrouded from my view the familiar path and the lights of home;
> When with deliberate intent I have turned my back on truth and peace;
> When in the midst of the crowd I have sought refuge among the strangers;
> When things to do have peopled my days with mounting anxiety and ever-deepening frustration;
> When in loneliness I have sat in the thicket of despair too weak to move, to lift my head;

Thou hast searched for and found me!

I cannot escape Thy Scrutiny!
I would not escape Thy Love!
—From *The Inward Journey* by Howard Thurman

❧ According to the Baltimore catechism, "Prayer is the raising of the mind and heart to God." In using this ancient formula it is important to keep in mind that it is not *we* who do the lifting. In every kind of prayer the raising of the mind and heart to God can be the work only of the Spirit. In prayer inspired by the Spirit we let ourselves flow with the lifting movement and drop all reflection. Reflection is an important preliminary to prayer, but it is not prayer. Prayer is not only the offering of interior acts to God: it is the offering of ourselves, of who and what we are.

The action of the Spirit might be compared to a skillful nurse teaching the adopted children of a wealthy household how to behave in their new home. Like waifs pulled in off the street and seated at the banquet table in the elegant dining hall, we require a lot of time to learn and practice the proper table manners. Because of our earthy background, we tend to put our muddy feet on the table, break the chinaware and spill the soup in our laps. To assimilate the values of our new home, profound changes in our attitudes and behavioral patterns are required. For this reason we may experience our nurse as constraining in the beginning and heavy on the "don't." And yet she always seems to be encouraging in the midst of correction; never condemnatory, never judgmental, always inviting us to amendment of life.

The practice of contemplative prayer is an education imparted by the Spirit.

—From *Open Mind, Open Heart* by Thomas Keating

Hymn: Lord, Save Thy World

Lord, save thy world: in bitter need
Thy children lift their cry to thee;
We wait thy liberating deed
To signal hope and set us free.

Lord, save thy world: our souls are bound
In iron chains of fear and pride;
High walls of ignorance around
Our faces from each other hide.

Lord, save thy world: we strike in vain
To save ourselves without thine aid;
What skill and science slowly gain
Is soon to evil ends betrayed.

Lord, save thy world: but thou hast sent
The Savior whom we sorely need;
For us his tears and blood were spent,
That from our bonds we might be freed.

Then save us now, by Jesus' power,
And use the lives thy love sets free
To bring at last the glorious hour
When all shall find thy liberty.
—Albert Frederick Bayly

20: *Power to Give Life*

I. Invocation
Jesus, who has come that we may experience
life in its fullest dimensions, give us now that
life, and let it ever be in us a river rushing forth
to life eternal. Through Christ. Amen.

II. Psalm 36

III. Reading and Reflection

IV. Daily Scripture Readings
Monday	John 17:1-19
Tuesday	Romans 6:1-14
Wednesday	John 10:22-30
Thursday	Matthew 16:21-28
Friday	Luke 8:40-56
Saturday	John 12:44-50

Sunday A. Ezekiel 37:1-14; Romans 8:6-11;
Psalm 116:1-9; John 11:(1-16),
17-45

B. Jeremiah 31:31-34; Hebrews 5:7-
10; Psalm 51:10-17; John 12:20-33

C. Isaiah 43:16-21; Philippians 3:8-
14; Psalm 126; John 12:1-8

V. Reflection: Silent and Written

VI. Prayers: For the Church, for Others, for Myself

VII. Hymn: "O Christ, the Healer"

VIII. Benediction
And now, my Lord, may the same power dis-
played in your resurrection reside always in me,
raising me up to immortality, now and forever.
Amen.

Readings for Reflection

❧ The signs which will persuade me of this are the evidences which I see around me or hear about from those whose witness I trust, that the life of oneness with God is not impossible for me, that if I choose I can experience the love, joy and peace which flow from it. The atheist French lawyer, who out of curiosity paid a visit to the curé of Ars, at that time the talk of Paris, returned home a believer. When asked what had induced him to abandon his atheism he relied, "I've seen God in a man."
—From *The Heart in Pilgrimage* by Christopher Bryant

❧ Jesus became a *sacrament* for me, the cause of my salvation, he brought my time in hell to an end, and put a stop to my inner disintegration. He washed me patiently in the waters of baptism, he filled me with the exhilarating joy of the Holy Spirit in confirmation, he nourished me with the bread of his word. Above all, he forgave me, he forgot everything, he did not even wish me to remember my past myself.

When, through my tears, I began to tell him something of the years during which I betrayed him, he lovingly placed his hand over my mouth in order to silence me. His one concern was that I should muster courage enough to pick myself up again, to try and carry on walking in spite of my weakness, and to believe in his love in spite of my fears. But there was one thing he did, the value of which cannot be measured, something truly unbelievable, something only God could do.

While I continued to have doubts about my own salvation, to tell him that my sins could not be forgiven, and that justice, too, had its rights, he appeared on the Cross before me one Friday towards midday.

I was at its foot, and found myself bathed with the blood which flowed from the gaping holes made in his flesh by the nails. He remained there for three hours until he expired.

I realized that he had died in order that I might stop turning to him with questions about justice, and believe instead, deep within myself, that the scales had come down overflowing on the side of love, and that even though all... through unbelief or madness, had offended him, he had conquered for ever, and drawn all things everlastingly to himself.

—From *In Search of the Beyond* by Carlo Carretto

❧ When you pray, you open yourself to the influence of the Power which has revealed itself as Love. The Power gives you freedom and independence. Once touched by this Power, you are no longer swayed back and forth by the countless opinions, ideas and feelings which flow through you. You have found a center for your life that gives you a creative distance so that everything you see, hear and feel can be tested against the source.

—From *With Open Hands* by Henri J. M. Nouwen

❧ Prayer, of course, has to do with God. God is both initiator and recipient of this underreported but extensively pursued activity. But prayer also has to do with much else: war and government, poverty and sentimentality, politics and economics, work and marriage. Everything, in fact. The striking diagnostic consensus of modern experts that we have a self problem is matched by an equally striking consensus among our wise ancestors on a strategy for action: the only way to get out of the cramped world of the ego and into the large world of God without denying or suppressing or mutilating the ego is through prayer. The only way to escape from self-annihilating and society-destroying egotism and into self-enhancing community is through prayer. Only in prayer can we escape the distortions and constrictions of the self and enter the truth and expansiveness of God. We find there, to our surprise, both self and society whole and blessed. It is the old business of losing your life to save it; and the life that is saved is not only your own, but everyone else's as well.

—From *Earth and Altar* by Eugene H. Peterson

❧ Prayer is political action. Prayer is social energy. Prayer is public good. Far more of our nation's life is shaped by prayer than is formed by legislation. That we have not collapsed into anarchy is due more to prayer than to the police. Prayer is a sustained and intricate act of patriotism in the largest sense of that word—far more precise and loving and preserving than any patriotism served up in slogans. That society continues to be livable and that hope continues to be resurgent are attributable to prayer far more than to business prosperity or a flourishing of the arts. The single most important action contributing to whatever health and strength there is in our land is prayer.
—From *Earth and Altar* by Eugene H. Peterson

❧ The single most widespread American misunderstanding of prayer is that it is private. Strictly and biblically speaking, there is no private prayer. *Private* in its root meaning refers to theft. It is stealing. When we privatize prayer we embezzle the common currency that belongs to all. When we engage in prayer without any desire for or awareness of the comprehensive, inclusive life of the kingdom that is "at hand" in both space and time, we impoverish the social reality that God is bringing to completion.
—From *Earth and Altar* by Eugene H. Peterson

❧ The powers are strong, but Christ is stronger still. The defeat of the powers is sure. We live in that life that overcomes the world, and we should expect to see the overthrow of the kingdom of darkness and the inauguration of the Lamb's rule of righteousness wherever we go.
—From *Money, Sex and Power* by Richard J. Foster

❧ Most Christians are convinced that prayer is more than the outward performance of an obligation, in which we tell God things he already knows. It is more than a kind of daily waiting attendance on the exalted Sovereign who receives his subjects' homage morning and evening. And although many Christians experience in pain and regret that their prayer gets no further than this lowly stage, they are sure, nonetheless, that there should be more to it. In this field there lies a hidden treasure, if only I could find it and dig it up. This seed has the power to become a mighty tree bearing blossoms and fruit, if only I would plant and tend it. This hard and distasteful duty would yield the freest and most blessed kind of life, if only I could open and surrender myself to it. Christians know this, or at least they have an obscure intimation of it on the basis of prior experiences of one kind or another, but they have never dared to follow these beckoning paths and enter the land of promise. The birds of the air have eaten up the sown word, the thorns of everyday life have choked it; all that remains of it is a vague regret in the soul. And if, at particular times throughout life, they feel an urgent need for a relationship with God which is different from the incessant repetition of set prayers, they feel clumsy and lacking in ability, as if they had to speak in a language without having mastered its grammar. Instead of fluent conversation they can only manage a few, halting scraps of the heavenly idiom. Like a stranger in a foreign land, unacquainted with the language, they are almost inarticulate children once again, wanting to say something but unable to do so.

—From *Prayer* by Hans Urs von Balthasar

ॐ This is a fundamental axiom of soteriology and it implies that there can be no other basis for Christian discipleship than the resurrection. It is the ascending and exalted Head of the Church and of mankind who distributes the charisms and missions of discipleship (Eph. 4:7 f). Out of the fullness of his victory the Son endows the different kinds of men with different modes of sharing in his temporal sufferings and in Calvary's profound mystery of judgment. Such participation, as the Lord wishes, can go to the extremes of powerlessness, spiritual darkness, forsakenness and rejection; since these things are a sharing in the cross, they may go beyond what can be experienced and endured at the natural level. They can be so intense that the subject seems to lose all spiritual light whatever, all prospect and hope of redemption and resurrection. And yet, infallibly, this is all a result of that light; it presupposes it, objectively and even subjectively. For the light is never withdrawn from a believer unless, having already experienced it, he consents, at least implicitly, to be deprived of it.

—From *Prayer* by Hans Urs von Balthasar

Hymn: O Christ, the Healer

O Christ, the healer, we have come
To pray for health, to plead for friends.
How can we fail to be restored
When reached by love that never ends?

From every ailment flesh endures
Our bodies clamor to be freed;
Yet in our hearts we would confess
That wholeness is our deepest need.

How strong, O Lord, are our desires,
How weak our knowledge of ourselves!
Release in us those healing truths
Unconscious pride resists or shelves.

In conflicts that destroy our health
We recognize the world's disease;
Our common life declares our ills.
Is there no cure, O Christ, for these?

Grant that we all, made one in faith,
In your community may find
The wholeness that, enriching us,
Shall reach the whole of humankind.
—Fred Pratt Green

Palm Sunday
21: The Cost of Right Choices

I.   Invocation
     O God, whose very presence causes us to choose
     whom we will serve, help us to joyfully choose
     always for you. Let us not be tossed about by
     conflicting motives but live solely for you. In the
     power of Christ's name. Amen.

II. Psalm 56

III. Reading and Reflection

IV. Daily Scripture Readings
     Monday   Acts 14:19-28
     Tuesday   1 Peter 2:21-25
     Wednesday   1 Corinthians 1:3-11
     Thursday   Isaiah 53:1-6
     Friday   Isaiah 53:7-9
     Saturday   Isaiah 53:10-12
     Sunday   A. Isaiah 50:4-9a; Philippians 2:5-11;
                   Psalm 118; Matthew 21:1-11
                B. Isaiah 50:4-9a; Philippians 2:5-11;
                   Psalm 118:19-29; Mark 11:1-11
                C. Isaiah 50:4-9a; Philippians 2:5-11;
                   Psalm 118:19-20; Luke 19:28-40

V.   Reflection: Silent and Written

VI. Prayers: For the Church, for Others, for Myself

VII. Hymn: "I Want a Principle Within"

VIII. Benediction
     As I go now to face the confusion and allurements
     of the world's systems, help me to separate the
     precious from the worthless, that I may be your
     worthy disciple. Amen.

Readings for Reflection

🎗 In his pictures Aerlius painted all faces after the manner and appearance of the women he loved, and so too everyone paints devotion according to [one's] own passions and fancies. A man given to fasting thinks himself very devout if he fasts, although his heart may be filled with hatred. Much concerned with sobriety, he doesn't dare to wet his tongue with wine or even water but won't hesitate to drink deep of his neighbor's blood by detraction and calumny. [A woman] thinks [herself] devout because [she] daily recites a vast number of prayers, but after saying them [she] utters the most disagreeable, arrogant, and harmful words at home and among the neighbors. Another [person] gladly takes a coin out of his purse and gives it to the poor, but he cannot extract kindness from his heart and forgive his enemies. Another forgives [her] enemies but never pays [her] creditors unless compelled to do so by force of law. All these [people] are usually considered to be devout, but they are by no means such. Saul's servants searched for David in his house but Michal had put a statue on his bed, covered it with David's clothes, and thus led them to think that it was David himself lying there sick and sleeping. In the same manner, many persons clothe themselves with certain outward actions connected with holy devotion and the world believes that they are truly devout and spiritual whereas they are in fact nothing but copies and phantoms of devotion.
—From *Introduction to the Devout Life* by St. Francis de Sales

🎗 Do we buy a particular home on the basis of the call of God, or because of the availability of money? Do we buy a new car because we can afford it, or because God instructed us to buy a new car? If money determines what we do or do not do, then money is our boss. If God determines what we do or do not do, then God is our boss. My money might say to me, "You have

enough to buy that," but my God might say to me, "I don't want you to have it." Now, who am I to obey?
—From *Money, Sex and Power* by Richard J. Foster

❧ Prayer is the action that gets us in touch with and develops the most comprehensive relationship—self, God, community, creation, government, culture. We are born into the web of relationships and continue in it throughout our lifetimes. But we often don't feel like it. We feel isolated, cut off, fragmented, out of touch. We do not tolerate such isolation very well and move out to overcome it: we call up a neighbor, join a club, write a letter, get married. The disparate attempts accumulate. The self is less isolated. Society is less fragmented. The facts add up. But if we do not pray, they do not add up to enough: in prayer and only in prayer are we able to enter the complexity and depth of the dynamic and interrelated whole. A failure to pray is not a harmless omission; it is a positive violation of both the self and the society.
—From *Earth and Altar* by Eugene H. Peterson

❧ Have I rejoiced with and for my neighbor in virtue or pleasure? grieved with [her] in pain, for him in sin?

Have I received his infirmities with pity, not anger?

Have I thought or spoke unkindly of or to [her]? Have I revealed any evil of anyone, unless it was necessary to some particular good I had in view? Have I then done it with all the tenderness of phrase and manner consistent with that end? Have I anyway appeared to approve them that did otherwise?

Has goodwill been, and appeared to be, the spring of all my actions toward others?

Have I duly used intercession? Before, after, speaking to any? For my friends on Sunday? For my pupils on Monday? For those who have particularly desired it, on Wednesday and Friday? For the family in which I am, every day?
—John Wesley (*Classics of Western Spirituality* Series)

❧ Honest, direct confrontation is a true expression of compassion. As Christians, we are *in* the world without being *of* it. It is precisely this position that renders confrontation both possible and necessary. The illusion of power must be unmasked, idolatry must be undone, oppression and exploitation must be fought, and all who participate in these evils must be confronted. This is compassion. We cannot suffer with the poor when we are unwilling to confront those persons and systems that cause poverty. We cannot set the captives free when we do not want to confront those who carry the keys. We cannot profess our solidarity with those who are oppressed when we are unwilling to confront the oppressor. Compassion without confrontation fades quickly into fruitless sentimental commiseration.

But if confrontation is to be an expression of patient action, it must be humble. Our constant temptation is to fall into self-righteous revenge or self-serving condemnation. The danger here is that our own witness can blind us. When confrontation is tainted by desire for attention, need for revenge, or greed for power, it can easily become self-serving and cease to be compassionate.

—From *Compassion: A Reflection on the Christian Life* by Donald P. McNeill, Douglas A. Morrison, and Henri J. M. Nouwen

❧ Reverence is a gentle virtue; it is also strong. Reverence is a tender virtue; it is also tough. Reverence is a patient virtue; it is also persistent. Reverence bears no ill will toward others; it is able to bear the ill will of others when necessary. Reverence is a virtue that prepares us well to belong to one another; it reaches out to those who have given messages of not wishing to belong.

When we approach others with gentle reverence, we bring gifts and share theirs with us.

—From *Growing Strong at Broken Places* by Paula Ripple

Hymn: I Want a Principle Within

I want a principle within
Of watchful, godly fear,
A sensibility of sin,
A pain to feel it near.
I want the first approach to feel
Of pride or wrong desire,
To catch the wandering of my will,
And quench the kindling fire.

From thee that I no more may stray,
No more they goodness grieve,
Grant me the filial awe, I pray,
The tender conscience give.
Quick as the apple of an eye,
O God, my conscience make;
Awake my soul when sin is nigh,
And keep it still awake.

Almighty God of truth and love,
To me thy power impart;
The mountain from my soul remove,
The hardness from my heart.
O may the least omission pain
My reawakened soul,
And drive me to that blood again,
Which makes the wounded whole.
—Charles Wesley

22: *The Living Christ*

I. Invocation
    O God, whose Son declared himself to be the resurrection and the life, give me now a sense of the presence of the One who is alive forever more. I pray. Amen.

II. Psalm 23

III. Reading and Reflection

IV. Daily Scripture Readings
    Monday   Acts 3:11-16
    Tuesday   Acts 4:1-12
    Wednesday   Acts 5:17-32
    Thursday   Acts 2:22-36
    Friday   Ephesians 1:15-23
    Saturday   2 Corinthians 4:7-18
    Sunday   A. Acts 10:34-43; Colossians 3:1-4; Psalm 118:14-24; John 20:1-18
               B. Isaiah 25:6-9; Acts 10:34-43; Psalm 118:14-24; Mark 16:1-8
               C. Acts 10:34-43; 1 Corinthians 15:19-26; Psalm 118:14-24; John 20:1-18

V. Reflection: Silent and Written

VI. Prayers: For the Church, for Others, for Myself

VII. Hymn: "Ascended Christ, Who Gained the Glory"

VIII. Benediction
    Lord Jesus, I have heard your knocking at the door of my life. Come in and abide with me. I throw open the door to you, my Lord. Come in! And never leave me. Amen.

Readings for Reflection

❧ I find myself reflecting on the last supper of Jesus. We seldom recognize a final occasion when it is happening. Only in retrospect do we recognize that it was the last. Then we recall every moment, every gesture and try to draw from it what we will carry with us the rest of our lives. So easily we take for granted the meals of every day. They are so regular and common, so ordinary as long as they continue. But when it is the last one, all of the previous ones are drawn into it and it becomes a singularity, a once and never again. It becomes a rare, precious moment to be treasured forever.
—From *Gathering the Fragments* by Edward J. Farrell

❧ The Day of Resurrection has dawned upon us, the day of true light and life, wherein Christ, the life of believers, arose from the dead. Let us give abundant thanks and praise to God, that while we solemnly celebrate the day of our Lord's resurrection, He may be pleased to bestow on us quiet peace and special gladness; so that being protected from morning to night by His favoring mercy, we may rejoice in the gift of our Redeemer. Amen.
—Mozarabic Sacramentary

❧ Paul told the Colossians that the indwelling presence of Christ in the believer—the fruit of the Spirit—was a mystery before Pentecost. Too many Christians live like it still is. Why is it so difficult to talk simply and clearly about what it means to have God dwelling in us?

Let me risk a description of what has been the experience of some of us at least. When we say that Christ pervades all the aspects of our human nature, it does not mean that he effects a takeover of our will. He did not do that before we became his children; he does not do it now. It does mean that when we set our hearts in the direction of what we know to be God's heart in the matter—and begin to model our behavior in that direction—the Spirit within immediately reinforces our finite strength with infinite strength. The synthesis is so smooth, it is sometimes impossible to tell where our strength ends and his begins.

—From *Radiance of the Inner Splendor* by Lloyd John Ogilvie

ᨱ The Opening

Alone, O Lord, alone with thee,
Where none could speak nor hear nor see,
The bar I've placed across my heart
I'd lift, and bid the doors to part—
On rusty hinges open wide
And let just once your love inside;
And when I'd turn to close the door
And put the bar in place once more,
My heart so filled with thee I'd find
The doors could not be closed behind.
—Shirley Gupton Lynn in *For Everything There Is a Season* compiled by Karen Greenwaldt

ᨱ Grant that the remembrance of the blessed Life that once was lived out on this common earth under these ordinary skies may remain with me in all the tasks and duties of this day. Let me remember—

His eagerness, not to be ministered unto, but to minister:

His sympathy with suffering of every kind:

His meekness of bearing, so that, when reviled, He reviled not again:

His steadiness of purpose in keeping to His appointed task:

His simplicity:

His self-discipline:

His serenity of spirit:

His complete reliance upon Thee, His Father in Heaven.

And in each of these ways give me grace to follow in His footsteps.

Almighty God, Father of our Lord Jesus Christ, I commit all my ways unto Thee. I make over my soul to Thy keeping. I pledge my life to Thy service. May this day be for me a day of obedience and of charity, a day of happiness and of peace. May all my walk and conversation be such as becometh the gospel of Christ. Amen.

—From *A Diary of Private Prayer* by John Baillie

ï➤ You who read these words already know this inner Life and Light. For by this very Light within you, is your recognition given. In this humanistic age we suppose [we are] the initiator and God is the responder. But the Living Christ within us is the initiator and we are the responders. God the Lover, the accuser, the revealer of light and darkness presses within us. "Behold I stand at the door and knock." And all our apparent initiative is already a response, a testimonial to his secret presence and working within us.

—From *A Testament of Devotion* by Thomas R. Kelly

Hymn: Ascended Christ, Who Gained the Glory

Ascended Christ, who gained
The glory that we sing,
Anointed and ordained,
Our prophet, priest, and king:
By many tongues
The church displays
Your power and praise
In all our songs.

No titles, thrones, or powers
Can ever rival yours;
No passing mood of ours
Can turn aside your laws:
You reign above
Each other name
Of worth or fame,
The Lord of love.

Now from your Father's side
You make your people new;
Since for our sins you died,
Our lives belong to you:
From our distress
You set us free
For purity
And holiness.

You call us to belong
Within one body here;
In weakness we are strong,
And all your gifts we share:
In you alone
We are complete,
And at your feet
With joy bow down.

All strength is in your hand,
All power to you is given;
All wisdom to command
In earth and hell and heaven:
Beyond all words
Creation sings
The King of kings
And Lord of lords.
—Christopher Idle

23: *Life in Christ*

I.   Invocation

O Jesus, who called Lazarus from his tomb and presented him alive to his friends, call me, I pray, from the tombs which seek to stifle the life I have. Remove from me the grave clothes which yet hinder my free movement in your Spirit. Through the power of your name. Amen.

II.   Psalm 126

III.   Reading and Reflection

IV.   Daily Scripture Readings

Monday	Romans 6:1-11
Tuesday	Ephesians 2:1-10
Wednesday	Galatians 2:11-21
Thursday	John 17:1-5
Friday	Romans 6:15-23
Saturday	Romans 8:18-30
Sunday	A. Acts 2:14a, 22-32; 1 Peter 1:3-9; Psalm 16:5-11; John 20:19-31
	B. Acts 4:32-35; 1 John 1:1–2:2; Psalm 133; John 20:19-31
	C. Acts 5:27-32; Revelation 1:4-8; Psalm 2; John 20:19-31

V.   Reflection: Silent and Written

VI.   Prayers: For the Church, for Others, for Myself

VII.   Hymn: "Make Me a Captive, Lord"

VIII.   Benediction

In these moments with you, my Lord, I have heard your call to life. O glorious call that awakens me, I am yours and yours alone. Amen.

Readings for Reflection

🔊 *Watch and Pray* "I invite you to spend the night in converse with me. Will you refuse?"

"I ask you to stay awake to contemplate Me, to tell me that you love Me—to adore Me: to pray for all [people]: to ask pardon of Me for those who are sinning at this moment, and who stay awake for the purpose of sinning."

If I neglect to stay awake and am too lazy to rise, (1) I am refusing to lay myself at the feet of Our Lord, and keep him company, we two together, when he is calling me to do so. (2) I am preferring to sleep rather than to be alone with Our Lord, in intimate converse and union with him.

—From *Meditations of a Hermit* by Charles de Foucauld

🔊 "Christ in me" means something quite different from the weight of an impossible ideal, something far more glorious than the oppression of a pattern for ever beyond all imitation. "Christ in me" means Christ bearing me along from within, Christ the motive-power that carries me on, Christ giving my whole life a wonderful poise and lift, and turning every burden into wings. All this is in it when the apostle speaks of "Christ in you, the hope of glory" (Col. 1:27). Compared with this, the religion which bases everything on example is pitifully rudimentary. This, and this alone, is the true Christian religion. Call it mysticism or not—the name matters little: the thing, the experience, matters everything. To be "in Christ," to have Christ within, to realize your creed not as something you have to bear but as something by which you are borne, this is Christianity. It is more: it is release and liberty, life with an endless song at its heart. It means feeling within you, as long as life here lasts, the carrying power of Love Almighty; and underneath you, when you come to die, the touch of everlasting arms.

—From *A Man in Christ* by James Stewart

❧ Most benign Lord Jesus, grant me Your grace, that it may always be with me and work with me and preserve me unto the end. Grant that I may always desire and will what is most pleasing and acceptable to You. Let Your will be my will, and let my will always follow Your will and best conform with it. Let there be always in me one will and one desire with You, and grant that I may have no power to will or not to will except as You will or do not will. Grant that I may die to all things in the world, and that for You I may love to be despised and be a man unknown in this world. Grant me, also, above all things that can be desired, that I may rest in You and fully in You bring peace to my heart. You, Lord, are the truest peace of the heart, and the perfect rest of body and soul, and without You all things weary and disturb. Wherefore, in that peace which is in you, one high, one blessed and one endless Goodness, shall I find my rest. So be it.
—From *The Imitation of Christ* by Thomas à Kempis

❧ I've always dreamed of solitude, the hermit's life, a cabin in the woods or a tiny chalet on the edge of a mountain. I've always dreamed of deserts and silence. But I've resisted the dream, with the exception of one time when I offered myself the luxury of a retreat with a hermit: four hours by foot, far from any living creature and a hermit happy to see me. We talked a lot.
—From *With Open Heart* by Michel Quoist

❧ The world has found itself in a harsh spiritual crisis and a political impasse. All the celebrated technological achievements of progress, including the conquest of outer space, do not redeem the twentieth century's moral poverty. . . . We have placed too much hope in politics and social reforms, only to find out that we were being deprived of our most precious possession: our spiritual life. It is trampled by the party mob in the East, by the commercial one in the West. [History] . . . will demand from us a spiritual blaze; we shall have to rise to a new height of vision, to a new level of life, where our physical nature will not be cursed, as in the Middle Ages, but even more importantly, our spiritual being will not be trampled upon, as in the Modern Era.

—From *A World Split Apart* by Aleksandr Solzhenitsyn

❧ Power touches us all. We cannot get away from it even if we wanted to. All human relationships involve the use of power. Therefore, rather than seek to run from it or to deny that we use it, we would do well to discover the Christian meaning of power and learn how to use it for the good of others. All who follow Christ are called to the "ministry of power."

—From *Money, Sex and Power* by Richard J. Foster

❧ Interestingly, the social dimension of spirituality can be expressed negatively as well as positively. It includes what we do *not* do, as well as what we do. "Doing no harm" brought the element of avoidance into the Christian's frame of reference. Our problem today is that this too easily seems like legalism. To read Wesley this way, however, is again to miss the point. Wesley's prohibitions were not binders so much as they were boundaries. He knew that antinomianism resulted in spiritual inertia and moral chaos. He saw the use of law so necessary to guide the believer in the way of righteousness.

—From *Devotional Life in the Wesleyan Tradition* by Steve Harper

❧ Where does the life of prayer lead? Toward the end of the journey inward, after one has met Christ and shared his cross, one enters a strange land of loneliness. Peace seems to precede it. I think it is the peace that comes through having been crucified. There is a moment of resurrection, as if one has been taken off the cross. The wounds are not healed, but they no longer hurt.

—From *Soul of My Soul* by Catherine de Hueck Doherty

❧ We must act as each is fully persuaded in his [or her] own mind. Hold you fast that which you believe is most acceptable to God, and I will do the same. I believe the episcopal form of Church government to be scriptural and apostolical. If you think the Presbyterian or Independent is better, think so still and act accordingly. I believe infants ought to be baptized, and that this may be done either by dipping or sprinkling. If you are otherwise persuaded, be so still, and follow your own persuasion. It appears to me that forms of prayer are of excellent use, particularly in the great congregation. If you judge extemporary prayer to be of more use, act suitable to your own judgment....If thou love God and all [humanity], I ask no more. "Give me thine hand."

—John Wesley

❧ By salvation I mean, not barely, according to the vulgar notion, deliverance from hell or going to heaven, but a present deliverance from sin; a restoration of the soul to its primitive health, its original purity; a recovery of the divine nature; the renewal of our souls after the image of God...

True religion is the loving God with all our heart, and our neighbour as ourselves; and in that love abstaining from all evil and doing all possible good to all [persons].

—John Wesley

Hymn: Make Me a Captive, Lord

Make me a captive, Lord,
And then I shall be free.
Force me to render up my sword,
And I shall conqueror be.
I sink in life's alarms
When by myself I stand;
Imprison me within thine arms,
And strong shall be my hand.

My heart is weak and poor
Until it master find;
It has no spring of action sure,
It varies with the wind.
It cannot freely move
Till thou has wrought its chain;
Enslave it with thy matchless love,
And deathless it shall reign.

My power is faint and low,
Till I have learned to serve;
It wants the needed fire to glow,
It wants the breeze to nerve.
It cannot drive the world,
Until itself be driven;
Its flag can only be unfurled
When thou shalt breathe from heaven.

My will is not my own,
Till thou hast made it thine;
If it would reach a monarch's throne,
It must its crown resign.
It only stands unbent
Amid the clashing strife,
When on thy bosom it has leant,
And found in thee its life.
—George Matheson

Third Sunday of Easter
24: *Companionship with the Living Lord*

I. Invocation
    Merciful and loving God, I come seeking quiet communion with you. In this place apart from confusion and stress, grant me stillness of heart and quietness in thy presence. Amen.

II. Psalm 121

III. Reading and Reflection

IV. Daily Scripture Readings
Monday	Ezekiel 36:22-36
Tuesday	Genesis 17:1-8
Wednesday	Genesis 39:19-23
Thursday	Philippians 4:1-9
Friday	Colossians 2:6-15
Saturday	Acts 4:23-37
Sunday	A. Acts 2:14a, 36-41; 1 Peter 1:17-23; Psalm 116:12-19; Luke 24:13-35
	B. Acts 3:12-19; 1 John 3:1-7; Psalm 4; Luke 24:35-48
	C. Acts 9:1-20; Revelation 5:11-14; Psalm 30:4-12; John 21:1-19

V. Reflection: Silent and Written

VI. Prayers: For the Church, for Others, for Myself

VII. Hymn: "O Come and Dwell in Me"

VIII. Benediction
    O God, as I prepare to leave this quiet place, give me a sense of your power and your glory, that I may take it everywhere you send me today. Amen.

Readings for Reflection

🕭 When you are sad, tired, lonely and full of suffering, take refuge in the sanctuary of your soul and there you will find your Brother, your Friend, Jesus, who will console you, support you and strengthen you.

—From *Meditations of a Hermit* by Charles de Foucauld

🕭 [One] who dares not say an ill-natured word or do an unreasonable thing because he [or she] considers God as everywhere present performs a better devotion than [one] who dares not miss the church. To live in the world as a stranger and a pilgrim, using all its enjoyments as if we used them not, making all our actions as so many steps toward a better life, is offering a better sacrifice to God than any forms of holy and heavenly prayers.

To be humble in our actions, to avoid every appearance of pride and vanity, to be meek and lowly in our words, actions, dress, behavior, and designs—all in imitation of our blessed Saviour—is worshiping God in a higher manner than do they who have only stated times to fall low on their knees in devotions. [A person who is contented] with necessities that he [or she] may give the remainder to those who need it; who dares not spend any money foolishly, [considering] it as a talent from God which must be used according to [God's] will, praises God with something that is more glorious than songs of praise.

—From *A Serious Call to a Devout and Holy Life* by William Law

🕭 Spiritual guidance is not therapy, nor is it the giving of advice. Its aim is to provide assistance in both clarification and discernment. It involves sitting down on a regular basis with someone you trust in order to examine, adjust, and recommit yourself to the disciplines that give substance to your journey. It might be that your spiritual guide is someone you do not normally see, but from whom you feel you will gain wisdom. Or it might be that you find a person who is a spiritual companion to you at the same time that you are a spiritual companion to him. It is incidental whether the relationship lasts a year or a lifetime. The important thing is that the relationship be one in which you are able to talk comfortably and reflectively about the unfolding process of your spiritual journey, knowing that it is in the living out of this spiritual journey that Christ is made known through you to others.

—From *Mutual Ministry* by James C. Fenhagen

   🙠 Yet, for all of this lukewarmness, we hunger. And we know well enough that there is a response. There is an answering back to the Grace of God on your part and on mine that is all-important. We know, too, that the redeeming of our time calls for nothing less than the blazing up out of our prostrate bodies of an authentic, original, passionate, interior life in answer to the Living Flame that confronts us.

—From *Together in Solitude* by Douglas Steere

   🙠 Our study of money leads us to one inescapable conclusion: we who follow Jesus Christ are called to a vow of simplicity. This vow is not for the dedicated few but for all. It is not an option to take or leave depending on our personal preference. All who name Christ as Lord and Savior are obliged to follow what he says, and Jesus' call to discipleship in money can be best summed up in the single word *simplicity*. Simplicity seeks to do justice to our Lord's many-faceted teachings about money— light and dark, giving and receiving, trust, contentment, faith.

Simplicity means unity of heart and singleness of purpose. We have only one desire: to obey Christ in all things. We have only one purpose: to glorify Christ in all things. We have only one use for money: to advance his kingdom upon the earth. Jesus declares, "If thine eye be single thy whole body shall be full of light" (Matt. 6:22, KJV).

—From *Money, Sex and Power* by Richard J. Foster

❧ Meeting [Jesus] does not inevitably lead to his becoming our personal savior. We must *make* room in our life for him; we must *choose* him and *accept* him as our savior by claiming his presence. We must *let* him be Lord of our lives. That decision involves opening ourselves to Jesus, and receiving him into the most intimate dimensions of our lives. Because Jesus comes to us in love, he refuses to exploit or manipulate us, to be coercive or invasive, for to do so would contradict the very nature of love. If we would be loved by others, we must let them love us. We must be vulnerable and reachable enough that others can get close enough to love us, including Jesus. So Jesus approaches the threshold of our being with beckoning love, and he waits for us to open our life to him from the inside. . . .

To enter into that intimate relationship where Jesus becomes our savior is to let Jesus be with us and within us, person to person, on the emotional and volitional levels of our being. It is to respond to the contagion of his presence. It is to let down whatever defenses we have in place so that we come together heart to heart, so that the spirit in him touches and resonates with the spirit in us. It is to meet him with our deepest feelings and fears, with our aspirations and imaginations, with our desires and loyalties, with our creative energies and self-understanding. It is to meet him with our shadow-side and our hidden face, risking his acceptance of all we are—even those things about ourselves we have rejected and tried to disguise. It is to meet him with the expectation that what happens between him and us will enlarge life with fulfillment and beauty. It is to enjoy with him that same pervasive sense of well-being and excitement that quickens in us when we spend unhurried time with good friends or when we share intimate moments of oneness with those we love. It is to meet him with gratitude and a sense of wonder over the gift of himself that Jesus offers.

—From *Forever Beginning* by Donald J. Shelby

๕ How can you live in the same house with someone (forever!) without the same likes and dislikes?

How can you sit at table together with different plans—or worse, opposing ones?

"I died on the cross for you and you don't move a finger for me," Jesus would have the right to say to me. And:

"I'm faithful, I've never betrayed you. And you? Betray me is all you do.

"I love poverty. What about you? What do you love?

"I consented to be humiliated, ridiculed, defeated, while you are afraid of what others will think of you. You tremble if someone criticizes you in the paper!"

Isn't this so?

The journey is long and its name is exodus.

The exodus is the journey made by human beings to learn God's tastes by experience.

It is God's school, the apprenticeship of the kingdom, the child's growing up to become like the parent.
—From *Why, O Lord?* by Carlo Carretto

๕ We do not begin life on our own. We do not finish it on our own. Life, especially when we experience by faith the complex interplay of creation and salvation, is not fashioned out of our own genetic lumber and cultural warehouses. It is not hammered together with the planks and nails of our thoughts and dreams, our feelings and fancies. We are not self-sufficient. We enter a world that is created by God, that already has a rich history and is crowded with committed participants—a world of animals and mountains, of politics and religion; a world where people build houses and raise children, where volcanos erupt lava and rivers flow to the sea; a world in which, however carefully we observe and watch and study it, surprising things keep on taking place (like rocks turning into pools of water). We keep on being surprised because we are in on something beyond our management, something over our heads.

In prayer we realize and practice our part in this intricate involvement with absolutely everything that is, no matter how remote it seems to us or how indifferent we are to it. This prayer is not an emotional or aesthetic sideline that we indulge in after our real work is done; it is the connective tissue of our far-flung existence. The world of creation interpenetrates the world of redemption. The world of redemption interpenetrates the world of creation. The extravagantly orchestrated skies and the exuberantly fashioned earth are not background to provide a little beauty on the periphery of the godlike ego; they are the large beauty in which we find our true home, room in which to live the cross and Christ expansively, openhearted in praise.
—From *Earth and Altar* by Eugene H. Peterson

Hymn: O Come and Dwell in Me

O come and dwell in me,
Spirit of power within,
And bring the glorious liberty
From sorrow, fear, and sin.

Hasten the joyful day
Which shall my sins consume,
When old things shall be done away,
And all things new become.

I want the witness, Lord,
That all I do is right,
According to thy mind and word,
Well-pleasing in thy sight.

I ask no higher state;
Indulge me but in this,
And soon or later then translate
To thine eternal bliss.
—Charles Wesley

Fourth Sunday of Easter
25: The True Shepherd

I. Invocation
True shepherd of our souls, who calls his own by name, help us this hour to hear and to heed your voice. We know no other voice, and no other voice will we follow. Amen.

II. Psalm 80

III. Reading and Reflection

IV. Daily Scripture Readings
Monday   Jeremiah 23:1-8
Tuesday   Ezekiel 11:14-21
Wednesday   Jeremiah 31:10-14
Thursday   John 10:1-18
Friday   1 Peter 5:1-11
Saturday   Acts 20:17-38
Sunday   A. Acts 2:42-47; 1 Peter 2:19-25; Psalm 23; John 10:1-10
            B. Acts 4:8-12; 1 John 3:18-24; Psalm 23; John 10:11-18
            C. Acts 13:15-16, 26-33; Revelation 7:9-17; Psalm 23; John 10:22-30

V. Reflection: Silent and Written

VI. Prayers: For the Church, for Others, for Myself

VII. Hymn: "Savior, Like a Shepherd Lead Us"

VIII. Benediction
In this moment of quietness I have heard your call, my Lord. Now, lead on, and I will follow. Amen.

Readings for Reflection

❧ Let me stand to-day—
>
> for whatever is pure and true and just and good:
>
> for the advancement of science and education and true learning:
>
> for the redemption of daily business from the blight of self-seeking:
>
> for the rights of the weak and the oppressed:
>
> for industrial co-operation and mutual help:
>
> for the conservation of the rich traditions of the past:
>
> for the recognition of new workings of Thy Spirit in the minds of the [people] of my own time:
>
> for the hope of yet more glorious days to come.

To-day, O Lord—
>
> let me put right before interest:
>
> let me put others before self:
>
> let me put the things of the spirit before the things of the body:
>
> let me put the attainment of noble ends above the enjoyment of present pleasures:
>
> let me put principle above reputation:
>
> let me put Thee before all else.

O Thou the reflection of whose transcendent glory did once appear unbroken in the face of Jesus Christ, give me to-day a heart like His—a brave heart, a true heart, a tender heart, a heart with great room in it, a heart fixed on Thyself; for His name's sake. Amen.

—From *A Diary of Private Prayer* by John Baillie

❧ If I did not simply live from one moment to the next, it would be impossible for me to keep my patience. I can see only the present, I forget the past and I take good care not to think about the future. We get discouraged and feel despair because we brood about

the past and the future. It is such folly to pass one's time fretting, instead of resting quietly on the heart of Jesus.
—Thérèse of Lisieux

꒛ Perhaps no one has captured the exuberant spirit of simple caring and sharing better than the Christian philosopher Aristides, whose words (written in A.D. 125) are so moving that they are best quoted in full:

> They walk in all humility and kindness, and falsehood is not found among them, and they love one another. They despise not the widow, and grieve not the orphan. He that hath distributeth liberally to him that hath not. If they see a stranger, they bring him under their roof, and rejoice over him as if he were their own brother: for they call themselves brethren, not after the flesh, but after the Spirit of God; but when one of their poor passes away from the world, and any of them see him, then he provides for his burial according to his ability; and if they hear that any of their number is imprisoned or oppressed for the name of their Messiah, all of them provide for his needs, and if it is possible that he may be delivered, they deliver him. And if there is among them a [person] that is poor and needy, and they have not an abundance of necessaries, they fast two or three days that they may supply the needy with their necessary food.

This model of simplicity speaks to our condition. How desperately we need today to discover new creative ways of caring and sharing with any in need.
—From *Freedom of Simplicity* by Richard J. Foster

꒛ Ministers of the gospel have many occupational hazards and diseases and these have frequently been diagnosed with telling power. But all too seldom have the ministers been reminded of the unmatched spiritual opportunity that has been almost uniquely lavished on them by God, namely the opportunity of being confronted hour after hour with human problems that are utterly beyond their own strength to unravel, and which drive them back to listen for, and to draw upon a deeper wisdom and strength than they are able in themselves to supply. How often are ministers drawn back into the supernatural life of God, back into what Tauler calls "suffering in God" by their own weakness and the sheer abysmal personal needs of those who call on them for help?

—From *Together in Solitude* by Douglas V. Steere

❧ Trinity Sunday

Lord, who hast form'd me out of mud,
And hast redeem'd me through thy blood,
And sanctifi'd me to do good;

Purge all my sins done heretofore:
For I confess my heavy score,
And I will strive to sin no more.

Enrich my heart, mouth, hands in me,
With faith, with hope, with charity;
That I may run, rise, rest with thee.

—George Herbert (*Classics of Western Spirituality* Series)

Hymn: Savior, Like a Shepherd Lead Us

Savior, like a shepherd lead us,
Much we need thy tender care;
In thy pleasant pastures feed us,
For our use thy folds prepare.
Blessed Jesus, blessed Jesus!
Thou has bought us, thine we are.
Blessed Jesus, blessed Jesus!
Thou has bought us, thine we are.

We are thine, do thou befriend us,
Be the guardian of our way;
Keep thy flock, from sin defend us,
Seek us when we go astray.
Blessed Jesus, blessed Jesus!
Hear, O hear us, when we pray.
Blessed Jesus, blessed Jesus!
Hear, O hear us, when we pray.

Thou hast promised to receive us,
Poor and sinful though we be;
Thou hast mercy to relieve us,
Grace to cleanse and power to free.
Blessed Jesus, blessed Jesus!
We will early turn to thee.
Blessed Jesus, blessed Jesus!
We will early turn to thee.

Early let us seek thy favor,
Early let us do thy will;
Blessed Lord and only Savior,
With thy love our bosoms fill.
Blessed Jesus, blessed Jesus!
Thou hast loved us, love us still.
Blessed Jesus, blessed Jesus!
Thou hast loved us, love us still.
—Attr. to Dorothy A. Thrupp

26: *Staying Close to God*

I. Invocation
    O God, whose nature invites us always to stay close by you, help us now to make your word our home, that we may be your true disciples. Through Jesus Christ, who is the word, the way, and the life. Amen.

II. Psalm 34

III. Reading and Reflection

IV. Daily Scripture Readings
    | Monday | Psalm 18:1-19 |
    | Tuesday | Matthew 7:21-28 |
    | Wednesday | Mark 12:28-34 |
    | Thursday | James 1:19-26 |
    | Friday | Colossians 1:15-29 |
    | Saturday | Ephesians 3:14-21 |

    Sunday
    A. Acts 7:55-60; 1 Peter 2:2-10; Psalm 31:1-8; John 14:1-14
    B. Acts 8:26-40; 1 John 4:7-12; Psalm 22:25-31; John 15:1-8
    C. Acts 14:8-18; Revelation 21:1-6; Psalm 145:13b-21; John 13:31-35

V. Reflection: Silent and Written

VI. Prayers: For the Church, for Others, for Myself

VII. Hymn: "Christ Is Alive"

VIII. Benediction
     And now, my Lord, send me from this sacred place, still keeping me close to you. May the journey of this day bring me closer, ever closer to you. Amen.

Readings for Reflection

❧ Picturing God must precede any speaking about God, for our pictures accompany all our words and they continue long after we fall silent before God. Images—the language of the psyche—are the coin of life; they touch our emotions as well as our thoughts; they reach down into our bodies as well as toward our ideas. They arrive unbidden, startling, after our many years of effort to craft them.
—From *Picturing God* by Ann Belford Ulanov

❧ We keep our pictures of God secret from each other and often even from ourselves. For what would others think if we talked of God as a stalking animal, sniffing us like prey, or as an alien, a foreigner whose breath is upon our face, or whose foot is on our neck? What of a God so palpable and near that only an abstract symbol can make it bearable, like Jung's mandala, to some so calming and capacious, to others only dead artifacts? What of God, as the psalmist says, with great wings under which we hide? Or God's grace like a large lap into which we crawl, a breast upon which we lean? Or God a warrior calling us out to fight? Or God as Jesus sitting in the back pew of your church...?
—From *Picturing God* by Ann Belford Ulanov

❧ We are that which we love. Neither larger nor smaller than the size of the objects of our desire. And that is why Christians become known by revealing to each other their dreams. To dream is to see love and desires transformed into symbols, words. It should not be frightening, then, that God, who is love, speaks to us through our *dreams*. And may we, from our part, speak to God through *prayer*, which is nothing more than the confession of our dream of love before the altar.
—From *I Believe in the Resurrection of the Body* by Rubem Alves

❧ Meister Eckhart wrote, "As thou art in church or cell, that same frame of mind carry out into the world, into its turmoil and fitfulness." Deep within us all there is an amazing inner sanctuary of the soul, a holy place, a Divine Center, a speaking Voice, to which we may continuously return. Eternity is at our hearts, pressing upon our time-torn lives, warming us with intimations of an astounding destiny, calling us home unto Itself. Yielding to these persuasions, gladly committing ourselves in body and soul, utterly and completely, to the Light Within, is the beginning of true life. It is a dynamic center, a creative Life that presses to birth within us. It is a Light Within which illumines the face of God and casts new shadows and glories upon the face of [humanity]. It is a seed stirring to life if we do not choke it. It is the Shekinah of the soul, the Presence in the midst. Here is the Slumbering Christ, stirring to be awakened, to become the soul we clothe in earthly form and action. And He is within us all.
—From *A Testament of Devotion* by Thomas R. Kelly

❧ When we get a vision of the God of whom Jesus speaks we will want fellowship with this one who combines the best qualities of a good father and a good mother. We are children. There is no question about Abba's receiving us. All we need to do is acknowledge our childishness and come. This is the reason why the broken and simple, the poor in spirit, the anxiety-ridden, the mourning, the meek, the unsatisfied and unfulfilled, the hungry and thirsty, the persecuted and ridiculed find it so easy to turn to the God Jesus reveals. Those who are doing quite well on their own and think that they have life securely within their grasp don't like to admit their ultimate helplessness and come as children before Abba. They don't feel the need of it. It also may be beneath their dignity.
—From *Companions on the Inner Way* by Morton T. Kelsey

❧ Think of the number of people who have been encouraged in this way by the simple writings and profound life of Brother Lawrence. How vastly enriched we are that he was finally persuaded, almost against his will, to write down how he had learned *The Practice of the Presence of God*. His famous words still throb with life and joy, "The time of business does not with me differ from the time of prayer; and in the noise and clatter of my kitchen, while several persons are at the same time calling for different things, I possess God in as great tranquillity as if I were upon my knees at the blessed sacrament."

—From *Freedom of Simplicity* by Richard J. Foster

❧ "There is a place of quiet rest," the poet Cleland McAfee wrote, "near to the heart of God. A place where sin cannot molest." It can be a place to meet the One whom Helmut Thielike called *The Waiting Father*. No one can live well without such places; but many try.

—From *Restoring Your Spiritual Passion* by Gordon MacDonald

❧ It is this linking of piety and mercy which gave Wesleyan spirituality its life and its ministry. It saved the United Societies from becoming ingrown and self-sufficient. Wesley made the world his parish and wanted his followers to do the same. Consequently, Wesley's interpreters nearly two hundred years later have seen his social ethic as an extension of his individual ethic. Or to put it another way, here we see the Wesleyan synthesis—his ability to take two ideas which seem like opposites on the surface, and put them together to form a stronger unity than existed when they were kept separate.

   This is exactly what happened in early Methodist spirituality. Their wedding of piety and mercy forged a more effective instrument in God's hand than they could ever have been if they had opted for one form of spirituality to the exclusion of the other. The same thing is true for our time. Holiness of heart *and* life remain the twin peaks of vital spirituality.

—From *Devotional Life in the Wesleyan Tradition* by Steve Harper

Hymn: Christ Is Alive

Christ is alive! Let Christians sing.
His cross stands empty to the sky.
Let streets and homes with praises ring.
His love in death shall never die.

Christ is alive! No longer bound
To distant years in Palestine,
He comes to claim the here and now
And dwell in every place and time.

Not throned afar, remotely high,
Untouched, unmoved by human pains,
But daily, in the midst of life,
Our Savior in the Godhead reigns.

In every insult, rift, and war,
Where color, scorn, or wealth divide,
He suffers still, yet loves the more,
And lives, though ever crucified.

Christ is alive, and comes to bring
Good news to this and every age,
Till earth and all creation ring
With joy, with justice, love, and praise.
—Brian Wren

27: *Love One Another*

I. Invocation
    Ever-loving God, who having loved us loves us
    still, help us to hear again your word, "By this
    shall they know you are my disciples; that you
    love one another." Turn our hostility into hospi-
    tality and our callousness into care. Through
    Christ, we pray. Amen.

II. Psalm 128

III. Reading and Reflection

IV. Daily Scripture Readings
     Monday   Romans 12:9-21
     Tuesday   Colossians 3:12-17
     Wednesday   Galatians 5:1-15
     Thursday   1 John 2:7-17
     Friday   1 John 3:1-18
     Saturday   1 John 4:7-21
     Sunday   A. Acts 17:22-31; 1 Peter 3:13-22;
                     Psalm 66:8-20; John 14:15-21
                 B. Acts 10:44-48; 1 John 5:1-6; Psalm
                     98; John 15:9-17
                 C. Acts 15:1-2, 22-29; Revelation
                     21:10, 22-27; Psalm 67; John 14:
                     23-29

V. Reflection: Silent and Written

VI. Prayers: For the Church, for Others, for Myself

VII. Hymn: "Forgive My Foes? It Cannot Be"

VIII. Benediction
       In this hour, loving God, you have touched me
       with love. Send me now to be your touch-of-
       love for another. May the love of Jesus flow
       through me, a current of healing and life. Amen.

Readings for Reflection

જ It is contemplation (*contemplatio*) that leads us most powerfully into compassion. It is true that, because of the solidarity of the human race and the more profound oneness of the baptized in Christ, whenever any one of us rises through contemplation to new levels of consciousness the whole human family is raised. Any bit of leaven will leaven the entire mass.
—From Basil Pennington in *Living with Apocalypse* edited by Tilden H. Edwards

જ Hunger, in its stark and highly visible forms, touches a chord in us because our own bodies, our own experience, enable us to relate in some way to the hungry. Our experience of God's goodness in our own lives, and in so much that we know of [God's] goodness to others, equally convinces us that we are not doomed to sit by helplessly while we watch our hungry sisters and brothers die. Hunger, like the poverty which causes it, is not inevitable. *We can make a difference.* We can know a joy God intends for us—that of being both host and guest at the banquet of life.
—From *How You Can Be a Peacemaker* by Mary Evelyn Jegen, SND

જ Hospitality does not seek power over others. Cruelty does. Cruelty deliberately causes harm, especially by crushing a person's self-respect. By manipulating a disparity of power, cruelty sets up a relationship wherein the stronger becomes the victimizer of the weaker. As long as the difference in power is maintained, cruelty will be maintained. To the extent that the difference in power is eliminated, to that extent cruelty will be eliminated. Philip Hallie's studies of cruelty led him to discover that the opposite of cruelty is not liberation from the disparity of power. Rather, he found that the opposite of cruelty is hospitality, a sharing of power.
—From *To Walk Together Again* by Richard M. Gula

❧ I Need to be More Loving

Almighty God,
I know so little of what love in its fullness can be.
My love is marred by jealousy,
    scarred by envy,
        limited by selfishness.
I withhold love at the slightest provocation,
    and withdraw myself from involvement with others
        for fear of being hurt.

Still, I know something of what love can be like.
I can remember being forgiven generously and freely
        by someone I had wronged.
I can remember being comforted and cared for
    when, bruised and battered, I crept home.
I can remember being made strong
        by the realization that someone cared.
I am grateful for such experiences,
    for they tell me what love is about.
And if the Lord Jesus be right,
        to know what love is like
    is to know what you are like.

If we humans can manifest unselfishness and concern,
    is it not because such experiences are of the very
        nature of that which is most important?
For out of the heart of the Lord Jesus
    came the evidences of his love
        for all kinds of people
    and his refusal to give up on any of us.
I am grateful for that love and for that refusal,
    for in him I have hope.
I can even hope
    that I may catch more of his Spirit in my life.
Will you help me to be more outgoing,
        less sensitive to slights,
        and more alert to the feelings of others?
Will you help me to be less quick to judge
        and less righteous in my indignation?

Will you help me to be more open to life
and to other people?
Will you give me confidence enough to be less
defensive and less ready to react to rebuffs?
Give me steadiness and firmness
and true commitment to the life of faith. *Amen.*
—From *A Book of Uncommon Prayer* by Kenneth G.
Phifer

❧ O God, bless every member of this household.
Now as I pray this prayer, let me not still harbour
in my heart a wrongful feeling of jealousy or bitterness or anger towards any of them.
—From *A Diary of Private Prayer* by John Baillie

❧ Yet I would not think only of myself or pray only for
myself, as now I seek Thy presence. I would remember
before Thee all my human brothers and sisters who
need Thy help. Especially to-night I think—

of those who are faced by great temptation:
of those who are faced by tasks too great for their
powers:
of those who stand in any valley of decision:
of those who are in debt or poverty:
of those who are suffering the consequences of
misdeeds long ago repented of:
of those who, by reason of early surroundings,
have never had a fair chance in life:
of all family circles broken by death;
of all missionaries of the Kingdom of Heaven in
far-away corners of the earth:
of those who lift high the lamp of truth in lonely
places. . . .

Dear Father of [humankind] make me the human
channel, so far as in me lies, through which Thy divine
love and pity may reach the hearts and lives of a few of
those who are nearest to me. Amen.
—From *A Diary of Private Prayer* by John Baillie

🙠 Love will make demands on us. It will question us from within. It will disturb us. Sadden us. Play havoc with our feelings. Harass us. Reveal our superficialities. But at last it will bring us to the light.

The light that flashes forth from love is the thirst for martyrdom.

Jesus instituted true martyrdom, and his friends and followers will love martyrdom too.

The primacy of martyrdom will be the apex of their scale of values.

Martyrdom begins by telling you: "Today your martyrdom will be to detach yourself from your wealth. You will have to be detached if you want to be happy, for wealth will destroy your peace of mind, especially when you see your fellow-man going hungry."

Tomorrow it will tell you: "Don't be an idolater. Cast away your idols! God alone is your God." And you will have to do this to slake the thirst for freedom that love has given you.

Thenceforth this process of purification will be endless, working its way down deeper and deeper to reach the roots of your selfishness, pride and folly.

—From *Why, O Lord?* by Carlo Carretto

Hymn: Forgive My Foes? It Cannot Be

Forgive my foes? it cannot be:
My foes with cordial love embrace?
Fast bound in sin and misery,
Unsaved, unchanged by hallowing grace,
Throughout my fallen soul I feel
With man this is impossible.

Great Searcher of the mazy heart,
A thought from thee I would not hide,
I cannot draw th'envenomed dart,
Or quench this hell of wrath and pride,
Jesus, till I thy Spirit receive,
Thou know'st, I never can forgive.

Come, Lord, and tame the tiger's force,
Arrest the whirlwind in my will,
Turn back the torrent's rapid course,
And bid the headlong sun stand still,
The rock dissolve, the mountain move,
And melt my hatred into love.

Root out the wrath thou dost retain;
And when I have my Savior's mind,
I cannot render pain for pain,
I cannot speak a word unkind,
An angry thought I cannot know,
Or count mine injurer my foe.
—Charles Wesley

28: *That All May be One*

I. Invocation
    Our Lord, before your trials of suffering you prayed that all your disciples might be one in Spirit. Grant that we may be bound together in love for one another and in obedience to you, that the world may see and believe. In Jesus, our Lord. Amen.

II. Psalm 133

III. Reading and Reflection

IV. Daily Scripture Readings
Monday	1 Peter 1:13-25
Tuesday	Titus 3:1-11
Wednesday	Philemon 1-25
Thursday	Hebrews 13:1-25
Friday	2 Timothy 1:1-14
Saturday	1 Thessalonians 1:2-10

    Sunday
    A. Acts 1:6-14; 1 Peter 4:12-14; 5:6-11; Psalm 68:1-10; John 17:1-11
    B. Acts 1:15-17, 21-26; 1 John 5:9-13; Psalm 1; John 17:11b-19
    C. Acts 16:16-34; Revelation 22:12-14, 16-17, 20; Psalm 97; John 17:20-26

V. Reflection: Silent and Written

VI. Prayers: For the Church, for Others, for Myself

VII. Hymn: "Jesus, United by Thy Grace"

VIII. Benediction
    Enlarge my heart, dear Lord, that I may truly love you and live in harmony with all my fellows. In Jesus' name. Amen.

Readings for Reflection

❧ Therefore, in all we are called to do in the way of holding human society together, the greatest blessing is this: although humanly we have to distinguish between righteousness and unrighteousness, these distinctions go no further than our own opinion. Would you go so far as to damn people for eternity? Do you want to take over the work of God? Is it then . . . that *you* would make eternal decrees?
—From *Thy Kingdom Come: A Blumhardt Reader* edited by
  Vernard Eller

❧ Jesus' command of love is tough. People throughout the ages have tried to make it work. Some people have died for it; almost all have known the discouragement of failing to make it work. What does this love demand? Of all the attempts to bring some insight into what love demands, I have found those which explore the notion of "hospitality" to be the most helpful. The New Testament word for this kind of love which is commanded, and which is the love that reconciles, is *agape*. The Greek word, however, does not seem to work for most people today. Who knows what it means? "Hospitality" works. Everyone seems to have some idea of what it means.
—From *To Walk Together Again* by Richard M. Gula

❧ The divine ratification we need is that which comes with the good news that God really does love all people without exception, that God loves "us," and, most importantly, that God loves me! The heartwarming part of the Good News is that we do not have to come to this stunning truth all by ourselves. As we make our efforts to reach out and be open to this loving God, God is already there helping us. This is grace: "I am here; I am with you; I love you; I will never let you go!"

In retrieving our experiences of God and images of God, we are forced to confront the basic question that penetrates to the nature of our relationship to God: Is the Mystery within which we live, and to which we are inescapably bonded, ultimately gracious or indifferent? Are we grounded in a reality that cares for us or not? That is for us or against us? The Christian response to these questions is that the hallmark of God is graciousness. God cares for us. God is for us. This takes us to heart of the reality we call grace.

—From *To Walk Together Again* by Richard M. Gula

   The covenant-call to be God's people, far from being primarily an invitation to special privilege, is first of all a summons to special responsibility. God calls a people to live in response to the needs of others, to live in right relationship with God, to bring justice and mercy to the land, and to lead the way toward peace and freedom. The covenant binds Israel to trust in God alone, not putting confidence in false prophets or false securities (Ezk 13:16; Jr 6:14; 8:10-12; Is 7:1-9; 30:1-4).

—From *Seeking God's Peace in a Nuclear Age: A Call to Disciples of Christ*

   For whatever the actual state of the empirical church, we know that in that sphere human beings are beckoned into new relationships with one another, and that this beckoning is more than a command; it is gospel. We can begin there, and thus also in the larger community beyond this sphere of explicit faith, to turn toward one another. The face of forgiveness, acceptance, and love that has been shown using the compassionate countenance of the God of Golgotha can be reflected in the faces that we show to one another. We can also begin there—and thus beyond the bounds of this fellowship as well—to live out of a trust that overcomes the ancient addiction to suspicion that infects our race. We can begin there—and thus also in the larger community of humankind—to seek and find intimations of the communality that is our de facto status as creatures, though we resist it strenuously and take refuge in the illusion of self-sufficiency. We can begin there—and

thus find the necessary support for the same praxis within the life of the world—to defy the barriers to peace and justice that arise when human beings are conditioned to regard other human beings as "the enemy," or to think them less than fully human.
—From *Imaging God* by Douglas John Hall

❧ Two-thirds of the people of this earth have not heard the wonderful news of Christ's liberating Gospel. Are you not moved with the desire to do more than ever before to reach out to help? This is no time for business as usual. Nearly two and one-half billion people stand culturally outside the reach of a Christian witness. These "hidden peoples" will never be reached through the Church as it now stands. No Christian is within their cultural sphere of influence. We must find new creative ways to reach out to the hidden peoples if we ever hope to fulfill Christ's commission to disciple all nations. Such a task will demand vast outlays of time and resources.

The Covenant that came out of the 1974 International Congress on World Evangelism held in Lausanne, Switzerland, states, "The goal should be, by all available means and at the earliest possible time, that every person will have the opportunity to hear, understand, and receive the good news." Our hearts resonate with this high and holy goal. But it will never be realized without drastic and sacrificial lifestyles changes. The Covenant continues, "We cannot hope to attain this goal without sacrifice. All of us are shocked by the poverty of millions and disturbed by the injustices which cause it. Those of us who live in affluent circumstances accept our duty to develop a simple life-style in order to contribute more generously to both relief and evangelism."

Ecologists and economists shout out to us that simplicity is a new necessity. The great host of hidden people shout out to us that simplicity is a new necessity. Will we hear their cry?
—From *Freedom of Simplicity* by Richard J. Foster

Hymn: Jesus, United by Thy Grace

Jesus, united by thy grace
And each to each endeared,
With confidence we seek thy face
And know our prayer is heard.

Help us to help each other, Lord,
Each other's cross to bear;
Let all their friendly aid afford,
And feel each other's care.

Up unto thee, our living Head,
Let us in all things grow;
Till thou hast made us free indeed
And spotless here below.

Touched by the lodestone of thy love,
Let all our hearts agree,
And ever toward each other move,
And ever move toward thee.

To thee, inseparably joined,
Let all our spirits cleave;
O may we all the loving mind
That was in thee receive.

This is the bond of perfectness,
Thy spotless charity;
O let us, still we pray, possess
The mind that was in thee.
—Charles Wesley

Pentecost Sunday
29: Life in the Spirit

I. Invocation
Ever-watchful God, who knows the heart and
secret desires of all persons, search my heart, I
pray. See if there be any harm in me, and lead
me in your way—forever. I pray in the name of
your own gentle Spirit. Amen.

II. Psalm 104

III. Reading and Reflection

IV. Daily Scripture Readings
Monday	Ephesians 4:17-32
Tuesday	Ephesians 3:14-21
Wednesday	Ezekiel 39:21-29
Thursday	2 Corinthians 1:3-11
Friday	2 Corinthians 8:1-15
Saturday	1 Corinthians 13:1-13

Sunday
A. Acts 2:1-21; 1 Corinthians 12:3b-13; Psalm 104:24-34; John 20:19-23
B. Ezekiel 37:1-14; Romans 8:22-27; Psalm 104:24-34; John 16:4b-15
C. Acts 2:1-21; Romans 8:14-17; Psalm 104:24-34; John 14:8-17, 25-27

V. Reflection: Silent and Written

VI. Prayers: For the Church, for Others, for Myself

VII. Hymn: "Like the Murmur of the Dove's Song"

VIII. Benediction
Come upon me, Spirit of the living God. Melt
all hardness of heart. Use me for your own pur-
poses wherever you are sending me now. Amen.

Readings for Reflection

❧ While there are obvious political, economic, social and technological dimensions to the issues of nuclear war, it must be recognized that the issues posed are first and foremost of a religious and ethical nature. Through the scriptures we have received a vision of God's intention to overcome all hostility and alienation, and to bring *shalom* to all creation. Our calling is to be faithful to that divine revelation and that vision. From the standpoint of biblical faith, nuclear issues are religious issues. The vision of God's concern for human suffering and God's wrath against those who cause oppression and destruction must become our guiding vision if we would claim to be God's people.

—From *Seeking God's Peace in the Nuclear Age: A Call to Disciples of Christ*

❧ You cannot command or compel people into holiness, you cannot increase their spiritual stature one cubit by any kind of force or compulsion. You can do it only by sharing your life with them, by making them feel your goodness, by your love and sacrifice for them.

—From *The Double Search* by Rufus M. Jones

❧ I feel an urgency at this stage in my life to name the human expressions and vivid manifestations of our life in the Spirit. I believe that nothing human is foreign to the Spirit, that the Spirit embraces all. Our mundane experiences contain all the stuff of holiness and of human growth in grace. Our world is rife with messages and signatures of the Spirit. Our encounters with one another are potential sites of the awakening and energizing that characterize the Spirit. But so much goes unnoticed. We fail so often to recognize the light that shines through the tiny chinks and the dusty panes of our daily lives. We are too busy to name the event that is blessed in its ordinariness, holy in its uniqueness, and grace-filled in its underlying challenge.

—From *Every Bush Is Burning* by Joan Puls

The holiness of God is all around us, but it is not something easily recognized. Although the experience of the holy is direct (we know we have encountered something out of the ordinary), it is reflected in people whose lives are as complex as our own. In Mother Teresa of Calcutta, the world experienced a vision of holiness; but as soon as she came to the world's attention, she was criticized for her failure to challenge the system that produced the conditions of poverty and hunger to which she was responding. The criticism, I suspect, was accurate; but rather than diminishing the holiness Mother Teresa reflected, it simply reminded us of her humanity. Holiness and perfection are not synonyms.

—From *Invitation to Holiness* by James C. Fenhagen

Prayer leads you to see new paths and to hear new melodies in the air. Prayer is the breath of your life which gives you freedom to go and stay where you wish and to find the many signs which point out the way to a new land. Praying is not simply some necessary compartment in the daily schedule of a Christian or a source of support in time of need, nor is it restricted to Sunday morning or as a frame to surround mealtimes. Praying is living.

—From *With Open Hands* by Henri J. M. Nouwen

I Need to Feel Whole

O God, what is Spirit?
How do I worship in spirit and in truth?
I am such a solid, earthly creature,
    my feet planted firmly on the ground,
    my life based upon material things.
I like to touch and feel and see before I believe.
I am accustomed to dealing with houses, land, and
        money, with bread, meat, and potatoes,
        with objects handled, weighed, and valued
        by my own standards.

I am uncomfortable with what cannot be analyzed
    or dissected or given a market value.
What is Spirit?

Yet, O Lord, the very things I handle and see
    lose meaning when they become ends in
        themselves.
They are all given meaning by the things of the spirit,
    by love and hope and faith.
I know when I come down to it,
    if I have all kinds of earthly goods
        and have not love,
    I have nothing.
I need the mystery beyond the tangible.
I need the things of the spirit
    to give meaning to the material things I prize.
I cannot divide life up,
    you have made it whole.
If I avoid love, diminish hope, deny faith,
    my appreciation of my house and land,
    my meat and potatoes, shrinks,
And I become a little man
    with little aims and little power.

So help me to see that I worship in spirit and in truth,
    not just through the use of the right words
        in the right place at the right time.
I worship in spirit and in truth
    as life assumes wholeness.

I worship in spirit
    as life takes on shape and form,
    and I glory in it all.
I worship in truth insofar as I know that
    no life can be separated from your Spirit.
I worship as I offer it all unto you. *Amen.*
—From *A Book of Uncommon Prayer* by Kenneth G.
    Pfifer

❧ In the New Testament, we glimpse how those early
Christians were "trying on" their new life in Christ. For
most of them, the changes were radical departures

from their former patterns of life. Moreover, the early Christians daily faced the subtle and insidious pressures of the pagan world as well as the threats of oppression and death, so living the new life was a struggle for them. That is why we find repeated encouragement and challenge from the leaders in the church to stay faithful: "Put off your old nature which belongs to your former manner of life . . . and be renewed in the spirit of your minds, and put on the new nature, created after the likeness of God in true righteousness and holiness" (Eph. 4:22-24, RSV). Or this word: "As obedient children, do not be conformed to the passions of your former ignorance, but as he who called you is holy, be holy yourselves in all your conduct" (1 Pet. 1:14-15, RSV).

Temptations, frustrations, and pressures beset believers today, and our new life in Christ can be easily compromised and betrayed. In fact, it may be as difficult—if not more so—to live out a new life in our day than it was in the first century. This, paradoxically, because the pressures are more subtle, the temptations are cloaked with respectability, and the gray areas of compromise are almost the norm. It is neither easy nor simple to translate our commitment to Christ into the living of our days. It does not happen instantaneously or automatically, but it is instead a process of growth and development, including reversals, retreats, detours, beginning over, and moving ahead. We need such an understanding of our journey at the very outset because there are those who claim otherwise, who promote the new life in Christ as a kind of idyllic state of spiritual perfection in which there are no doubts, uncertainties, stumblings, or times of falling away. Such claims are simply not true, are very misleading, and result in unnecessary anguish and discouragement.
—From *Forever Beginning* by Donald J. Shelby

&. Recently, I have experienced great physical reformation in intensive physiotherapy. In a series of ten sessions with a highly trained physiotherapist, my body has undergone remarkable changes. Tightened tendons, conditioned by years of bad habits of posture and relating to my body, have been stretched and released. A hump in my back, formed by long hours slouched over my writing desk, has been removed. Constricted muscles in my stomach which were pulling me down into a stooped posture have been liberated so that I can stand up straight. Forty-nine years of self-conditioning of my body are being reversed. Over the months of therapy I have grown an inch! I do not have to be the physical person I was for the rest of my life. The body is like plastic and under the skilled hands of the therapist, I have been liberated to stand, walk, and sit differently.

I have shared this personal experience as an illustration that none of us needs to remain the person we are. What that series of treatments did to my body, Christ has done and continues to do with my personality. I am not the personality I was; nor am I the person I will be. Seldom a day goes by without the Lord's impact.

—From *Radiance of the Inner Splendor* by Lloyd John Ogilvie

❧ Give me, O Lord, purity of lips, a clean and innocent heart, and rectitude of action. Give me humility, patience, abstinence, chastity, prudence, justice, fortitude, temperance. Give me the spirit of wisdom and understanding, the spirit of counsel and strength, the spirit of knowledge and godliness, and of Thy fear. Make me ever to seek Thy face with all my heart, all my soul, all my mind; grant me to have a contrite and humbled heart in Thy presence—to prefer nothing to Thy love. Most high, eternal, and ineffable Wisdom, drive away from me the darkness of blindness and ignorance; most high and eternal Strength, deliver me; most high and eternal Fortitude, assist me; most high and incomprehensible Light, illuminate me; most high and infinite Mercy, have mercy on me. *Amen.*
—A Gallican Sacramentary

Hymn: Like the Murmur of the Dove's Song

Like the murmur of the dove's song,
Like the challenge of her flight,
Like the vigor of the wind's rush,
Like the new flame's eager might:
Come, Holy Spirit, come.

To the members of Christ's body,
To the branches of the Vine,
To the church in faith assembled,
To her midst as gift and sign:
Come, Holy Spirit, come.

With the healing of division,
With the ceaseless voice of prayer,
With the power of love and witness,
With the peace beyond compare:
Come, Holy Spirit, come.
—Carl P. Daw, Jr.

30: God in Three Persons

I. Invocation
    Almighty and everlasting God, help us to know
    you in the three glorious expressions of your
    being—Father, Son, and Holy Spirit—that we
    may share in your one and eternal glory. Amen.

II. Psalm 80

III. Reading and Reflection

IV. Daily Scripture Readings
     Monday   Deuteronomy 6:4-25
     Tuesday   John 5:19-29
     Wednesday   1 Corinthians 12:1-13
     Thursday   Ephesians 1:1-14
     Friday   Colossians 1:1-14
     Saturday   John 16:1-11
     Sunday   A. Deuteronomy 4:32-40; 2 Corin-
                   thians 13:5-14; Psalm 33:1-12;
                   Matthew 28:16-20
                B. Isaiah 6:1-8; Romans 8:12-17;
                   Psalm 29; John 3:1-17
                C. Proverbs 8:22-31; Romans 5:1-5;
                   Psalm 8; John 16:12-15

V. Reflection: Silent and Written

VI. Prayers: For the Church, for Others, for Myself

VII. Hymn: "Come, Thou Almighty King"

VIII. Benediction
       Keep me steadfast, my God, in faith and service,
       that in me the fullness of your glory may take
       bodily expression. I pray. Amen.

Readings for Reflection

🍂 "My Father and I will come and abide in you." Few of us really comprehend the meaning of these words of Christ. Besides our baptism, besides the food of the Eucharist which sustains us along the way, besides the psychological assurance and the spiritual reality of forgiveness in the sacrament of reconciliation, what exactly do these words mean to us?

Christ assures us that the Trinity dwells in us. To the Eastern mind, this is the very essence of faith, and of our life as Christians. It is the starting point, to be returned to again and again, like a fountain of crystal clear water.

—From *Soul of My Soul* by Catherine de Hueck Doherty

🍂 No one had ever imagined that life would be born from death, and that the Messiah would have reigned from the gallows. This required something more than logic, even that of all the theologians put together.

It was a revelation. And what a revelation!

Believing that henceforth we should win by losing defied all sense. Believing that God intended to inaugurate the kingdom of love freely given, the kingdom in which the poor were to be first and the rich overthrown in their uselessness and stupidity; believing in such an inversion of values would have been beyond our wildest imagination!

The Spirit had to come.

And the Spirit did come.

And then we believed.

—From *Why, O Lord?* by Carlo Caretto

🍂 You believe there is such a thing as *light*, whether flowing from the sun or any other luminous body. But you cannot comprehend either its nature or the manner wherein it flows. How does it move from Jupiter to the earth in eight minutes, two hundred thousand miles in a moment? How do the rays of the candle brought into the room instantly disperse into every corner? Here are three candles, yet there is but one light. Explain this, and I will explain the Three-One God.

The knowledge of the Three-One God is interwoven with all true Christian faith, with all vital religion.
—John Wesley

➡ Goodness! How difficult it is to believe in the sort of Messiah that Jesus of Nazareth represents!

To believe that we win by losing our very selves!

To believe that love is everything.

To believe that power is a great danger, wealth slavery, comfortable life a misfortune.

It is not easy.

This is why you hear [people] in the street say, "If there was a God there would not be all this suffering."

Two thousand years have gone, and there are still Christians whose doctrinal notions belong to those ancient days when the power and existence of God was revealed by displays of strength and the victory of armies. And especially by wealth and having more possessions.

The real secret had not then been received.

Nor is it received very easily even today.

Hence the blasphemy in general circulation denying the kingdom's visibility, given the ordeal of suffering and death.

The old teaching that we, the Church, must be strong still feeds our determination to possess the land and dominate the world.

We must make ourselves felt. We must keep our enemies down. We must scowl. We must win, and to win we need money, money, money. And to have money we need banks, we need the means and we need clever bankers. How can we do good without means, without money? Let's have a big meeting, and then any opposition will be shamed into silence. Well, we must defend our rights, the rights of the Church. We must defeat our enemies.

Enemies, always enemies on the Church's horizon!
Yet Jesus has told us in no uncertain terms that we no
longer have any enemies, since they are the same
people we are supposed to love, and love specially.

Can it be that we have not understood?

Don't we read the Gospel in our churches?

How long shall we wait before following the teaching of Jesus?

—From *Why, O Lord?* by Carlo Carretto

🙠 Since God is far beyond our limited comprehension,
we can understand why different people view God in
different ways. Several of these ways can be widely
convincing since they are based on quite evident aspects of reality. Even the most skeptical or scientifically
rigorous person is likely to accept one or more of the
following views. There is certainly a fundamental,
sustaining force or energizing power in all of reality. We
can think of God as this ground of being. There is that
which holds reality together in unity and order, that
sustains spontaneity within a framework of regularity.
There are also unrealized potentialities in persons, nature, and society. We can think of God as a power
establishing and sustaining these possibilities, or as the
creative process in all reality. We can see God as the
source of values such as truth, beauty, goodness, and
love. In all these respects God is here now, as well as
everywhere always. God is continuously active in all of
reality. We cannot remove ourselves from God's presence.

—From *Explorations in Meditation and Contemplation* by
Harvey Seifert

🙠 Was nothing changed by the passage of Jesus of
Nazareth?

Have we made no effort to grasp his motives for
substituting humility for pride, simplicity for complication, poverty for wealth, service for power?

Should not the holy wars, the crusades, the ranks
of Christians drawn up to defend the privileges of the
Church, be over and done with by now?

You see, it is hard to understand and even harder to live the true privilege of those who follow Christ: the privilege of the cross.

The fact of the matter is that in my old pagan heart I have got to grasp the meaning of the Beatitudes.

They sound so unconvincing to the sort of Christians we are, who have received baptism like the squirt of a water pistol.

—From *Why, O Lord?* by Carlo Carretto

᠅ Daily we enter the Trinity through our journey inward. There I find the God who dwells in my heart. Immediately, I open wide my arms to embrace my brother and sister with this renewed life! I touch God, I touch you, and I am cruciform as a Christian is meant to be. I pick you up and bring you with me, not into myself but upwards. I lift you up to the Trinity.

—From *Soul of My Soul* by Catherine de Hueck Doherty

Hymn: Come, Thou Almighty King

Come, thou almighty King,
Help us thy name to sing,
Help us to praise!
Father all-glorious
O'er all victorious,
Come and reign over us,
Ancient of Days!

Come, thou incarnate Word,
Gird on thy mighty sword,
Our prayer attend!
Come, and thy people bless,
And give thy word success;
Spirit of holiness,
On us descend!

Come, holy Comforter.
Thy sacred witness bear,
In this glad hour:
Thou who almighty art,
Now rule in every heart,
And ne'er from us depart,
Spirit of power!

To thee, great One in Three,
Eternal praises be,
Hence, evermore:
Thy sovereign majesty
May we in glory see,
And to eternity
Love and adore!
—Anonymous

31: The Authority of Jesus Christ

I. Invocation
Our Lord Jesus, whose word is always authority, speak to me now, that I may hear your special word for me today. By Christ. Amen.

II. Psalm 103

III. Reading and Reflection

IV. Daily Scripture Readings
Monday	Colossians 1:15-20
Tuesday	Acts 3:1-10
Wednesday	Acts 5:1-16
Thursday	Acts 5:33-42
Friday	Acts 9:1-19
Saturday	Acts 12:1-11
Sunday	A. Genesis 12:1-9; Romans 3:21-28; Psalm 33:12-22; Matthew 7:21-29
	B. 1 Samuel 16:1-13; 2 Corinthians 4:5-12; Psalm 20; Mark 2:23–3:6
	C. 1 Kings 8:22-23, 41-43; Galatians 1:1-10; Psalm 100; Luke 7:1-10

V. Reflection: Silent and Written

VI. Prayers: For the Church, for Others, for Myself

VII. Hymn: "Christ, Whose Glory Fills the Skies"

VIII. Benediction
I have heard your call to me in this hour, and I bind your word to my heart as the guide and rule of life. Speak to others through me, I pray. Amen.

*If the Sunday between May 24 and 28 follows Trinity Sunday, use Week 14.

Readings for Reflection

❧ As members of churches we are also members of other groups and institutions—political parties, economic organizations, regional and national associations. Each of these constituencies has its vested interests, its value systems, and its authority figures. We cannot deny our participation in these groups; in fact, it is of the utmost importance that these memberships be acknowledged, lest we become unconsciously possessed by them. But the challenge before us as followers of Jesus Christ is to make conscious decisions as Christians, honoring our commitment to him above the claims and assumptions of every other authority.

—From *Seeking God's Peace in a Nuclear Age: A Call to Disciples of Christ*

❧ The Jerusalem Bible does fairly well at translating the Greek word of Jesus' attitude toward Peter. *Emblepas* has the character of a fixed gaze or spiritual discernment. Again our own contemplation is the best way to touch the mystery of those eyes and that look. What would it be like to have God look into our eyes? Perhaps the terror of realizing our absolute nakedness, then the deeper terror of seeing God see depths and dark places and glorious possibilities in us totally beyond our awareness. Then the incredible peace of loving acceptance transforms terror into the relief of being totally known and the joy and promise of what we can be.

—From *Healing of Purpose* by John E. Biersdorf

❧ In the debates, charges, and countercharges that have already been stimulated by the Roman Catholic Bishops' pastoral on the economy, the holy will most certainly emerge. When we speak about how a society organizes its resources, whom it is responsive to, and what its vision is, we are talking about a Kingdom vision. As the gap between rich and poor becomes wider, we are being prepared for a radical shift in consciousness that will make it possible for us to see what most of us cannot see now. This will occur, I believe, as the holy emerges in ways we least expect.

—From *Invitation to Holiness* by James C. Fenhagen

❧ The role and contribution of women in human society is not just an issue that is confronting Western society. It is an issue of exploding consequences in Islamic and many Third World societies. Because our understanding of sexuality—of what it means to be male and female—is fundamental to our understanding of humanity, it draws us to the very core of God's vision of creation. The conflicts we experience over abortion, homosexuality, and gender are deeply divisive, causing hurt and crippling injury in more ways than we can imagine. The holiness we look for will not be seen in who can shout the loudest, or make the more coercive claim for the principles they will defend to the death; but rather, holiness will appear in those people who can take us beyond where we are now and allow us to see in them something new. The holy might appear in people we least expect. Indeed, the holy might emerge in us.

—From *Invitation to Holiness* by James C. Fenhagen

❧ The biblical use of the world "righteousness" is the moral equivalent of what we mean when we speak of holiness. It incorporates such concerns as a passion for justice and a concern for truth along with the need to live an ethically responsible life. It involves reflecting in what we *do* the Christian moral vision by which we understand who we are. Righteousness is the human expression of holiness embodying a vision rooted in moral perspective. In the New Testament the same word is used for righteousness that is used for justification. As New Testament scholar John Koenig puts it, righteousness is God making things right.

—From *Invitation to Holiness* by James C. Fenhagen

☙ He comes to us as One unknown, without a name, as of old, by the lake side, He came to those men who knew Him not. He speaks to us the same word: "Follow thou me!" and sets us to the tasks which He has to fulfill for our time. He commands. And to those who obey Him, whether they be wise or simple, He will reveal Himself in the toils, the conflicts, the sufferings which they shall pass through in His fellowship, and, as an ineffable mystery, they shall learn in their own experience Who He is.

—From *The Quest for the Historical Jesus* by Albert Schweitzer

☙ Christian joy is joy in obedience, joy in loving God and keeping [God's] commandments; and yet not in keeping them as if we were thereby to fulfill the terms of the covenant of works, as if by any works or righteousness of ours, we were to procure pardon and acceptance with God. Not so: we are already pardoned and accepted, through the mercy of God in Christ Jesus. Not as if we were by our own obedience to procure life, life from the death of sin: this also we have already from the grace of God. Us "hath he quickened, who were dead in sins," and now we are "alive to God, through Jesus Christ our Lord." But we rejoice in walking according to the covenant of grace, in holy love and happy obedience. We rejoice in knowing that, "being justified through his grace," we have "not received that grace of God in vain," that God having freely (not for the sake of our willing or running, but through the blood of the Lamb) reconciled us to himself, we run, in the strength which [God] hath given us, the way of [God's] commandments.

"But can Christ be in the same heart where sin is?" Undoubtedly he can. Otherwise it never could be saved therefrom. Where the sickness is, there is the physician,

Carrying on his work within,
Striving till he cast out sin.

Christ indeed cannot *reign*, where sin *reigns*, neither will he *dwell* where any sin is *allowed*. But he *is* and

dwells in the heart of every believer, who is *fighting against* all sin, although it be not yet purified, according to the purification of the sanctuary.
—John Wesley

Hymn: Christ, Whose Glory Fills the Skies

Christ, whose glory fills the skies,
Christ, the true, the only light,
Sun of Righteousness, arise,
Triumph o're the shades of night;
Day-spring from on high, be near;
Day-star in my heart appear.

Dark and cheerless is the morn
Unaccompanied by thee;
Joyless is the day's return,
Till thy mercy's beams I see;
Till they inward light impart,
Cheer my eyes and warm my heart.

Visit then this soul of mine;
Pierce the gloom of sin and grief;
Fill me, Radiancy divine,
Scatter all my unbelief;
More and more thyself display,
Shining to the perfect day.
—Charles Wesley

32: Christ's True Family

I. Invocation
O God, loving parent of us all, we approach you in confidence that though father and mother forsake us, you will never forsake us, and that Jesus is a friend who sticks with us closer than a brother. O glorious bond. Amen.

II. Psalm 40

III. Reading and Reflection

IV. Daily Scripture Readings
Monday	Hosea 6:1-6
Tuesday	Hosea 11:1-9
Wednesday	Matthew 13:53-58
Thursday	Matthew 21:12-17
Friday	John 17:20-26
Saturday	Matthew 12:46-50
Sunday	A. Genesis 22:1-18; Romans 4:13-18; Psalm 13; Matthew 9:9-13
	B. 1 Samuel 16:14-23; 2 Corinthians 4:13–5:1; Psalm 57; Mark 3:20-35
	C. 1 Kings 17:17-24; Galatians 1:11-24; Psalm 113; Luke 7:11-17

V. Reflection: Silent and Written

VI. Prayers: For the Church, for Others, for Myself

VII. Hymn: "Help Us Accept Each Other"

VIII. Benediction
My Lord, you said your mother, brothers, and sisters were all those who did your will. Help me this day to accomplish your will for my life that you and I may be one. Amen.

Readings for Reflection

❧ In the face of the needy, the sufferer, the enemy, we see the face of the incarnate God. What we do to the needy, the sufferer, the enemy, we do to God. Moreover, our every action as Christians either expresses or denies the intention of Christ who, in indwelling our humanity, lives not only in all other persons, but in each of us as well. Conversion to the way of Christ demands the radical change which follows our acknowledgement of this indwelling: "It is no longer I who live, but Christ who lives in me" (Ga 2:20). "To me to live is Christ" (Ph 1:21. The Christian life is a continuing effort to release the divine impulse through all that we say and do.

—From *Seeking God's Peace in a Nuclear Age: A Call to Disciples of Christ*

❧ In a world endangered by the threat of nuclear annihilation and pulled apart by opposing political ideologies, gross economic inequities, and polarizing rhetoric, the church is called to be reconciler and peacemaker. The church is not limited by political boundaries; it transcends national identities in celebrating the unity of the human family in God's creation.

—From *Seeking God's Peace in a Nuclear Age: A Call to Disciples of Christ*

❧ Some time ago when I was browsing through St. John's gospel, I came across these reassuring words of Jesus: "Whoever believes in me will do what I do— yes, he will do even greater things" (Jn 14:12). That is surely an exaggeration, I thought. It cannot be true. This has to be understood as hyperbolic language. Doing greater things than Jesus has done! But when I studied the context and began to think about it, the full impact of Jesus' statement dawned on me. Jesus meant what he said, and its message has weighty implications.

Jesus has just declared, "Whoever has seen me has

seen the Father." He goes on to say that he is in the Father and the Father in him. Also his teaching is not his own teaching, but the Father's. Jesus' activity, in other words, what he does and says, reveals the Father. Then he continues:

> The Father, who remains in me, does his own work. Believe me when I say that I am in the Father and the Father is in me. If not, believe because of the things I do. I am telling you the truth: whoever believes in me will do what I do— yes, he will do even greater things, because I am going to the Father. And I will do whatever you ask for in my name, so that the Father's glory will be shown through the Son (Jn 14:10-13).

Whatever Jesus does—the preaching on the kingdom, the manifestation of his power, his service to the people— is all work done by the Father. In the same way the Father will work in Jesus' disciples. Jesus is going to heaven, but in the disciples the same work of the Father will go on. The disciples, therefore, will do what Jesus did—yes, even greater things than he did.
—From *Inheriting the Master's Cloak* by John Wijngaards

&. This is the truth.
The will of God is fulfilled in spite of us . . . and even with us sometimes.
—From *Why, O Lord?* by Carlo Carretto

&. Yes, the kingdom is fulfilled, and even if hindered it is still fulfilled.
There will still be power-seekers even in Christian clothing.
But there will also be saints.
Many people will go on clinging to the old Adam's way of thinking, concentrating on righteousness and formal worship, but deep in the hearts of those visited by the Spirit of Jesus there will be an explosion, the novelty of the kingdom will erupt there and little by little, day by day, good will gain the upper hand over

evil, mercy over revenge, willingness to serve over selfish prideful interest.

Above all there will be more and more of those who joyfully receive the scandalous words Jesus said to the brigand who made his confession beside him on the cross: "today you will be with me in paradise" (Luke 23:43).

So drastic an absolution for so real a sinner may seem a bit forced.

Not to be shocked by it means you have indeed made a great leap forward in understanding mercy.

This is the leap into the kingdom of grace freely given, the kingdom which even prostitutes and publicans will enter ahead of you if you have trusted in your own presumed righteousness.

This is the kingdom of the poor, the triumph of those on the margin of society, the oppressed, the last and the least.

This is the kingdom the currency of which is forgiveness, where the banks amass only those treasures produced by human love and suffering.

This is the kingdom where the race for money and comfort does not exist, only the race for mutual service and love of your neighbor.

This is the kingdom where the highest status is martyrdom.

How extraordinary, to see all our values reversed, to see the mighty tumble from their thrones, as Mary sings in the Magnificat!
—From *Why, O Lord?* by Carlo Carretto

Hymn: Help Us Accept Each Other

Help us accept each other
As Christ accepted us;
Teach us as sister, brother,
Each person to embrace.
Be present, Lord, among us,
And bring us to believe
We are ourselves accepted
And meant to love and live.

Teach us, O Lord, your lessons,
As in our daily life
We struggle to be human
And search for hope and faith.
Teach us to care for people,
For all, not just for some,
To love them as we find them,
Or as they may become.

Let your acceptance change us,
So that we may be moved
In living situations
To do the truth in love;
To practice your acceptance,
Until we know by heart
The table of forgiveness
And laughter's healing art.

Lord, for today's encounters
With all who are in need,
Who hunger for acceptance,
For righteousness and bread,
We need new eyes for seeing,
New hands for holding on;
Renew us with your Spirit;
Lord, free us, make us one!
—Fred Kaan

33: Signs of God's Kingdom

I. Invocation
Our Lord Jesus, who turned water into wine as a sign of the new Kingdom, in you the old has passed away. Behold! You make all things new. Give us today a superabundance of the bread and drink you provide, that all our noble desires may be satisfied. Through your strong name. Amen.

II. Psalm 84

III. Reading and Reflection

IV. Daily Scripture Readings
Monday	Matthew 3:1-10
Tuesday	Matthew 18:21-35
Wednesday	Matthew 20:1-16
Thursday	Matthew 20:20-28
Friday	Luke 9:46-62
Saturday	Acts 7:54–8:8
Sunday	A. Genesis 25:19-34; Romans 5:6-11; Psalm 46; Matthew 9:35–10:8
	B. 2 Samuel 1:1, 17-27; 2 Corinthians 5:6-10, 14-17; Psalm 46; Mark 4:26-34
	C. 1 Kings 19:1-8; Galatians 2:15-21; Psalm 42; Luke 7:36–8:3

V. Reflection: Silent and Written

VI. Prayers: For the Church, for Others, for Myself

VII. Hymn: "O Church of God, United"

VIII. Benediction
O Lord, as at Cana's wedding you filled empty jars with new wine so I ask that you fill me. O glorious provision. Amen.

Readings for Reflection

&❧ The actress Lillah McCarthy describes how she went in great misery to see George Bernard Shaw, just after she had been deserted by her husband:

> I was shivering. Shaw sat very still. The fire brought me warmth . . . How long we sat there I do not know, but presently I found myself walking with dragging steps with Shaw beside me . . . up and down Adelphi Terrace. The weight upon me grew a little lighter and released the tears which would never come before . . . He let me cry. Presently I heard a voice in which all the gentleness and tenderness of the world was speaking. It said: "Look up, dear, look up to the heavens. There is more in life than this. There is much more."

Whatever his own faith in God or lack of it, Shaw points here to something that is fundamental to the spiritual Way. He did not offer smooth words of consolation to Lillah McCarthy, or pretend that her pain would be easy to bear. What he did was more perceptive. He told her to look out for a moment from herself, from her personal tragedy, and to see the world in its objectivity, to sense its wonder and variety, its "thusness." And his advice applies to all of us. However oppressed by my own or others' anguish, I am not to forget that there is more in the world than this, there is much more.

—From *The Orthodox Way* by Kallistos Ware

&❧ The dream of course is just a dream, even if it is the messianic dream. But what the Gospel calls the kingdom is fact—realized in us a little at a time in all the beauty of its design, the marvel of its structures, the fertility of life and the inexhaustible loving creativity of God.

The kingdom of God is the final project of the Absolute, the end of creation, the future of the human being, the answer to people's questions and the revealing of all mysteries.

All things converge on the kingdom Christ came to announce. This is the definitive response to what we see, the meaning of the history in which we are involved, the object of our final expectation.

The kingdom is our future: heaven and earth are its space, the visible and the invisible its reality-in-becoming, God and ourselves its actualizers. The kingdom of God is at the centre of God's heart and of human awareness.

For the poor, the unimportant, the oppressed the kingdom is perfectly intelligible. For the rich, the sated, the sensual it is mysterious and not anything they want to seek.

As Jesus was to say, the kingdom of God is good news to the poor (Luke 4:18; cf. Isa. 61:1): the poor can understand what it means, though of course it is destined to come about and no power on earth can prevent it doing so.

Pride—another name of idolatry—refuses to believe in the kingdom but is constantly in collision with it, since the kingdom lies in everybody's path. The cause of the collision is always an idol embodying pride, and the word of God mocks idols, saying they have "eyes, but never see . . . hands, but never touch, feet, but never walk" (Ps. 115:5-7).

To make pride see the error of its ways it has to be defeated, and all security destroyed.

There is only God!

This is the cornerstone of the kingdom.

Nothing can disturb the design, the perfection of the kingdom, nothing can change the will of God.

At the very most you can remain on the outside. But everything is so arranged that to stay outside is a continuous hell, and the anguish of loneliness will be enough to change your mind and, with all due respect, ask to be allowed to enter.

—From *Why, O Lord?* by Carlo Carretto

❧ *Who can resist God?*

You are certainly free to do so but there is precious little advantage in it.

I do not think resisting God for long would be feasible. All round the kingdom which God's love has designed and willed is an "anti-kingdom," the dominion of "evil," of "Satan the divider," of the "Liar." And it is so horrible that—if I may proffer my personal opinion—I do not think anyone would willingly choose to make it his or remain forever under its sway.

—From *Why, O Lord?* by Carlo Carretto

❧ We are trying to make our communities another Nazareth, where Jesus can come and rest awhile.

—From *Words to Love By* by Mother Teresa

❧ Praying, therefore, means being constantly ready to let go of your certainty and to move on further than where you now are. It demands that you take to the road again and again, leaving your house and looking forward to a new land for yourself and your fellowman. This is why praying demands poverty, that is, the readiness to live a life in which you have nothing to lose so that you always begin afresh. Whenever you willingly choose this poverty you make yourself vulnerable, but you also become free to see the world and to let the world be seen in its true form.

—From *With Open Hands* by Henri J. M. Nouwen

❧ Where are the gentle spirits and the prayerful souls among our leaders? When will we trust the qualifications of credible lifestyle and courageous witness as much as articulation of programmes and financial expertise? When will we die to the styles of government and authority that characterize our secular society and choose the style of the gospel? So that what is most evident in those who direct and encourage us is their pilgrim status, their ability to listen and to learn and to change, and their global sensitivity. Persons who can share their own spiritual adventure and who release and affirm others to do the same.

—From *Every Bush Is Burning* by Joan Puls

Hymn: O Church of God, United

O church of God, united
To serve one common Lord,
Proclaim to all one message,
With hearts in glad accord.
Christ ever goes before us;
We follow day by day
With strong and eager footsteps
Along the upward way.

From every land and nation
The ordered ranks appear;
To serve one valiant leader
They come from far and near.
They chant their one confession,
They praise one living Lord,
And place their sure dependence
Upon his saving word.

Though creeds and tongues may differ,
They speak, O Christ, of thee;
And in thy loving spirit
We shall one people be.
Lord, may our faithful service
And singleness of aim
Proclaim to all the power
Of thy redeeming name.

May thy great prayer be answered
That we may all be one,
Close bound, by love united
In thee, God's blessed Son:
To bring a single witness,
To make the pathway bright,
That souls which grope in darkness
May find the one true light.
—Frederick B. Morley

Sunday between June 19 and 25
(if after Trinity Sunday—otherwise turn to next Sunday)

34: God Calls and Provides

I. Invocation
    O God, who calls those who will to follow along with you, show us our duty today, and give us bread for our journey. Through Jesus Christ. Amen.

II. Psalm 8

III. Reading and Reflection

IV. Daily Scripture Readings
    Monday   1 Corinthians 2:1-13
    Tuesday   Matthew 9:35–10:15
    Wednesday   Matthew 10:16-23
    Thursday   Matthew 10:24-33
    Friday   Matthew 10:34-42
    Saturday   John 21:15-23
    Sunday   A. Genesis 28:10-17; Romans 5:12-19; Psalm 91:1-10; Matthew 10:24-33
                 B. 2 Samuel 5:1-12; 2 Corinthians 5:18–6:2; Psalm 48; Mark 4:35-41
                 C. 1 Kings 19:9-14; Galatians 3:23-29; Psalm 43; Luke 9:18-24

V. Reflection: Silent and Written

VI. Prayers: For the Church, for Others, for Myself

VII. Hymn: "O God Who Shaped Creation"

VIII. Benediction
    I am thine, O Lord. I have heard thy voice! And having heard, I will go wherever you send me and to whatever task. Only go with me, my Lord; I cannot make the journey alone. Amen.

Readings for Reflection

❧ This pervasive sense of togetherness is like the mutuality that develops in marriage. Now more intensely, now less, we have the feeling that *mine* and *thine* are inappropriate, *our* is the proper adjective. If God has chosen to be the Beginning and Beyond of every aspect of our lives, then every aspect of our lives is something we share with God. I suspect this is the implication of the self-disclosure of God recorded in Exodus 3:14. There Moses, having asked God for God's name, receives the enigmatic answer, "I am who I am."

The point seems to be that the mere name *God* is not much of an identifier. Only over time, through experience, in trust, will the mystery reveal who and what it is. Moreover, this revelation will depend on our capacity to appreciate it. Communication, even between God and us, is a two-way flow of traffic. God can only transmit effectively if we are good receivers. And the full sort of revelation or transmission that the biblical notion of covenant implies is much more than just mind to mind. It is heart to heart: sharing of time on the model of a marriage.

—From *How to Make It Through the Day* by John Carmody

❧ The explicitly Christian references to the *imago* symbol can be summarized succinctly in two interrelated ideas. First, they affirm that Jesus as Christ is himself the image of God. Second, they affirm that those who through hearing, baptism and the work of the divine Spirit are being incorporated into the life of the Christ— that is, believers—are being conformed to the image as revealed and embodied in Christ, and thus renewed according to the original intention of the Creator.

—From *Imaging God* by Douglas John Hall

❧ When we begin to confine God to specifically religious areas of life, we are forced to turn away from the ordinary experiences of life in order to be touched by the gracious reality of God. Yet this is not the way it was for Jesus. The fundamental message of Jesus about God is that human life is the home of God. Do not look anywhere else. All the parables of Jesus are stories about experiencing God. These stories are filled with very human characters and very human experiences. Yet none of them ever mention "God" directly.

What the theologians seem to be saying today, and what so many people searching for God force us to admit, is that if it makes sense to speak of God at all, then we must be able to experience God in the center of our lives where we spend most of our time and expend most of our energy. To realize that God is there in the center of our lives at the deepest dimension of every human moment means that God is never far from us. To experience God in the depths is to be aware that we are related to a larger mystery within which we live. St. Paul understood this well when he expressed the following in his speech in the Areopagus of Athens:

> Yet God is actually not far away from any one of us; as someone has said, "In him we live and move and have our being" (Acts 17:27-28).

For this reason, our relationship to God and response to God cannot be relegated to special activities or special moments. Our relationship and response to God are going on all the time, whether we want them to or not.

—From *To Walk Together Again* by Richard M. Gula

ᔊ It will come as the greatest of surprises when one day the word will be heard: "These were my lowliest ones, and you did not feed them!" Why did you not feed them? We thought they were devils. They were in prison, and you did not visit them! Why did you not visit them? We thought they were devils! Now *they* are the lowly ones of God who are languishing in misery; and I say: *There* is the heaven of Jesus Christ, *there* is the God who leaves the ninety-nine righteous ones in the wilderness and seeks the lost sheep.

—From *Thy Kingdom Come: A Blumhardt Reader* edited by Vernard Eller

꙳ Long before Jesus told his parables to help us understand things, God the Father had told one of cosmic dimensions and as deep as the abyss: the parable of life . . .

The listener was immersed in this parable without any possibility of escape, for its "words" were made of things themselves and these could in no way be denied.

"Who can gainsay the sun?" asks the sundial indicating the visible passing hour.

When the sky speaks—above your head with its billions of stars; and the earth you tread speaks—the sensible basis of living experience: how can you escape logic which surrounds you?

How can you ignore the harmony and beauty of things, or disregard the energy and power of storms and earthquakes?

How can you escape the "absent presence" of a secret entity, the designer of a creative will and indisputable unity, of which you yourself are aware of being a part?

—From *Why, O Lord?* by Carlo Carretto

꙳ A year ago I had a wonderful period of uninterrupted time with my mother. She is eighty-three years old. Mother had a new red dress made for the occasion, spent the morning at the hairdressers, cleaned the house, had the coffee on the stove, and was all ready for my arrival.

We sat and talked like we had not talked for years, and like we might never talk again. She got out some of the old scrapbooks and albums, and entrusted to me a photo that is now one of my most cherished possessions. It was a picture of my father when he was my age. Years before she had put it away to give to me in such a moment. My eyes devoured the photo for marks of the heredity we shared. I traced the lines and contours in my father's face now evident in my own. . . .

Have you been looking for and detecting the inescapable marks of an emerging family likeness to your own heredity? Paul's code name *fruit*, far from being archaic, is the flash of an eloquent symbol to remind us that all the graces and characteristics of God are to be modeled in the daily life and relationships of [God's] children.

Are we doing it? Are we giving the world a symmetrical, authentic, fully-formed image of Christ? There is still time. Spiritual growth is not a matter of chronology alone. It's a matter of spirit. Of heart. Of who you are to the next person you meet. In the next crisis you face. In the next moment you live.

—From *Radiance of the Inner Splendor* by Lloyd John Ogilvie

ᴥ Each of us seeks a treasure. It is elusive and difficult to achieve. It attracts us even when we aren't sure of its contents. The longing for it sustains us on rough and dangerous terrain. In the searching we already possess the sought-for. We journey all the days of our lives, with hope in our hearts, led by the Spirit. One day there dawns the realization that we must give all we possess in exchange for the pearl of great price. In the end, the one "who searches hearts" knows our spirit and our intention, and it is God's glory that is revealed in us.

—From *Every Bush Is Burning* by Joan Puls

Hymn: O God Who Shaped Creation

O God who shaped creation
At earth's chaotic dawn,
Your word of power was spoken,
And lo! the dark was gone!
You framed us in your image,
You brought us into birth,
You blessed our infant footsteps
And shared your splendored earth.

O God, with pain and anguish
A mother sees her child
Embark on deadend pathways,
Alluring, but defiled;
So too your heart is broken
When hate and lust increase,
When worlds you birthed and nurtured
Spurn ways that lead to peace.

Although your heart is broken
When people scorn your ways,
You never cease your searching
Through evil's darksome maze;
And when we cease our running,
Your joys, O God, abound
Like joy of searching woman
When treasured coin is found.

O God, when trinkets tarnish
And pleasures lose their charm,
When, wearied by our wandering,
We seek your opened arm,
With motherlike compassion
You share your warm embrace;
You set for us a banquet
And heal us through your grace.

In mercy and compassion
Your goodness is revealed;
With tenderness you touch us,
And broken hearts are healed.
You claim us as your children,
You strip our prideful shame;
With freedom born of mercy
We bless your holy name!
—William W. Reid, Jr.

35: Consequences of Following Jesus Christ

I.   Invocation
     We know, O Lord, that if we follow close to
     you, nothing shall be able to separate us from
     your love. Give us the grace today to make your
     word our home, that we may know you more
     clearly and serve you ever more. Amen.

II. Psalm 28

III. Reading and Reflection

IV. Daily Scripture Readings
Monday	Matthew 12:46-50
Tuesday	Luke 14:25-33
Wednesday	Luke 22:24-30
Thursday	Luke 9:57-62
Friday	Joshua 24:16-28
Saturday	Romans 14:13-23

     Sunday   A. Genesis 32:22-32; Romans 6:3-
                11; Psalm 17:1-7, 15; Matthew 10:
                34-42
              B. 2 Samuel 6:1-15; 2 Corinthians
                8:7-15; Psalm 24; Mark 5:21-43
              C. 1 Kings 19:15-21; Galatians 5:1,
                13-25; Psalm 44:1-8; Luke 9:51-62

V.   Reflection: Silent and Written

VI. Prayers: For the Church, for Others, for Myself

VII. Hymn: "Be Thou My Vision"

VIII. Benediction
     My Lord, I come to this moment knowing alto-
     gether too well that my feet are prone to wan-
     der and my heart prone to coldness. Go with
     me, my Lord. Keep my feet to your path and
     my heart aflame with your Spirit. Amen.

Readings for Reflection

❧ Hope in God and in the triumph of God's purpose is the central thrust of biblical eschatology. Concern with the *ending* of history (the time, the manner) is minimal in scripture; concern with the *End* of history is a dominant theme. The End is God's goal for the entire enterprise, Jesus' term for the End was God's reign, the kingdom of heaven. To him that reign was at hand, as near as the readiness of women and men to receive it (Mk 1:15). Most people, of course, were not ready, and they sent him to a cross. But in preaching Jesus as the Christ, the Messiah, the church continues to point toward the coming of God's new age.

—From *Seeking God's Peace in a Nuclear Age: A Call to Disciples of Christ*

❧ Some of Jesus' disciples are asked to enter fully into his passion and death. There is to be no limit to the love and solidarity they extend. Their lives and deaths are gifts to the rest of us as we struggle to realize the full meaning of spiritual discipleship. Our minds are baffled by the seeming loss and our hearts are broken by the depths of their courage and sacrifice. Blessed are we when our lives are touched in a human way by the event of martyrdom. Wayward are we if the effects of such sacrifice are lost and forgotten.

—From *Every Bush Is Burning* by Joan Puls

❧ How great are the needs of Your creatures on this earth, oh God. They sit there, talking quietly and quite unsuspecting, and suddenly their need erupts in all its nakedness. Then, there they are, bundles of human misery, desperate and unable to face life. And that's when my task begins. It is not enough simply to proclaim You, God, to commend You to the hearts of others. One must also clear the path towards You in them, God, and to do that one has to be a keen judge of the human soul. A trained psychologist. Ties to father and mother, youthful memories, dreams, guilt feelings, inferiority complexes and all the rest block the way. I embark on a slow voyage of exploration with everyone who comes to me. And I thank You for the great gift of being able to read people. Sometimes they seem to me like houses with open doors. I walk in and roam through passages and rooms, and every house is furnished a little differently and yet they are all of them the same, and every one must be turned into a dwelling dedicated to You, oh God. And I promise You, yes, I promise that I shall try to find a dwelling and a refuge for You in as many houses as possible. There are so many empty houses, and I shall prepare them all for You, the most honoured lodger. Please forgive this poor metaphor.

—From *An Interrupted Life: The Diaries of Etty Hillesum 1941-1943*, translated from the Dutch by Arno Pomerans

✒ There are countless ways in which this (spiritual journey) may happen: sometimes under conditions which seem to the world like the very frustration of life, of progress, of growth. Thus boundless initiative is chained to a sick bed and transmuted into sacrifice; the lover of beauty is sent to serve in the slum, the lover of stillness is kept on the run all day, the sudden demand to leave all comes to the one who least expects it, and through and in these apparent frustrations the life of the spirit emerges and grows.

—From *The Spiritual Life* by Evelyn Underhill

✒ The joy that Jesus offers his disciples is his own joy, which flows from his intimate communion with the One who sent him. It is a joy that does not separate happy days from sad days, successful moments from moments of failure, experiences of honor from experiences of dishonor, passion from resurrection. This joy is a divine gift that does not leave us during times of illness, poverty, oppression, or persecution. It is present even when the world laughs or tortures, robs or maims, fights or kills. It is truly ecstatic, always moving

us away from the house of fear into the house of love, and always proclaiming that death no longer has the final say, though its noise remains loud and its devastation visible. The joy of Jesus lifts up life to be celebrated.
—From *Lifesigns* by Henri J. M. Nouwen

❧ The Quest

I asked for bread!
  Life led me to a plain,
  And put a plough at hand,
  And bade me toil until my bread I earned.

I asked for drink!
  Life led me to a sand
  As dry as tearless grief—
  Forced me to find the springs of sympathy.

I asked for joy!
  Life led me to a street,
  And had me hear the cries
  Of wayward souls who waited to be freed.

I asked for words!
  Life led me to a wood,
  Set me in solitude
  Where speech is still and wisdom comes by prayer.

I asked for love!
  Life led me to a hill,
  And bound me to a cross
  To bear and lift and to be hanged upon.
—Chester B. Emerson

❧ I find that it is better to love badly and faultily than not to try to love at all. God does not have to have perfect instruments, and the Holy One can use our feeble and faltering attempts at love and transform them. My task is to keep on trying to love, to be faithful in my continuing attempt, not necessarily to be successful. The quality of my love may well be the most important element of my spiritual guidance.

The kind of love that the Divine Lover would have me give is not an instinctive drive. We have flashes of desire and moments of desiring to embody it, and at those moments we are carried on eagle's wings, but our task is to walk in this way without tiring of this love, even when we feel little inspiration in our loving. Genuine Christian love is forged against the anvil of our selfishness and possessiveness, of our anger and our fear, and this involves suffering. No one needs to wear hair shirts or chains, cultivate lice, or live on cabbage leaves in order to pick up crosses and follow Jesus. All we have to do is come to God and ask that we be forged into adequate instruments of divine love.

It is important to remember that love is more than a feeling. It is active and transitive. The real test of my loving is not that I feel loving, but that the other person feels loved by me. Love is what I do to create this sense of feeling cared for. It is independent of my personal feelings.

—From *Companions on the Inner Way* by Morton T. Kelsey

❧ Church members occasionally object to the inclusion of a prayer of confession in the order of worship for the congregation. "It makes people feel bad," they say. "Confessing our offenses and our negligence stirs up guilt feelings and contributes to low self-esteem. People come to church to feel better, not to feel worse."

Christian confession, however, is a means of grace. When we confess who we really are to the One who already knows us and loves us as we really are, we have a chance at self-esteem grounded in personal integrity. God's acceptance and forgiveness does not say that everything we have done and left undone is all right. It says that we can pick up from here and move on. Freed from the burden of guilt, we can live with our real, sinful selves, accepting ourselves because God accepts us and esteeming ourselves because if God prizes us, how can we do otherwise?

—From *In Spirit and in Truth* by Martha Graybeal Rowlett

Hymn: Be Thou My Vision

Be thou my vision, O Lord of my heart;
Naught be all else to me, save that thou art.
Thou my best thought, by day or night,
Waking or sleeping, thy presence my light.

Be thou my wisdom, and thou my true word;
I ever with thee and thou with me, Lord;
Thou and thou only, first in my heart,
Great God of heaven, my treasure thou art.

Great God of heaven, my victory won,
May I reach heaven's joys, O bright heaven's Sun!
Heart of my own heart, whatever befall,
Still be my vision, O Ruler of all.
—Translated by Mary E. Byrne, versed by Eleanor H.
   Hull, alt.

Sunday between July 3 and July 9

36: A Disciple's Mission and Reward

I. Invocation
Almighty God, in this hour, grant me grace that amidst the changes, miseries, or pleasures of life I may keep my mind fixed upon you and improve in grace every day till I am received into your kingdom of eternal happiness. Amen.

II. Psalm 35

III. Reading and Reflection

IV. Daily Scripture Readings

Monday	Matthew 10:1-15
Tuesday	Romans 1:1-7
Wednesday	John 1:6-13
Thursday	Colossians 1:9-23
Friday	Colossians 1:24-29
Saturday	1 Peter 1:1-9
Sunday	A. Exodus 1:6-14, 22–2:10; Romans 7:14-25a; Psalm 124; Matthew 11:25-30
	B. 2 Samuel 7:1-17; 2 Corinthians 12:1-10; Psalm 89:20-37; Mark 6:1-6
	C. 1 Kings 21:1-3, 17-21; Galatians 6:7-18; Psalm 5:1-8; Luke 10:1-12, 17-20

V. Reflection: Silent and Written

VI. Prayers: For the Church, for Others, for Myself

VII. Hymn: "Hope of the World"

VIII. Benediction
And now, O Lord, assist me to be diligent in labor and wise in my dealings, that I may one day hear the glorious, "Well done, faithful servant; enter into the joy of your Lord." Amen.

Readings for Reflection

ﳨ For most people in the twentieth century perfection is a lost goal . . . To have individuals attain a level of perfection which would make them inhuman in this world not only implies a defective doctrine of sin, but also eliminates the very anxious, discontented and passionate qualities which make for benevolent change in the world. To keep from being laughable folly, perfection must be a gift and a goal for Christians—never an attainment or a possession.

If repentance is the porch of religion, faith the door, then it is perfect holiness which is religion itself. This ever growing experience is completely dependent on the fusion of grace and faith. This process is the business of the church, the community in which Christ is forming and shaping his people. One has assurance, not of perfection (as Wesley sometimes taught), but of justification by grace. Perfection is never assured in this life (as Wesley often admits), but it is the goal of the dynamic process of sanctification which ends finally in the perfection planned for and provided by God.

—From *A Blueprint for Church Renewal* by Blaine Taylor

ﳨ It is always tempting for those who—probably against their wills—are caught up in the prophetic tradition of truth-telling to begin straightaway to locate the causes of what is wrong outside the sphere of faith and church. But the uncanny thing about biblical religion is that it refuses to permit easy divisions of the world into guilty and innocent; and even more unsettling is that it seldom identifies the innocent ones it occasionally speaks of with the community of belief as such. More often, the innocent are those being neglected or hurt by "the elect!" Therefore, those who want to get to the bottom of things in biblical terms must reckon with the prospect that they will themselves have to feel the sting of the divine *krisis* (judgment) in the process; that they will have to discover anew how "we ourselves are

wrong," our Christianity notwithstanding. For "the time has come for the judgment to begin with the household of God" (I Pet. 4:17).
—From *Imaging God* by Douglas John Hall

❧ The work we do is only our love for Jesus in action. And that action is our wholehearted and free service—the gift of the poorest of the poor— to Christ in the distressing disguise of the poor.

If we pray the work . . .
    if we do it to Jesus
    if we do it for Jesus
    if we do it with Jesus . . .
that's what makes us content.
—From *Words to Love By* by Mother Teresa

❧ A disciple experiences a joy and peace so deep within that he or she is compelled to share it with others. When this hidden mission begins to emerge in us, we find other people who also know that they have been haunted by Jesus and are drawn to each other to grow together in him.

When we begin to follow Jesus, we allow him to live more consciously in our lives. In surprising and simple ways, he is always speaking to us. He is at the heart of the world and at the heart of each of us, especially at the fragile center where we are afraid—of ourselves, of others, of God. Fragile people are such a revelation of God.
—From *Gathering the Fragments* by Edward J. Farrell

❧ To understand the Christian religion with all of its widely varying forms of worship and expression—its mystical, its prophetic, its mutual caring outreach to the world's needs—one must return to the divine love at the heart of things that undergirds us all and, above all, one must realize that we are not in this alone.

Arthur Gossip, a hard-bitten pastor in a slum church in Glasgow, tells of how, at the end of a long day of

visiting his parishioners, he arrived late in the afternoon at a five-story tenement where the last family on his list for that day lived at the very top. He was done in and said to himself, "It's too far up. I'll come tomorrow." He was about to turn away when a pair of stooped gray shoulders seemed to brush past him and start up the stairs with the word, "Then I'll have to go alone." Arthur Gossip added, "We went together."
—From *Gleanings* by Douglas V. Steere

❧ Two men were part of a small Lenten sharing group in their church. They were discussing personal commitment to Christ and how we translate it into our everyday life, our relationships, our business affairs. One man asked, "What would happen to me if I should undertake to carry on my business as Christ would want me to? It might mean financial ruin."

There was a moment of silence, and then one of the other men replied, "And what will happen if you don't? What *kind* of ruin do you want?"
—From *Meeting the Messiah* by Donald J. Shelby

❧ Be serious and frequent in the examination of your heart and life. . . . Every evening review your carriage through the day; what you have done or thought that was unbecoming your character; whether your heart has been instant upon religion and indifferent to the world? Have a special care of two portions of time, namely, morning and evening; the morning to forethink what you have to do, and the evening to examine whether you have done what you ought.

Let every action have reference to your whole life, and not to a part only. Let all your subordinate ends be suitable to the great end of your living. Exercise yourself unto godliness.
—John Wesley

❧ Grant me, O Lord, to know what I ought to know, to love what I ought to love, to praise what delights thee most, to value what is precious in thy sight, to hate what is offensive to thee. Do not suffer me to judge according to the sight of my eyes, nor to pass sentence according to the hearing of the ears of ignorant [people]; but to discern with a true judgment between things visible and spiritual, and above all, always to inquire what is the good pleasure of Thy will.

—Thomas à Kempis

Hymn: Hope of the World

Hope of the world, thou Christ of great compassion,
Speak to our fearful hearts by conflict rent.
Save us, thy people, from consuming passion,
Who by our own false hopes and aims are spent.

Hope of the world, God's gift from highest heaven,
Bringing to hungry souls the bread of life,
Still let thy spirit unto us be given,
To heal earth's wounds and end all bitter strife.

Hope of the world, afoot on dusty highways,
Showing to wandering souls the path of light,
Walk thou beside us lest the tempting byways
Lure us away from thee to endless night.

Hope of the world, who by the cross didst save us
From death and dark despair, from sin and guilt,
We render back the love thy mercy gave us;
Take thou our lives, and use them as thou wilt.

Hope of the world, O Christ o'er death victorious,
Who by this sign didst conquer grief and pain,
We would be faithful to thy gospel glorious;
Thou art our Lord! Thou dost forever reign.

—Georgia Harkness

37: God's Plan for the Church

I. Invocation
O Lord Jesus, who comes always seeking a bride without spot or wrinkle, grant that we may prepare ourselves to welcome you as our faithful groom. O glorius union. Amen.

II. Psalm 46

III. Reading and Reflection

IV. Daily Scripture Readings

Monday	Isaiah 55:1-13
Tuesday	Isaiah 1:10-17
Wednesday	Isaiah 1:21-26
Thursday	Romans 15:1-13
Friday	Ephesians 4:1-16
Saturday	John 17:20-26

Sunday   A. Exodus 2:11-22; Romans 8:9-17; Psalm 69:6-15; Matthew 13:1-9, 18-23
B. 2 Samuel 7:18-29; Ephesians 1:1-10; Psalm 132:11-18; Mark 6:7-13
C. 2 Kings 2:1, 6-14; Colossians 1:1-14; Psalm 139:1-12; Luke 10:25-37

V. Reflection: Silent and Written

VI. Prayers: For the Church, for Others, for Myself

VII. Hymn: "God the Spirit, Guide and Guardian"

VIII. Benediction
My Lord, you once said many are called to enter your kingdom but few are chosen. Help me today to hear your call—and to so live as to be numbered among the few who enter into the fullness of your love. Amen.

Readings for Reflection

❧ Personal commitment to human beings in love is the hallmark of the church. In his conflict with the Moravians, Wesley thought them mystical and ineffective precisely because they were unwilling to perform the work of service and love which were marks of the primitive church. Wesley turned his back on them "because they not only do not practice but utterly despise and decry self-denial and the daily cross; because they, upon principle, conform to the world in wearing gold and gay or costly apparel" and (fundamentally) "because they are by no means zealous of good works; or at least, only to their own people . . . because they make inward religion swallow up outward in general." Nothing is more common in his journals than his call to the service and love of all peoples.

—From *A Blueprint for Church Renewal* by Blaine Taylor

❧ The gospel calls us to count up the cost of our witness. Part of this process is the assessing of our power as well. In God's grace the Church discovers that its members are not helpless victims of alien powers but bearers of gifts, competencies, and influence for effecting change. Just as Moses was told to use the rod in his hand and the disciples were bidden to feed the multitude with the lunch they had, so we are expected to use what we have. One of the functions of the Church is to help its members discover and release their power in ways that promote the cause of the Kingdom. Professionals and nonprofessionals, trained and untrained workers, rich and poor—all are influencing their context either by reinforcing the status quo or promoting change. The issue is not simply one of getting power but of becoming aware of how we use the power we have, and then developing expertise to make an impact on our communities for good. The Church is the sleeping giant. What a powerful witness we could be if the parts of the body came to a new awareness of the power that is at work within and around us!

—From James A. Forbes, Jr. in *Living with Apocalypse* edited by Tilden Edwards

❧ Those who love cross histories and heritages, continents and careers. They are deepened and hollowed out by mutual burdens and by a common cup of suffering. They wait with hope for love's direction. Freed by love's own dynamic, to be sifted and to die, to be made whole and human. Love is creative and those who partake are enlarged and made fruitful. They give birth to new networks and new visions.

—From *Every Bush Is Burning* by Joan Puls

❧ We live limited lives until we "cross over" into the concrete world of another country, another culture, another tradition of worship. I was stretched and challenged in so many ways by travelling and encountering people in India. . . . I have been enriched by the opportunities of sharing prayer and faith with persons of many denominations. Welcomed into a prayer meeting by Quakers. Served the eucharist by Anglican Africans and Lutheran women. Experiencing community in prayer with evangelicals and Protestant nuns and Orthodox priests. History comes alive and what is foreign becomes familiar. Vague images take flesh and understanding and appreciation grow. I have left forever a small world to live with the tensions and the tender mercies of God's larger family.

—From *Every Bush Is Burning* by Joan Puls

❧ After this, what will evangelization entail for you in the context of the Church?

First, that you have to proclaim the Gospel by your whole life. The monk evangelizes by striving to live the evangelical counsels radically. By doing this, you will— really and truly—bring a little more peace, mercy, purity, gentleness and justice into the world. This is already a form of evangelization.

—From *The Jerusalem Community Rule of Life* by Pierre-Marie Delfieux

❧ The following statements are therefore true: "Good works do not make a good [person], but a good [person] does good works; evil works do not make a wicked [person], but a wicked [person] does evil works." Consequently it is always necessary that the substance or person . . . be good before there can be any good works, and that good works follow and proceed from the good person, as Christ also says, "A good tree cannot bear evil fruit, nor can a bad tree bear good fruit" (Matt. 7:18). It is clear that the fruits do not bear the tree and that the tree does not grow on the fruits, also that, on the contrary, the trees bear the fruits and the fruits grow on the trees. As it is necessary, therefore, that the trees exist before their fruits and the fruits do not make trees either good or bad, but rather as the trees are, so are the fruits they bear; so a [person] must first be good or wicked before he [or she] does a good or wicked work.

—Martin Luther.

❧ The love of this world, pleasure, and pride is a strong sweet wine by which the soul and the spirit are conquered. Noah and Lot were overcome by wine and lay in nakedness. Great honor, pleasure, and wealth are a strong wine that conquers soul and spirit. Because of it, one cannot come into the dwelling place of God, to a knowledge of God and holiness, and because of it one cannot distinguish what is holy or unholy, pure or impure; that is, one does not understand divine, heavenly things and one's people cannot learn properly from that one, that is, one's understanding and thoughts are not illuminated by the eternal light but are conquered by the wine of this world, and one goes into darkness. Following this repentance, that is following deep regret and sorrow for sins and following the true faith in Christ, forgiveness of sins results from the merits of

Jesus Christ alone. His merits no one can enjoy without repentance. Therefore, without repentance no forgiveness of sins results.
—From *True Christianity* by Johann Arndt (*Classics of Western Spirituality* series)

Hymn: God the Spirit, Guide and Guardian

God the Spirit, guide, and guardian,
Wind-sped flame and hovering dove,
Breath of life and voice of prophets,
Sign of blessing, power of love:
Give to those who lead your people
Fresh anointing of your grace;
Send them forth as bold apostles
To your church in every place.

Christ our Savior, sovereign, shepherd,
Word made flesh, love crucified,
Teacher, healer, suffering servant,
Friend of sinners, foe of pride:
In your tending may all pastors
Learn and live a shepherd's care;
Grant them courage and compassion
Shown through word and deed and prayer.

Great Creator, life-bestower,
Truth beyond all thought's recall,
Fount of wisdom, womb of mercy,
Giving and forgiving all:
As you know our strength and weakness,
So may those the church exalts
Oversee her life steadfastly
Yet not overlook her faults.

Triune God, mysterious being,
Undivided and diverse,
Deeper than our minds can fathom,
Greater than our creeds rehearse:
Help us in our varied callings
Your full image to proclaim,
That our ministries uniting
May give glory to your name.
—Carl P. Daw, Jr.

38: *Listening and Obeying*

I. Invocation
    O merciful God, help us to live always in the
    realization of the account we must one day give.
    May we pray rightly, listen keenly, and live as
    faithful stewards of your good gifts. With the
    assistance of your Spirit. Amen.

II. Psalm 62

III. Reading and Reflection

IV. Daily Scripture Readings
     Monday   Mark 9:1-8
     Tuesday   James 1:19-27
     Wednesday   James 4:1-10
     Thursday   Romans 6:15-23
     Friday   Philippians 2:12-18
     Saturday   John 14:15-24
     Sunday   A. Exodus 3:1-12; Romans 8:18-25;
                 Psalm 103:1-13; Matthew 13:24-
                 30, 36-43
              B. 2 Samuel 11:1-15; Ephesians 2:
                 11-22; Psalm 53; Mark 6:30-34
              C. 2 Kings 4:8-17; Colossians 1:21-
                 29; Psalm 139:13-18; Luke 10:38-
                 42

V. Reflection: Silent and Written

VI. Prayers: For the Church, for Others, for Myself

VII. Hymn: "The Voice of God Is Calling"

VIII. Benediction
       I have heard your word for my life today. I bind
       it to my heart, pledging my full obedience. Help
       me, my Lord, to keep this pledge. Amen.

Readings for Reflection

❧ Spiritual awareness for Christians, at its fullest, means seeing life through God's sound eye. We could use other senses to describe this awareness: hearing life through God's ear, touching life through God's strength, feeling life through God's compassion. Jesus revealed our incredible intimacy with the infinite One we call God, so we can dare to speak of being God's senses in the world. Saint Paul called us to live in the mind of Christ so fully that we can say with him, "Not I, but Christ, lives in me." The "I" that no longer lives then is the one that sees itself as an ultimately self-willed, self-centered being. The new "I" is one that lives moment by moment in the awareness that we are an intimate and unique expression of God's joy and compassion, living freely by grace, called to reverberate the joy and compassion, utterly interdependent with Creator and creation.

The test of any spiritual discipline is whether or not it assists this deep awareness for us. Without spiritual discipline we become easier prey to the old "I" that is full of possessiveness, fear, greed, anxiety, violence, indolence, untrustworthiness, willfulness, confusion, and all the other marks of life disconnected from our true being in God.

—From Tilden H. Edwards in *Living with Apocalypse* edited by Tilden H. Edwards

❧ The messianic dream is a proclamation from heaven and earth, a bridge between two banks, a tree on your parched path.

Inspiration comes from afar but you are the one to experience it.

You receive a proclamation but it is up to you to meditate on it. It comes from the far side but becomes a reality on your side.

I believe this is the way God calls to us, educates us. . . .

By listening, journeying, pausing, you make the dream more definite.

I have experienced this.

Learn to taste God, get used to God's logic, admire its contents.

Thousands over the centuries have slaked their thirst at this spring, thousands have found repose in the shade of this tree put by their road!

Listen.

—From *Why, O Lord?* by Carlo Carretto

&. Mother Teresa of Calcutta has a dream—that before they die all people will know that they are loved. She devotes her life to making this dream a reality.

She tells a story of walking past an open drain and catching a glimpse of something moving in it. She investigated and found a dying man whom she took back to a home where he could die in love and peace.

"I live like an animal in the streets," the man told her. "Now I will die like an angel."

"How wonderful to see a person die in love," she exclaims, "with the joy of love, the perfect peace of Christ on his face."

—From *Words to Love By* by Mother Teresa

&. With a power given from above we shout, "No!" to him who promises the whole world if we will only worship him. We crucify the old mechanisms of power—push, drive, climb, grasp, trample. We turn instead to the new life of power—love, joy, peace, patience, and all the fruit of the Spirit.

—From *Money, Sex and Power* by Richard J. Foster

&. Be still and know. Civilization is littered with unsolved problems, baffling impasses. The best minds of the world are at the end of their tether. The most knowledgeable observers of our condition are badly frightened. The most relevant contribution that Christians make at these points of impasse is the act of prayer—

determined, repeated, leisurely meetings with the personal and living God. New life is conceived in these meetings.
—From *Earth and Altar* by Eugene H. Peterson

❧ The closer we draw to others, the closer we draw to God. The farther away we move from God, the farther we move from others. . . . When we are willing to abandon ourselves and to fling ourselves outward in compassion and in service, we find that we have made room not just for others in our lives but also for God in our hearts. The energy that we had massed in our own little center is spent on others, leaving an open space where God may enter. From this same God-infused center also flows the renewing energy that allows us to keep loving and serving in the world. This is why John Wesley affirmed that true faith issues in good works. It is also why Baron von Hugel ordered his spiritual directee, Evelyn Underhill, to serve several days a week in a skid row soup kitchen when she was having trouble with her spiritual life.

True obedience, then, is both a listening to what we hear within us and to what we hear beyond us. It is being attentive to those we encounter in our daily lives. It is creating the empty, open space within us where we can hear God speak.
—From *The Potter and the Clay* by Thomas R. Hawkins

❧ One of the influences on our lives is the presence and call of God. God is with us, exerting an influence on us whether we choose to pay attention or not. When we choose to respond to God's offer of open communication, we choose to give power or weight to that relationship. We make an intentional move to give attention to the ideal possibilities that God offers to us. Without relinquishing our free will, we can freely choose to be Christian disciples. We can choose to live authentically in dialogue with God. Such open communion with God can creatively transform our lives. . . .

In a human friendship, communication and interaction are necessary if the relationship is to survive and grow. I need to know you in order to trust you. The only way we can get acquainted is by trusting each other enough to reveal ourselves. A little trust makes possible the first steps of friendship. This initial acquaintance makes possible more trust, which makes possible deeper friendship. So it is with prayer and faith. Faith expressed in prayer opens the way for the Spirit to nurture new faith, which in turn makes possible new adventures in prayer.

—From *In Spirit and in Truth* by Martha Graybeal Rowlett

Hymn: The Voice of God Is Calling

The voice of God is calling
Its summons in our day;
Isaiah heard in Zion,
So now we hear today:
"Whom shall I send to succor
My people in their need?
Whom shall I send to loosen
The bonds of shame and greed?

We heed, O Lord, your summons,
And answer: "Here are we!"
Send us upon your errand,
Let us your servants be.
Our strength is dust and ashes,
Our years a passing hour;
But you can use our weakness
To magnify your power.

From ease and plenty save us;
From pride of place absolve;
Purge us of low desire;
Lift us to high resolve;
Take us, and make us holy;
Teach us your will and way.
Speak, and behold! we answer;
Command, and we obey!
—John Haynes Holmes

Sunday between July 24 and 30
39: God's Ability to Provide

I.   Invocation
O God, creator of all humankind, I bring to you the cares and concerns of all your creatures. Look now to those who cry for help from every corner of the earth, for you alone are able to satisfy our deepest desires. Amen.

II.   Psalm 63

III.   Reading and Reflection

IV.   Daily Scripture Readings

Monday		Genesis 22:1-14
Tuesday		1 Timothy 6:11-19
Wednesday		Psalm 68:1-10
Thursday		John 10:1-18
Friday		Matthew 7:1-12
Saturday		1 Peter 5:1-11
Sunday	A.	Exodus 3:13-20; Romans 8:26-30; Psalm 105:1-11; Matthew 13:44-52
	B.	2 Samuel 12:1-14; Ephesians 3:14-21; Psalm 32; John 6:1-15
	C.	2 Kings 5:1-15ab; Colossians 2:6-15; Psalm 21:1-7; Luke 11:1-13

V.   Reflection: Silent and Written

VI.   Prayers: For the Church, for Others, for Myself

VII.   Hymn: "By Gracious Powers"

VIII.   Benediction
And now, my God, as I go to my place in the world, go with me. May the peace of sin forgiven and the power of your Holy Spirit work in me and through me to your glory. Amen

Readings for Reflection

❖ Now here I am in front of you, and you have your dreams too, or have had them. And I can tell you something.

That mistaken injection that paralyzed my leg was not a stroke of bad luck. It was a grace.

Let's be precise. There's no point in pious platitudes.

It was bad luck, yes. It was a misfortune. But God turned it into a grace.

I had a useless leg. I could not climb. So I got a jeep and became a meteorologist.

Through no wish of my own, there I was where I belonged: in the desert.

Instead of trudging through the snow I trudged through the sand.

Instead of mountain passes I came to know caravan routes. Instead of chamois I saw gazelles.

Life suddenly appeared to me as it was, an immense personal exodus. Now I saw the desert as an extraordinary environment of silence and prayer.

My crippled leg helped me to "stand firm" (Jas 1:12).

I the runner—now stood firm.

I who'd always tried to do two things at once—now I stood firm.

No doubt about it, it was a plus.

Deep down inside I began to understand that I hadn't been cheated.

Misfortune had thrust me upon new paths.

Brothers and sisters before me with your misfortunes, I testify to you of one thing only.

Today, thirty years after the incident that paralyzed my leg, I don't say it wasn't a misfortune.

I only say that God was able to transform it into a grace.

I have experienced in my flesh what Augustine says: "God permits evil, so as to transform it into a greater good."

—From *Why, O Lord?* Carlo Carretto

❦ O eternal God, though Thou art not such as I can see with my eyes or touch with my hands, yet grant me this day a clear conviction of Thy reality and power. Let me not go forth to my work believing only in the world of sense and time, but give me grace to understand that the world I cannot see or touch is the most real world of all. My life to-day will be lived in time, but eternal issues will be concerned in it. The needs of my body will be clamant, but it is for the needs of my soul that I must care most. My business will be with things material, but behind them let me be aware of things spiritual. Let me keep steadily in mind that the things that matter are not money or possessions, not houses or lands, not bodily comfort or bodily pleasure; but truth and honour and meekness and helpfulness and a pure love of Thyself . . . .

I, a pilgrim of eternity, stand before Thee, O eternal One. Let me not seek to deaden or destroy the desire for Thee that disturbs my heart. Let me rather yield myself to its constraint and go where it leads me. Make me wise to see all things to-day under the form of eternity, and make me brave to face all the changes in my life which such a vision may entail: through the grace of Christ my Saviour. Amen.

—From *A Diary of Private Prayer* by John Baillie

❦ The doctrine of the active presence of the transcendent God in all that is and all that happens is implied in the teaching of Jesus that the hairs of [our] head are numbered, that not a sparrow falls to the ground without the Father's knowledge and care. His injunction to his disciples not to worry about food and drink and dress but to seek the reign of God and trust God to take care of the rest implies God's active providence over human life. The eighteenth century spiritual writer de Caussade may serve to illustrate how this belief in God's providence can be made the keystone of a way of life. He teaches us to see everything that happens as coming to us from the hand of God. God addresses us through the people we meet and the work we do, through our hopes and fears, through our moods and dreams through the good [God] sends and the evil [God] permits. De Caussade speaks of the sacrament of the passing moment because in each fleeting moment we are confronted with an opportunity of responding to God who is present in that moment. No experience is so painful, no temptation so strong as to fall outside God's fatherly care.

—From *The River Within* by Christopher Bryant

    ⅍ Now let me tell you that the will of God is all that is necessary, and what it does not give you is of no use to you at all. My friends, you lack nothing. You would be very ashamed if you knew what the experiences you call setbacks, upheavals, pointless disturbances, and tedious annoyances really are. You would realize that your complaints about them are nothing more nor less than blasphemies—though that never occurs to you. Nothing happens to you except by the will of God, and yet [God's] beloved children curse it because they do not know it for what it is.

—From *Abandonment to Divine Providence* by Jean-Pierre de Caussade

    ⅍ I have not knowledge, wisdom, insight, thought,
      Nor understanding, fit to justify
   Thee in Thy work, O Perfect! Thou hast brought
   Me up to this; and lo! what Thou hast wrought,
      I cannot comprehend. But I can cry,
     "O enemy, the Maker hath not done;
   One day thou shalt behold, and from the sight shalt
    run."

   Thou workest perfectly. And if it seem
     Some things are not so well, 'tis but because
       They are too loving deep, too lofty wise,
    For me, poor child, to understand their laws.
   My highest wisdom, half is but a dream;
   My love runs helpless like a falling stream;
     Thy good embraces ill, and lo! its illness dies.

—George MacDonald

It would be impossible to meditate without coming to understand what poverty really is and what poverty of spirit involves. The knowledge that we are poor is one of the most healing and surprising experiences that meditation opens to us. It is also the sure confirmation that we are still on the journey; much more than spiritual success, the experience of poverty confirms that we are on course. In knowing poverty of spirit we know ourselves. We come progressively into a self-knowledge of a kind and of a depth that will always take us by surprise. . . .

Poverty of spirit is an essential human experience to pass through. If we don't pass through it, we don't break into reality. And that means that we neither break into the reality of ourselves or discover the destiny that each of us has in God. We call it *poverty* only because material poverty is a metaphor for us to understand this spiritual condition. It is called poverty because poverty is a state where we have touched rock-bottom (the ground of our being), where we have no further resources of our own while remaining dependent on our Creator. Theoretically or theologically there is nothing very special about that. The lived experience of it, however, is cataclysmic. It is knowing who we are. It is being simply realistic. Poverty of spirit is almost another term for reality. When we are genuinely poor we can see ourselves, our life and relationships in a bright, clear light. However, we resist this poverty instinctively and a kind of gravitational force pulls us away from it because we prefer the illusion of ourselves as being independent of our Creator. In that false light of independent status we develop the Luciferian, egotistical notion of having a *relationship* with God as a relationship of equals. We lose the humble realism of understanding that because of [God's] utter generosity we have *communion* with [God], which is something much greater than relationship. We live and move and have our being in [God]. The illusion of independence costs us the reality of the freedom of being a child of God.

—From *Light Within* by Laurence Freeman

Hymn: By Gracious Powers

By gracious powers so wonderfully sheltered,
And confidently waiting, come what may,
We know that God is with us night and morning,
And never fails to greet us each new day.

Yet is this heart by its old foe tormented,
Still evil days bring burdens hard to bear;
O give our frightened souls the sure salvation
For which, O Lord, you taught us to prepare.

And when this cup you give is filled to brimming
With bitter sorrow, hard to understand,
We take it thankfully and without trembling,
Out of so good and so beloved a hand.

Yet when again in this same world you give us
The joy we had, the brightness of your sun,
We shall remember all the days we lived through,
And our whole life shall then be yours alone.
—Dietrich Bonhoeffer, trans. by Fred Pratt Green

40: Establishing the Right Priorities

I. Invocation
Almighty God, create in us a clean heart, and renew a right spirit within us, that amid the din and confusion of this noisy world we may always chose the more excellent way. Through Christ. Amen.

II. Psalm 73

III. Reading and Reflection

IV. Daily Scripture Readings
Monday   Luke 10:38-42
Tuesday   Romans 8:18-25
Wednesday   2 Corinthians 6:1-13
Thursday   Revelation 19:1-8
Friday   Hebrews 10:19-39
Saturday   Colossians 3:5-17
Sunday   A. Exodus 12:1-14; Romans 8:31-39; Psalm 143:1-10; Matthew 14:13-21
            B. 2 Samuel 12:15b-24; Ephesians 4:1-6; Psalm 34:11-22; John 6:24-35
            C. 2 Kings 13:14-20a; Colossians 3:1-11; Psalm 28; Luke 12:13-21

V. Reflection: Silent and Written

VI. Prayers: For the Church, for Others, for Myself

VII. Hymn: "Dear Jesus, in Whose Life I See"

VIII. Benediction
My Lord, today I will make a thousand choices, big and small, consequential and trivial. In the midst of all these decisions, help me to choose the one thing needed for a richer, more vital life in you. Amen.

Readings for Reflection

❧ In other words, you choose your life, that is to say, you choose all the conditions of your life, when you choose the thoughts upon which you allow your mind to dwell. Thought is the real causative force in life, and there is no other. You cannot have one kind of mind and another kind of environment. This means that you cannot change your environment while leaving your mind unchanged, nor—and this is the supreme key to life and the reason for this pamphlet—can you change your mind without your environment changing too.

This then is the real key to life: if you change your mind your conditions must change too—your body must change, your daily work or other activities must change; your home must change; the color-tone of your whole life must change—for whether you be habitually happy and cheerful, or low-spirited and fearful, depends entirely on the quality of the mental food upon which you diet yourself.

Please be very clear about this. If you change your mind your conditions must change too. *We are transformed by the renewing of our minds*. So now you will see that your mental diet is really the most important thing in your whole life.
—From *Meditations on a Theme* by Anthony of Sourozh

❧ To have what we want is riches, but to be able to do without is power.
—George MacDonald

❧ *Re-collection*: those who have majored in the disciplines of the inner spirit have often seized upon that word as a description of what one does when there is a need for a restoration of spiritual passion. Hearing the word, I think of the act at the pool table. And I see it once again in the quiet but necessary actions of the heart: the recollection of the pieces of my being so that once again my inner self is a reservoir of spiritual passion, the energy that enables me to hear God's voice and to act as [God's] child.

"I used to dislike the term 'to re-collect' as in 'to recollect oneself,'" wrote Michel Quoist. "I thought it tired and deformed; it reminded me of angular, grey faces perched above scrawny necks more precarious than the tower of Pisa. But I rediscovered the term and find it quite marvelous now." Quoist continued:

> To recollect yourself is to recover all your scattered energies—those of the mind, the heart and the body. It is to reassemble all the pieces of yourself flung in the four corners of your past or the mists of your future, pieces clinging to the fringes of your desires. (Quoist, *With Open Heart*, p. 146)

Most of us have neither time nor place for recollection in this busy life of ours—and thus the exhaustion. Recollection becomes a matter of priority *only* when we have experienced one too many times the tastelessness of a passionless life.
—From *Restoring Your Spiritual Passion* by Gordon MacDonald

ᐁ When we begin to ask what the conditions of inner renewal are, we receive essentially the same answers from nearly all of those whom we have most reason to respect. One major answer is the emphasis upon discipline. In the conduct of one's own life it is soon obvious, as many have learned the hard way, that empty freedom is a snare and a delusion. In following what comes naturally or easily, life simply ends in confusion, and in consequent disaster. Without the discipline of time, we spoil the next day the night before, and without the discipline of prayer, we are likely to end by having practically no experience of the divine-human encounter. However compassionate we may be with others, we dare not be soft or indulgent with ourselves. Excellence comes at a price, and one of the major prices is that of inner control.

We have not advanced very far in our spiritual lives

if we have not encountered the basic paradox of free-dom, to the effect that we are most free when we are bound. But not just any way of being bound will suffice; what matters is the character of our binding. The one who would like to be an athlete, but who is unwilling to discipline his [or her] body by regular exercise and by abstinence, is not free to excel on the field or the track. . . . failure to train rigorously and to live abstemiously denies [that person] the freedom to go over the bar at the desired height, or to run with the desired speed and endurance. With one concerted voice the giants of the devotional life apply the same princi-ple to the whole of life with the dictum: *Discipline is the price of freedom.*
—From *The New Man for Our Time* by Elton Trueblood

❧ Today's global realities call for comfortable Christians to review their lifestyle. Guidelines for a simpler style of life cannot be laid down in universal rules; they must be developed by individuals and communities accord-ing to their own imagination and situation. A simpler lifestyle is not a panacea. It may be embarked upon for the wrong reasons, e.g., out of guilt, as a substitute for political action, or in a quest for moral purity. But it can also be meaningful and significant in some or all of the following ways:

1. As an *act of faith* performed for the sake of personal integrity and as an expression of a personal commitment to a more equitable distribution of the world's resources.

2. As an *act of self-defense* against the mind-and-body-polluting effects of overconsumption.

3. As an *act of withdrawal* from the achievement neurosis of our high-pressure, materialistic societies.

4. As an *act of solidarity* with the majority of human kind, which has no choice about lifestyle.

5. As an *act of sharing* with others what has been given to us, or of returning what was usurped by us through unjust social and economic structures.

6. As an *act of celebration* of the riches found in creativity, spirituality, and community with others, rather than in mindless materialism.

7. As an *act of provocation* (ostentatious *under-consumption*) to arouse curiosity leading to dialog with others about affluence, alienation, poverty, and social injustice.

8. As an *act of anticipation* of the era when the self-confidence and assertiveness of the underprivileged forces new power relationships and new patterns of resource allocation upon us.

9. As an *act of advocacy* of legislated changes in present patterns of production and consumption, in the direction of a new international economic order.

10. As an *exercise of purchasing power* to redirect production away from the satisfaction of artificially created wants, toward the supplying of goods and services that meet genuine social needs.

The adoption of a simpler lifestyle is meaningful and justifiable for any or all of the above reasons *alone*, regardless of whether it benefits the underprivileged. Demands for "proof of effectiveness" in helping the poor simply bear witness to the myth that "they the poor" are the problem, and "we the rich" have a solution. Yet, if adopted on a large scale, a simpler lifestyle will have significant socio-political side effects both in the rich and in the poor parts of the world. The two most important side effects are likely to be economic and structural adjustments and release of new resources and energies for social change.

—From David Crean in *Living Simply* edited by David Crean and Eric and Helen Ebbeson

੧ This life, therefore, is not godliness but the process of becoming godly, not health but getting well, not being but becoming, not rest but exercise. We are not now what we shall be, but we are on the way. The process is not yet finished, but it is actively going on. This is not the goal but it is the right road. At present, everything

does not gleam and sparkle, but everything is being cleansed.
—Martin Luther

Hymn: Dear Jesus, in Whose Life I See

Dear Jesus, in whose life I see
All that I would, but fail to be,
Let thy clear light forever shine,
To shame and guide this life of mine.

Though what I dream and what I do
In my weak days are always two,
Help me, oppressed by things undone,
O Thou whose deeds and dreams were one!
—John Hunter

41: Facing Life's Uncertainties

I.   Invocation
     Almighty God, who always moves with clarity of will and singleness of purpose, help me to live and work with certainty in an uncertain world. Light a lamp before me so that my feet do not stumble. Make my path clear so I may never wander from your chosen way. I pray in the name of Jesus who comes to make your way clear before our eyes. Amen.

II. Psalm 127

III. Reading and Reflection

IV. Daily Scripture Readings
     Monday   Isaiah 54:9-17
     Tuesday   Hebrews 10:1-10
     Wednesday   2 Peter 1:1-11
     Thursday   1 Peter 3:13-22
     Friday   1 Peter 4:12-19
     Saturday   John 17:1-19
     Sunday   A. Exodus 14:19-31; Romans 9:1-5; Psalm 106:4-12; Matthew 14:22-33
                   B. 2 Samuel 18:1,5, 9-15; Ephesians 4:25–5:2; Psalm 143:1-8; John 6:35, 41-51
                   C. Jeremiah 18:1-11; Hebrews 11:1-3, 8-19; Psalm 14; Luke 12:32-40

V.   Reflection: Silent and Written

VI. Prayers: For the Church, for Others, for Myself

VII. Hymn: "O God, Our Help in Ages Past"

VIII. Benediction
     Send me, Lord, as an evangel of hope and security to those whose paths will cross with mine this day. Amen.

Readings for Reflection

❧ Like many ideas, ["The sacrament of the present moment"] is a most obvious one—the moment we learn of it. It is simply this: most of us are very ordinary creatures with humdrum lives, work to be done, and with every day filled with a multiplicity of trivial decisions and tasks. Our lives are made up of a stream of petty affairs, some pleasant, many boring, and a lot unpleasant and often tragic. We must not exaggerate. There is a great deal of pleasure, even delight, in life. But there is also much that is irritating and tedious. Caussade says that everything in life is to be welcomed as the expression of the will of God, so we must "accept what we very often cannot avoid, and endure with love and resignation things which could cause us weariness and disgust. This is what being holy means." And "for most people the best way to achieve perfection is to submit to all that God wills for their particular way of life." Caussade tells us: "God speaks to every individual through what happens to them moment by moment." He goes on: "The events of each moment are stamped with the will of God . . . we find all that is necessary in the present moment." Again: "We are bored with the small happenings around us, yet it is these trivialities—as we consider them—which would do marvels for us if only we did not despise them." A key sentence in Caussade is: "If we have abandoned ourselves to God, there is only one rule for us: the duty of the present moment."

He insists, over and over again, that we must live from minute to minute. The past is past, the future is yet to be. There is nothing we can do about either, but we can deal with what is happening moment by moment.

—From John Beevers in *Abandonment to Divine Providence* by Jean-Pierre de Caussade

Suppose your whole world seems to rock on its foundations. Hold on steadily, let it rock, and when the rocking is over, the picture will have reassembled itself into something much nearer to your heart's desire.
—From *The Seven Day Mental Diet* by Emmet Fox

❧ Suffering—
   pain, humiliation, sickness and failure—
   is but a kiss of Jesus.

   Once I met a lady who had a terrible cancer.
   She was suffering so much.
   I told her,
   "Now you come so close to Jesus on the cross
   that he is kissing you."
   Then she joined hands and said,
      "Mother Teresa,
      please tell Jesus to stop kissing me."
   It was so beautiful.
   She understood.

   Suffering is a gift of God
   a gift that makes us most Christlike.
   People must not accept suffering as a punishment.
   —From *Words to Love By* by Mother Teresa

❧ The woman potter summarized not only the making of a pot but her basic belief about life:

   Both my hands shaped this pot. And, the place where it actually forms is a place of tension between the pressure applied from the outside and the pressure of the hand on the inside. That's the way my life has been. Sadness and death and misfortune and the love of friends and all the things that happened to me that I didn't even choose. All of that influenced my life. But, there are things I believe in about myself, my faith in God and the love of some friends that worked on the insides of me. My life, like this pot, is the result of what happened on the outside and what was going on inside of me. Life, like this pot, comes to be in places of tension. Life comes to be when we learn how to avoid looking for answers and finally learn how to ask the questions that will bring us to life.

There is a tendency in us to want to live tension-free. But, like the woman potter, I believe that this tension is God's gift to us, a gift that sometimes will not permit us to escape its presence. I believe that our creative energies are activated by just that kind of upsetting tension. It is in responding to this gnawing discomfort that we have the possibility of giving shape to dreams that are at once faithful to who we are and who we can become.

—From *Growing Strong at Broken Places* by Paula Ripple

❧ "You will know that I am among you and that I, the Lord, am your God . . ." (Joel 2:27).

Do you know who your God is?
Do you know that God is among you?
Do you know that the Lord watches over you?

Have you ever seen those portraits that have the eyes so contrived that no matter where you are in the room the eyes look at you? As you move from place to place, the eyes of the portrait are still looking at you.

God's vision of us is like that—except we can leave the presence of the portrait ever gazing upon us.

Our sense of God's presence spurs us on to holy living, living in fairness with our families, our colleagues, and everyone with whom we come in contact.

—From the journal of Richard Allen Ward

❧ And these words: You will not be overcome, were said very insistently and strongly, for certainty and strength against every tribulation which may come. [God] did not say: You will not be assailed, you will not be belaboured, you will not be disquieted, but [God] said: You will not be overcome. God wants us to pay attention to his words, and always to be strong in our

certainty, in well-being and in woe, for [God] loves us and delights in us.
—From *Showings* by Julian of Norwich (*Classics of Western Spirituality* Series)

Hymn: O God, Our Help in Ages Past

O God, our help in ages past,
Our hope for years to come,
Our shelter from the stormy blast,
And our eternal home!

Under the shadow of thy throne,
Still may we dwell secure;
Sufficient is thine arm alone,
And our defense is sure.

Before the hills in order stood,
Or earth received her frame,
From everlasting, thou art God,
To endless years the same.

A thousand ages, in thy sight,
Are like an evening gone;
Short as the watch that ends the night,
Before the rising sun.

Time, like an ever rolling stream,
Bears all who breathe away;
They fly forgotten as a dream
Dies at the opening day.

O God, our help in ages past,
Our hope for years to come;
Be thou our guide while life shall last,
And our eternal home.
—Isaac Watts

Sunday between August 14 and 20
42: The Mystery of God's Gifts

I. Invocation
    Lord Jesus, life of God hidden deep within, give us today your gift of life and nourish it until it is full-born in us. Through the power that is yours alone. Amen.

II. Psalm 145

III. Reading and Reflection

IV. Daily Scripture Readings
    Monday   Matthew 8:1-4
    Tuesday   Matthew 8:5-13
    Wednesday   Matthew 8:14-17
    Thursday   Matthew 9:18-26
    Friday   Matthew 9:27-34
    Saturday   Mark 10:46-52
    Sunday   A. Exodus 16:2-15; Romans 11:13-16, 29-32; Psalm 78:1-3, 10-20, Matthew 15:21-28
                 B. 2 Samuel 18:24-33; Ephesians 5:15-20; Psalm 102:1-12; John 6:51-58
                 C. Jeremiah 20:7-13; Hebrews 12:1-2, 12-17; Psalm 10:12-18; Luke 12:49-56

V. Reflection: Silent and Written

VI. Prayers: For the Church, for Others, for Myself

VII. Hymn: "How Like a Gentle Spirit"

VIII. Benediction
    And now, Lord Jesus, illumination of the mystery of God's unending love for me, give me the grace to shine today as one of your lesser lights, illuminating the way for others to come closer to you. Amen.

Readings for Reflection

❧ God's call is mysterious; it comes in the darkness of faith. It is so fine, so subtle, that it is only with the deepest silence within us that we can hear it.
—From *Letters from the Desert* by Carlo Carretto

❧ Be at peace with your own soul; then heaven and earth will be at peace with you. Enter eagerly into the treasure house that is within you, and so you will see the things that are in heaven; for there is but one single entry to them both. The ladder that leads to the kingdom is hidden within your soul. Flee from sin, dive into yourself, and in your soul you will discover the stairs by which to ascend.
—Isaac the Syrian

❧ If creation is like a woman's swelling womb, the child within—the human being—cannot but await with impatience the bursting of the waters, to look at last on the face of its begetter.

If the reality in which God has placed human beings is the garden of Eden, which they are to cultivate and tend, this garden is itself a sufficient initiation into the experience which ought ultimately to lead them to the fullness of truth.

Even if the garden happens to be the desert, the creature has the testimony of the stars to ripen hope and foster growth.

Only wait.

Of course, waiting is not easy and haste is ever the sin of Adam.
—From *Why, O Lord?* by Carlo Carretto

❧ One thing is certain: we are on earth as in a huge space where everything is light and dark at the same time, where everything is the sign of an invisible presence, and where a continual challenge comes from the splendid vault outstretched above in its astronomical distances.

Inaccessible far-away things question us endlessly, oblige us to look up at those luminous specks like starry holes piercing the black vault, which seem to say that there, above, is the repose we seek.

How often have I known that living picture in the desert night of the Sahara!

How often, lying wrapped in a blanket on the sand, have I passed hour after hour gazing at a starry dome ceaselessly speaking to me, questioning me, helping me to find my bearings in the dark!

Why do we live?

Why do things come to be?

Why do I plod along like a wandering shepherd?

Why this vast silence?

Why do stars look down as though indifferent to our suffering?

Withal, one thing is certain: this light, the sign of the truth we seek and the means by which we may catch a glimpse of it, has not got its roots on earth.

Light comes from up there, it comes from something stretching above me, something transcending me, something preceding me.

You can actually see this, physically.

Like it or not, the explanation I seek is not here on earth, though I may look for it here.

The earth goes on rotating on its axis, day after day, season after season, millennium after millennium, and vouchsafes no final answer to my justified questioning.

—From *Why, O Lord?* by Carlo Carretto

✪ Thus the feelings that well up when we do not the good we know we should are healthy and trustworthy. The loathing that a bad conscience brings is meant for the reform of the inconsistency that produces it. On the other hand, the serenity, peace, and joy of a good conscience are equally healthy and trustworthy. When we ring true to ourselves and others, we should enjoy our harmony. This may never be presumptuous. Always it must bow to the mystery of God. But it can and should be enjoyed—offered to God as one of the graces for which we most passionately give thanks.

—From *How to Make It Through the Day* by John Carmody

❧ When you are suffering, in flesh or in spirit, the natural response is to weep.

And what a lot of weeping there is!

If we could gather it all in one place it would fill a sea, a great ocean.

Then, when our eyes are dry for an instant, we ask, why? Why, Lord, all this weeping?

The answer does not come easily.

And again we begin to weep and our thoughts become all tangled and even more sorrowful, and we stumble about like wounded birds.

Then we start again asking: why?

Why?

—From *Why, O Lord?* by Carlo Carretto

❧ Here is something new indeed. You might say that the very experience of pain has brought us something we did not have before.

With the pain comes nothing less than knowledge of the Absolute, knowledge of God. Lord, "I knew you then only by hearsay; but now, having seen you with my own eyes . . ."

What has happened?

In experiencing suffering, what has happened in me?

—From *Why, O Lord?* by Carlo Carretto

❧ Ultimately, our acceptance of an obedience to the gospel and to a eucharistic style of living depends on a single factor. The living truth of our relatedness to the God of life. We submit ourselves when we trust and we love. Obedience is the offspring of a deep and intimate relationship between our own hearts and the God who embraces us and who shares with us a joyous delight in and passionate concern for all of creation. When God is the one in whom we live and move and have our being, then our spirits will reverberate and our lives echo that limitless love.

—From *Every Bush Is Burning* by Joan Puls

&. Holiness in human life is a reflection of the holiness of God and, therefore, has always been associated with religious experience. Holiness is a special word that suggests not so much a particular quality of the divine, as the essence of that transcendent mystery which for the believer stands at the center of human existence. The word holiness carries with it connotations of the numinous, and therefore includes the experience of awe and wonder and power—all of which cannot be clearly defined. Holiness always implies something more—pointing to that mystery which can never be contained. More than any other word in the history of language, it speaks of the essence of religious experience.

—From *Invitation to Holiness* by James C. Fenhagen

&. Jesus' life and death show us that God wants to share all with us. "He did not spare his own Son" (Rom 8:32). Sometimes the way we pray prevents us from realizing this and, to speak loosely, prevents God from sharing with us. This happens when we spend all our time in prayer doing the speaking to God, when we never pause to let God speak. We forget that in the time of prayer God is in full action, loving us with . . . immense love, by no means inactive or sleeping. We do not stop to let this sink in. A more appropriate way to pray is to allow plenty of time for God to do the acting.

—From *Living the Richness of the Cross* by John Dalrymple

Hymn: How Like a Gentle Spirit

How like a gentle spirit deep within
God reins our fervent passions day by day,
And gives us strength to challenge and to win
Despite the perils of our chosen way.

Let God be God wherever life may be;
Let every tongue bear witness to the call;
All humankind is one by God's decree;
Let God be God, let God be God for all.

God like a mother eagle hovers near
On mighty wings of power manifest;
God like a gentle shepherd stills our fear,
And comforts us against a peaceful breast.

When in our vain pretensions we conspire
To shape God's image as we see our own,
Hark to the voice above our base desire;
God is the sculptor, we the broken stone.

Through all our fretful claims of sex and race
The universal love of God shines through,
For God is love transcending style and place
And all the idle options we pursue.
—C. Eric Lincoln

43: The Centrality of Christ

I. Invocation
   Lord Jesus Christ, whose cross was raised on Golgotha's brow casting its long shadow over Jerusalem's soul, may the cross be raised at the center of my life, casting its shadow over all my desires and all my motives. In your strong name I pray. Amen.

II. Psalm 18:1-19

III. Reading and Reflection

IV. Daily Scripture Readings
Monday	John 1:19-28
Tuesday	John 14:1-11
Wednesday	Colossians 1:15-23
Thursday	John 6:66-71
Friday	John 12:20-36
Saturday	John 11:1-16

   Sunday   A. Exodus 17:1-7; Romans 11:33-36; Psalm 95; Matthew 16:13-20
             B. 2 Samuel 23:1-7; Ephesians 5:21-33; Psalm 67; John 6:55-69
             C. Jeremiah 28:1-9; Hebrews 12:18-29; Psalm 84; Luke 13:22-30

V. Reflection: Silent and Written

VI. Prayers: For the Church, for Others, for Myself

VII. Hymn: "How Can We Name a Love"

VIII. Benediction
   I bind myself today to the strong name of Jesus. My God, I call you to the center of my life. Come to me, stay with me, all the day long. Amen.

Readings for Reflection

❧ A person is a Christian because of Jesus. Through the paradoxical congruence between Jesus' life, death, and resurrection, and a person's experience, Jesus becomes a savior of power and might. For the Christian of lively faith, there breathes the dearest freshness in Jesus. He is a thesaurus, a treasury, never to be emptied. From cradle to grave, his mysteries shine golden with Johannine grace, glint green and white with Pauline grace aligned with springtime and Passover.
—From *The Heart of the Christian Matter* by John Carmody

❧ I believe Jesus of Nazareth fulfills our deepest human hopes and clarifies our deepest human fears, but somewhat strangely. For he takes our hopes far beyond what most of us consider realistic, telling us that we can live forever with God; and he brings our fears into an almost punishing light, telling us that we can utterly ruin ourselves and our world by loving badly.

Thus Jesus' life makes our lives dramatic. Like a story that soon will reach its climax, our time grows tense when we stretch it on Jesus' frame. The more intimately we know Jesus' life, the more it turns our significance, our lives, into a reflection of his death and resurrection. What are we dying for, what are we choosing against? What will we rise to, how shall our last numbers tally? When Jesus burst upon the Israelite scene, he laid down this most forceful challenge: "The time is fulfilled, and the kingdom of God is at hand; repent, and believe in the gospel" (Mk 1:14). I believe he continues to lay down this most forceful challenge wherever we allow him onto our scene.

So for me, the motive of Christian faith, its cause and source, is the power or allure of Jesus himself.
—From *The Heart of the Christian Matter* by John Carmody

❧ God probably granted me this experience so as to teach me to look beyond the spiritual characteristics and outward forms in search of the true center. And that can only be Jesus. I came to learn that the fact that we have been converted does not imply that we are following the path of true discipleship. On the contrary, I discovered that as evangelical believers we often use the statement, "I've been saved," as a cushion to rest on or even as a shield to protect ourselves from further penetration by the light of truth and from God's judgement. Consequently, the danger of hypocrisy and pharisaism is great. Assuming that one's life is in order, one proudly looks down on others, sometimes even being reluctant to take communion with "mere church-goers", who also attend lectures and concerts, i.e. those who still "belong to the world." One fails to realize that some of these churchgoers are more pleasing to God, since they are like the publican who prayed, "God, be merciful to me, a sinner."

—From *I Found the Key to the Heart of God* by Basilea Schlink

❧ For the Christian, therefore, holiness is the fruit of our association with Jesus. It seems to set us apart, not in the sense of being other-worldly, but rather in the sense of being grasped by the Kingdom vision that formed the center of Jesus' life and message. The call to holiness is a call to live in this world, but not of it—meaning that as we open ourselves to the relationship Jesus offers, we are more and more able to live from a perspective and a vision that transcends what we normally experience.

—From *Invitation to Holiness* by James C. Fenhagen

❧ Atheism, the attempt to be master of our fate and as many fates around us as we can decently manage, is not the bold swashbuckling affair of legend but a grim, tight-lipped business. These atheists are cramped, full of pretense, diminished beings. Either contemptuous or condescending toward the God whom they publically profess (their actual attitude toward the poor mirrors their inner attitude toward God), they depend on consumer goods or status positions, or peer opinions—always something impersonal or abstract—to validate their sense of worth. With no inner life they require external paraphernalia, personalized things or depersonalized persons, to get a sense of self. Narcissism is the most recent term for this secret atheism of the heart. It typifies the character structure of a society that has lost interest in God.

—From *Earth and Altar* by Eugene H. Peterson

&. To meet the Messiah in a yes-or-no encounter forces us to examine and to admit what we hold absolute, which is exactly what happened to the rich young ruler long ago. Jesus had—and still has—a disturbing way of putting everything into a different perspective. In his presence we cannot get by with "almost" or "maybe" or "later." A confrontation with Jesus is always a rigorous examination of the "musts" of our life. It is not unlike sifting through the ashes after a fire has destroyed our home and the possessions of a lifetime. In that aftermath we slowly relearn what we actually keep and what we value most. Or it is not unlike lying in the intensive care unit of a hospital after a massive coronary. In the silent darkness of early morning, we ask where all the hurrying and demanding, all the striving and spending bring us—at last.

—From *Meeting the Messiah* by Donald J. Shelby

&. Jesus Christ is a God whom we approach without pride, and before whom we humble ourselves without despair.

—Blaise Pascal

&. A healthy forgetter is developed by forgiveness. We cannot erase the memory cards of our failures in our brain computer until we have a profound experience of forgiveness. The authentic mark of truly mature persons is the capacity to forgive themselves. But that is a rare commodity. Years of experience of seeking to be a whole person and helping others with their self-esteem has led me to the conclusion that one of the greatest miracles of life is self-forgiveness. I have never known a person who has been able to do it without a healing experience of Christ's kindness.

—From *Radiance of the Inner Splendor* by Lloyd John Ogilvie

Hymn: How Can We Name a Love

How can we name a Love
That wakens heart and mind,
Indwelling all we know
Or think or do
Or seek or find?
Within our daily world,
In each familiar face
Where joy is found,
Love's echoes sound,
Hid in the commonplace.

If we awoke to life
Built on a rock of care
That asked no great reward
But firm, assured,
Was simply there,
We can, with parents' names,
Picture and then adore
Love's cosmic mind,
Our father kind,
Our mother strong and sure.

So in a hundred names
Daily we all can meet
Signals of love unknown
At work, at home,
Or in the street.
Yet on these terms alone
Faith would be weak and dim.
In Christ we see
Love's guarantee
And fix our hopes on him.
—Brian Wren

44: *True Discipleship*

I.   Invocation
     Good Teacher, help me in this hour to hear your clear call to discipleship. By the power of your Spirit grant me wisdom, courage and strength to live as your disciple all day long. Amen.

II. Psalm 1

III. Reading and Reflection

IV. Daily Scripture Readings
Monday	Philippians 2:1-8
Tuesday	Galatians 5:16-24
Wednesday	Matthew 5:1-11
Thursday	Matthew 5:12-16
Friday	Matthew 7:21-28
Saturday	Matthew 5:43-48

     Sunday   A. Exodus 19:1-9; Romans 12:1-13; Psalm 114; Matthew 16:21-28
              B. 1 Kings 2:1-4, 10-12; Ephesians 6:10-20; Psalm 121; Mark 7:1-8, 14-15, 21-23
              C. Ezekiel 18:1-9, 25-29; Hebrews 13:1-8; Psalm 15; Luke 14:1, 7-14

V.   Reflection: Silent and Written

VI. Prayers: For the Church, for Others, for Myself

VII. Hymn: "O Jesus, I Have Promised"

VIII. Benediction
     O my God, since you are with me, and I must now, in obedience to your commands, apply my mind to these outward things, I beg you to grant me the grace to continue in your presence. To this end, prepare me with your assistance, receive all my works, and possess all my affections. Amen.

Readings for Reflection

❧ Never think that in lowering yourself you have less power for good. On the contrary, in thus humbling yourself you are imitating me and using the same means that I used. You are walking in my *Way*, and therefore in the *Truth*, and you are in the right state to receive *Life* and impart it to others. The best means for this is always to imitate me. I came down to the level of [human beings] by my Incarnation, and to that of sinners by my Circumcision and Baptism. Be lowly, lowly, humble, humble. Let those that are in high places put themselves last in a spirit of lowliness and service, love . . . , humility, taking the lowest place so long as the divine will does not call you to another, for in that case you must obey. Obedience first of all— conformity to the will of God. If you are placed high, then keep yourself in humility of soul as though you were the last; occupy your high position as though you were there only to serve others and to lead them to salvation, and as if, though you may command them, you are rather serving them, for you command them only with the purpose of sanctifying them.
—From *Meditations of a Hermit* by Charles de Foucauld

❧ My Father, I commend myself to you, I give myself to you, I leave myself in your hands. My Father, do with me as you wish. Whatever you do with me, I thank you, I accept everything. I am ready for anything. I thank you always. So long as your will is done in me and in all creatures, I have no other wish, my God. I put my soul into your hands, giving it to you, my God, with all my heart's love, which makes me crave to abandon myself to you without reserve, with utter confidence. For are you not my Father?
—From *Meditations of a Hermit* by Charles de Foucauld

❧ At some thoughts [one] stands perplexed, above all at the sight of human sin, and . . . wonders whether to combat it by force or by humble love. Always decide: "I will combat it by humble love." If you resolve on that once for all, you can conquer the whole world. Loving humility is a terrible force: it is the strongest of all things, and there is nothing else like it.

—From *The Orthodox Way* by Kallistos Ware

❧ Now to complete the journey—the flight, as the Spanish mystic would say—love must be purified and transformed into charity.

What does this mean?

It is simple.

It means imitating Jesus on the road to Jerusalem.

Every situation must be reversed.

I who have used Jerusalem for my pleasures must sacrifice my pleasures for Jerusalem.

I who have made use of others for my amusement must make my life the tool of [others].

I who have been so afraid to suffer must accept Calvary with Jesus.

Like Jesus.

My exodus does not end when I die in my bed, but when I die on the cross of Christ.

Now *there* is something to fear. And we want to shout, "No one can go that far!"

And we would be right. But we know that the miracle worker is love itself.

God is God . . . the God of the impossible.

—From *Why, O Lord?* by Carlo Carretto

❧ Just allow people to see Jesus in you
to see how you pray
to see how you lead a pure life
to see how you deal with your family
to see how much peace there is in your family.
Then you can look straight into their eyes and say,
"This is the way."
You speak from life, you speak from experience.

—From *Words to Love By* by Mother Teresa

ᐤ The opposite of *foolish* in Scripture is *wise*. *Wise* refers to skill in living. It does not mean, primarily, the person who knows the right answers to things, but one who has developed the right responses (relationships) to persons, to God. The wise understand how the world works; know about patience and love, listening and grace, adoration and beauty; know that other people are awesome creatures to be respected and befriended, especially the ones that I cannot get anything out of; know that the earth is a marvelously intricate gift to be cared for and enjoyed; know that God is an ever-present center, a never-diminishing reality, an all-encompassing love; and know that there is no living being that does not reach out gladly and responsively to [God] and the nation/kingdom/community in which [God] has placed us.

The wise know that there is only one cure for the fool. Prayer that is as passionate for the salvation of others as it is for myself: "O that deliverance for Israel would come out of Zion!" Prayer that is convinced that there is no wellness until everyone is restored to a place of blessing: "When the Lord restores the fortunes of his people." And prayer that sees the community as a place not of acquisition, but of celebration: "Jacob shall rejoice, Israel shall be glad."

—From *Earth and Altar* by Eugene H. Peterson

ᐤ When I use "witness" and "martyr" together it is a play on words. "Witness" and "martyr" are at root the same word. I mean by "martyr" not one who dies in the process of witnessing but one whose witnessing costs something. This is its common meaning—one who sacrifices something of great value for the sake of principle. But unless one achieves the notoriety of a Martin Luther King, Jr., few in our society are so threatened by the witness of faithful disciples that they feel compelled to kill them. In our times, in contrast to the classic periods of persecution, it will be the manner of our lives rather than the manner of our deaths that counts for witness.

—From *Recovery of the Protestant Adventure* by Neill Q. Hamilton

❧ The suffering and death of Jesus Christ, his passion and cross, stand at the center of the Christian religion. The life of Jesus of Nazareth provided many graphic symbols, each of which might have been taken as the distinguishing sign of his movement: good shepherd, bread of life, light of the world, lamb of God, resurrection, transfiguration. None of these became the Christian sign. Instead, the sign of Jesus' suffering and death was accepted everywhere as the official mark of Christianity. We hang crucifixes on our walls, wear them around our necks, build our churches in the shape of the cross, put the cross on flags and medals. Almost certainly there will be a cross near the reader of these pages. It is the central symbol of Christianity and permeates our culture.

—From *Living the Richness of the Cross* by John Dalrymple

❧ From this you now see that works cannot make you righteous. First, you must be established in Christ through faith and be righteous in him before you can do any good work. See to it indeed that your righteousness is the grace and gift of God that comes before all your merit. How can a dead man walk, stand, or do anything good if someone does not first make him living? Thus, since you are dead in sins and dead before God you can do no work pleasing to God unless you are first made living in Christ.

Righteousness comes alone from Christ through faith, for faith is in [us] as a newborn, small, naked, and simple child that stands unclothed simply before [the] Redeemer and Sanctifier, and receives all from him who begot it, namely, righteousness, piety, holiness, grace, and the Holy Spirit.

Thus, if this naked, simple child is to be clothed with God's mercy, it must lift both its hands up and receive everything from God, grace together with all holiness and piety. Receiving this, it is made pious, holy, and blessed.

—From *True Christianity* by Johann Arndt (*Classics of Western Spirituality* Series)

Hymn: O Jesus, I Have Promised

O Jesus, I have promised
To serve thee to the end;
Be thou forever near me,
My Master and my Friend.
I shall not fear the battle
If thou art by my side,
Nor wander from the pathway
If thou wilt be my guide.

O let me feel thee near me!
The world is ever near;
I see the sights that dazzle,
The tempting sounds I hear;
My foes are ever near me,
Around me and within;
But Jesus, draw thou nearer,
And shield my soul from sin.

O let me hear thee speaking
In accents clear and still,
Above the storms of passion,
The murmurs of self-will.
O speak to reassure me,
To hasten or control;
O speak, and make me listen,
Thou guardian of my soul.

O Jesus, thou hast promised
To all who follow thee
That where thou art in glory
There shall thy servant be.
And Jesus, I have promised
To serve thee to the end;
O give me grace to follow,
My Master and my Friend.
—John E. Bode

45: Reconciliation

I. Invocation
My Lord and friend, in the quietness of this hour, reconcile my contrary motives and conflicting desires. Give me a singleness of purpose that I may come into your presence unashamed and sit under your gaze without blushing. Amen.

II. Psalm 130

III. Reading and Reflection

IV. Daily Scripture Readings

Monday	2 Corinthians 5:16-21
Tuesday	Romans 5:1-11
Wednesday	2 Corinthians 13:1-12
Thursday	Acts 10:34-43
Friday	Luke 6:37-42
Saturday	Luke 17:1-6
Sunday	A. Exodus 19:16-24; Romans 13:1-10; Psalm 115:1-11; Matthew 18:15-20
	B. Proverbs 2:1-8; James 1:17-27; Psalm 119:129-136; Mark 7:31-37
	C. Ezekiel 33:1-11; Philemon 1-20; Psalm 94:12-22; Luke 14:25-33

V. Reflection: Silent and Written

VI. Prayers: For the Church, for Others, for Myself

VII. Hymn: "Amazing Grace"

VIII. Benediction
And now, my Lord, I thank you for reconciling my inner conflicts and healing my brokenness. Send me, I pray, from this place as Christ's ambassador of reconciliation to those whom I meet this day. Amen.

Readings for Reflection

❧ Jesus is a very patient teacher. He never stops telling us where to make our true home, what to look for, and how to live. When we are distracted, we focus upon all the dangers and forget what we have heard. But Jesus says over and over again: "Make your home in me, as I make mine in you. Whoever remains in me, with me in them, bears fruit in plenty...I have told you this so that my own joy may be in you, and your joy may be complete" (John 15:4,5,11). Thus, Jesus invites us to an intimate, fruitful, and ecstatic life in his home, which is ours too.

—From *Lifesigns* by Henri J. M. Nouwen

❧ I release you from my hurt feelings. I free you from my reading of your motives. I withdraw my "justified" outrage and leave you clean and happy in my mind. In place of censure, I offer you all of God's deep contentment and peace. I will perceive you singing, with a soft smile of freedom and a glow of rich satisfaction. I bless you my brother. You are a shining member of the Family of God, and I will wait patiently for this truthful vision to come honestly to my mind.

—From *The Quiet Answer* by Hugh Prather

❧ To be immersed in the world means also to suffer fatal divisions between human beings. The self that is severed from its inborn connection with God readily becomes a "heart turned in upon itself." If the "divided self" characterizes our inner life, the "heart turned in upon itself" is a telling image of our alienation from one another. The self-seeking conveyed by Augustine's phrase fills our field of vision with the shapes of our own desires, eclipsing the profile of our neighbor's need. The "heart turned in upon itself" isolates us because it conceives of self-fulfillment in individual terms. It will not acknowledge that our truest fulfillment is found only within the texture of mutuality God has chosen for authentic human life.

It is difficult to imagine how greatly our immersion in the world pains God. This is not the pain of a regent disobeyed but the anguish of a loving parent spurned by a child in desperate want. We glimpse a vivid portrait of this divine passion in Psalm 81. After recounting the chapters of Israel's faithlessness in the wilderness, a voice still unknown to the psalmist utters this remarkable lament, "O that my people would heed me, that Israel would walk in my ways!" Here is the heart's desire of our God, and the wellspring of that reconciling love that would gather into one new creation all the scattered, shattered creatures so treasured by their Creator (see Eph. 1:9-10).

As we are awakened to the ingathering love of God, the brokenness that divides us from ourselves and others begins to mend.

—From "Editor's Introduction" by John Mogabgab in *Weavings*, January/February, 1990.

ᐧ What would not every lover of God and his [or her] neighbour do, what would [they] not suffer, to remedy this sore evil, to remove contention from the children of God, to restore or preserve peace among them? What but a good concience would [they] think too dear to part with, in order to promote this valuable end? And suppose we cannot "make (these) wars to cease in all the world," suppose we cannot reconcile all the children of God to each other, however let [us] do what [we] can, let [us] contribute, if it be but two mites, towards it.

—John Wesley

ᐧ We must not so stress our relationship with God that we forget our relationship with one another. And we must not so stress our relationship with one another that we have no need to look to God for forgiveness. Reconciliation involves both God and neighbors. Anyone committed to living a life of reconciliation must attend to the dynamics of love in relationship with God, others, self, and the world.

—From *To Walk Together Again* by Richard M. Gula

⌘ I was running under cloudless skies. And then suddenly I tripped, almost fell, pulled back this side of the sin, but was shaken and humiliated that I could come that close to sin. I thought I was emancipated and found I wasn't. I went to the class meeting—I'm grateful that I didn't stay away—went, but my [spiritual] music had gone. I had hung my harp on a weeping willow tree. As the others spoke of their joys and victories of the week, I sat there with the tears rolling down my cheeks. I was heartbroken. After the others had spoken, John Zink, the class leader, said: "Now, Stanley, tell us what is the matter." I told them I couldn't, but would they please pray for me?... they fell to their knees, and they lifted me back to the bosom of God by faith and love. When we got up from our knees, I was reconciled to my heavenly father, to the group, and to myself, I was reconciled. The universe opened its arms and took me in again. The estrangement was gone. I took my harp from the willow tree and began to sing again.

—From *A Song of Ascents* by E. Stanley Jones

⌘ Behind the meditations on the sufferings of Jesus during his passion has been the conviction that Jesus Christ died for our sins. It has been this fact, surely, which has made people concentrate so lovingly on the way Jesus suffered and died. If his death were not so important, then there would be little concentration on the manner of his death. But because his death was known to be completely central to Christian life, then there arose the loving concentration on the manner of his dying. Perhaps the reason for putting all that emphasis on how Jesus suffered is that people have found it difficult to say why Jesus' death was for our sins, so they transferred attention to the easily comprehended physical details of his death. We have been told, and we believe, that Jesus' death took place to redeem us from our sins, but once that is said it is difficult to go further in devotional pondering. It is easier to accept the fact without more questioning, and then to focus on the way Jesus died.

—From *Living the Richness of the Cross* by John Dalrymple

Hymn: Amazing Grace

Amazing grace! How sweet the sound
That saved a wretch like me!
I once was lost, but now am found;
Was blind, but now I see.

'Twas grace that taught my heart to fear,
And grace my fears relieved;
How precious did that grace appear,
The hour I first believed.

Through many dangers, toils and snares,
I have already come;
'Tis grace hath brought me safe thus far,
And grace will lead me home.

The Lord has promised good to me,
His word my hope secures;
He will my shield and portion be,
As long as life endures.

Yea, when this flesh and heart shall fail,
And mortal life shall cease,
I shall possess, within the veil,
A life of joy and peace.

When we've been there ten thousand years,
Bright shining as the sun,
We've no less days to sing God's praise
Than when we'd first begun.

—John Newton

Sunday between September 11 and 17
46: God's Unlimited Grace

I. Invocation
    O God, whose grace and mercy flow like an endless river from your great being, help me now to place myself in the path of your rushing love and limitless compassion, that I may find my spirit renewed. Amen.

II. Psalm 141

III. Reading and Reflection

IV. Daily Scripture Readings
    | Monday | Colossians 2:8-15 |
    | Tuesday | Ephesians 2:1-10 |
    | Wednesday | Romans 6:1-14 |
    | Thursday | Romans 8:1-11 |
    | Friday | 2 Timothy 2:1-13 |
    | Saturday | John 8:1-11 |
    | Sunday | A. Exodus 20:1-20; Romans 14:5-12; Psalm 19:7-14; Matthew 18:21-35 |
    | | B. Proverbs 22:1-2, 8-9; James 2:1-5,8-10,14-17; Psalm 125; Mark 8:27-38 |
    | | C. Hosea 4:1-3, 5:15–6:6; 1 Timothy 1:12-17; Psalm 77:11-20; Luke 15:1-10 |

V. Reflection: Silent and Written

VI. Prayers: For the Church, for Others, for Myself

VII. Hymn: "Seek the Lord"

VIII. Benediction
    O God, it is true that no eye has seen nor ear has heard what wonderful things you hold in store for your children; yet in these moments with you, I have seen more clearly and listened more deeply. I give you thanks. Amen.

Readings for Reflection

❧ I am bitterly ashamed, O God, that always I must be confessing to Thee my forgetfulness of Thee, the feebleness of my love for Thee, the fitfulness and listlessness of my desire. How many plain commandments of Thine have I this day disobeyed! How many little services of love have I withheld from Thee, O Christ, in that I withheld them from the least of these Thy brethren with whom I have had to do!
—From *A Diary of Private Prayer* by John Baillie

❧ Evening Prayer

> If I have wounded any soul today,
> If I have caused one foot to go astray,
> If I have walked in my own willful way—
>   Good Lord, forgive!
>
> If I have uttered idle words or vain,
> If I have turned aside from want or pain,
> Lest I myself should suffer through the strain—
>   Good Lord, forgive!
>
> If I have craved for joys that are not mine,
> If I have let my wayward heart repine,
> Dwelling on things of earth, not things divine—
>   Good Lord, forgive!
>
> If I have been perverse, or hard, or cold,
> If I have longed for shelter in Thy fold
> When Thou hast given me some part to hold—
>   Good Lord, forgive!
>
> Forgive the sins I have confessed to Thee,
> Forgive the secret sins I do not see,
> That which I know not, Father, teach Thou me—
>   Help me to live.
> —C. Maud Battersby

≈ *S. Matthew xxvi, 40.*
What? Could you not watch one
hour with me?

You do not say this only to your apostles, O my Lord, but to all of us who might watch with you, keep you company in the sadness of your Sacred Heart, console you with faithful love. But we do not do it. We go off to sleep; we lack courage and love, forgetting how precious is a vigil with you, forgetting that to watch at your feet is such an infinite privilege that even the Saints and Angels are unworthy of it, forgetting to rejoice in your presence as one rejoices in the presence of some much loved creature, and to long to console you with passionate love. If our longing was great and passionate enough to console and comfort you, we should never give in to this low, bestial temptation to sleep. If we felt, as we should, the infinite peace of praying at your feet, should we not always be there praying with you, not noticing how the time goes, fearing only one thing in our happiness—its end? Alas! my God, I am one of these low, base creatures, for how often do I fall asleep at your very feet when I should be praying with you. Forgive me, forgive me. Help me, my God, never to fall into this hateful coldness and infidelity. Many times have I fallen, I hate my fault, it is horrible to me. I ask your pardon, my God, with all my soul.

—From *Meditations of a Hermit* by Charles de Foucauld

≈ It was in [my] experience of suffering and the awareness of a healing presence in the midst of my pain and doubt, my physical immobility and dependency on others, that I realized the intimate connection between suffering and grace. I now join Samuel Miller in wondering why grace has been so dissociated from suffering in theology.

To be sure, [grace] is full of joy, a supernal joy of amazing buoyancy and light; and yet I think that grace and suffering must be seen together. It is by

grace that the world of nature is redeemed, and there is no redemption except by the cross. No poem is written, no picture painted, no music made, no sinner forgiven, no child born, no [person] loved, no truth known, no stone shaped, no peace attained, except grace took a risk, bore a burden, absorbed the evil, and suffered the pain. (*The Dilemma of Modern Belief*)
—From *Alive in Christ* by Maxie Dunnam

ò I feel immersed in God like a drop in the ocean, like a star in the immensity of night; like a lark in the summer sun or a fish in the sea.
—From *Love Is for Living* by Carlo Carretto

ò There is no greater act of love than of letting go in the dark and falling into the arms of our lover with total abandon; offering all for love.

Listen to what Father de Foucauld said in the desert. He really understood.

Father,
I abandon myself into your hands;
do with me what you will.
Whatever you may do, I thank you:
I am ready for all, I accept all.
Let only your will be done in me,
and in all your creatures.
I wish no more than this, O Lord.
Into your hands I commend my soul;
I offer it to you with all the love of my heart,
for I love you Lord, and so need to give myself,
to surrender myself into your hands, without reserve
and with boundless confidence,
for you are my Father.

That is how to pray when you are suffering. That is how to believe in God.
—From *Why, O Lord?* by Carlo Carretto

To speak of the thirst for holiness, then, is to speak of a moral vision and a capacity for love that comes from the source of creation itself. Holiness is that which expands our humanity, for it not only provides the context in which growth takes place, but provides a vision of what life is ultimately about and towards which we stumble and slowly make our way, owning our brokenness but rejoicing in the Grace that alone will make us whole.

—From *Invitation to Holiness* by James C. Fenhagen

Spend some time with children. Count among your friends and regular associates those who are poor. Learn from the sick and those who treat life as the gift it is. And observe true lovers, or better, become one. Such as these are sacraments of freedom in a world frightened by its own uncontrolled destructiveness and oppressed by its own denial of innocence and gentleness.

It was not by accident that Jesus placed a child in the midst of his adult followers and said: "Unless you become like this . . ." Spontaneous in your response to life, honest in your assessment of people, vulnerable to the world about you. Children are obedient to their element: innocent joy, eager trust, endless inquisitiveness.

—From *Every Bush Is Burning* by Joan Puls

Even the capacity to recognize our condition before God is itself a grace. We cannot always attain it at will. To learn meditation does not, therefore, mean learning an artificial technique for infallibly producing "compunction" and the "sense of our nothingness" whenever we please. On the contrary, this would be the result of violence and would be inauthentic. Meditation implies the capacity to receive this grace whenever God wishes to grant it to us.

—From *Contemplative Prayer* by Thomas Merton

Grace begins and ends prayer. Grace is what we call what is left over after the scouring of the self, the dying into self. Grace is what was there before we ever looked at ourselves in prayer. Grace gives us our initial impulse to pray. Further, grace sustains that beginning of our attentiveness, of our assiduousness, or even our mere muddling along, and does so when our prayers are blocked by self-judgment, met with no apparent answers, seem to lead nowhere. Some impulse, some effort, some intuition, some hope keeps us praying, despite failures, despite early successes that do not repeat themselves. That is grace, which we almost never recognize, at first anyway, as itself. But that is because grace comes to us in the flesh, through the spaces and forms and contents of our human life.

—From *Picturing God* by Ann Belford Ulanov

Hymn: Seek the Lord

Seek the Lord who now is present,
Pray to One who is at hand.
Let the wicked cease from sinning,
Evildoers change their mind.
On the sinful God has pity;
Those returning God forgives.
This is what the Lord is saying
To a world that disbelieves.

"Judge me not by human standards!
As the vault of heaven soars
High above the earth, so higher
Are my thoughts and ways than yours.
See how rain and snow from heaven
Make earth blossom and bear fruit,
Giving you, before returning,
Seed for sowing, bread to eat:

"So my word returns not fruitless;
Does not from its labors cease
Till it has achieved my purpose
In a world of joy and peace."
God is love! How close the prophet
To that vital gospel word!
In Isaiah's inspiration
It is Jesus we have heard!
— Fred Pratt Green

Sunday between September 18 and 24

47: Good Stewards

I. Invocation

My God, you saw me in my unformed substance and numbered my days before I had lived one of them. Be close to me now, my God, help me to love you without restraint and to manage all the affairs of my life to the end that when I stand to give account, I need not be ashamed. In the name of my Lord, I pray. Amen.

II. Psalm 3

III. Reading and Reflection

IV. Daily Scripture Readings

Monday	1 Corinthians 4:1-7
Tuesday	1 Corinthians 4:8-13
Wednesday	1 Thessalonians 1:1-10
Thursday	2 Thessalonians 1:1-4
Friday	Luke 12:35-40
Saturday	Luke 12:41-48
Sunday	A. Exodus 32:1-14; Philippians 1:21-27; Psalm 106:7-8, 19-23; Matthew 20:1-16
	B. Job 28:20-28; James 3:13-18; Psalm 27:1-6; Mark 9:30-37
	C. Hosea 11:1-11; 1 Timothy 2:1-7; Psalm 107:1-9; Luke 16:1-13

V. Reflection: Silent and Written

VI. Prayers: For the Church, for Others, for Myself

VII. Hymn: "How Shall They Hear the Word of God"

VIII. Benediction

Hold before my eyes, my Lord, the diminishing number of my fleeting days, that I may receive them as precious gifts and live them in faithfulness and fidelity to you. Amen.

Readings for Reflection

❧ There is a two way relationship between prayer and life. Prayer can be seen as the focusing and redirecting of an attitude to God and to our fellow [human beings] that runs through all that we do. On the other hand we can see our daily life as something which prayer purifies, directs and consecrates. This interrelationship of prayer and life was expressed by William Temple in his well known saying, "It is not that conduct is the end of life and worship helps it but that worship is the end of life and conduct tests it." Temple is here using worship in a broad sense to include all of life. For in worship, as the derivation of the word from worth implies, we declare what we value most. If in prayer I declare that I value God above all things and in my life I show that my own selfish interests come first I am making a nonsense of my praying. We declare how we value God as much by our actions, by the way we treat other people, by the manner in which we do our work, as by anything we say. If my actions are wrong or wrongly motivated prayer cannot make them right. If however, despite my failures and inconsistencies, I do on the whole want to put God above all things then prayer will help to purify my motives and clarify my judgment.

—From *The River Within* by Christopher Bryant

❧ At the end of the day, review your conversation during the day, and ask yourself some pertinent questions about it. "Did I say exactly what I meant?" "Did I seek to create any false impressions?" "Did I color my language any for effect?" "Did I make any claim for myself, my knowledge, my skill, my actions, my intentions, my attitudes, my relations which went beyond the reality?" Examine yourself as relentlessly as if it were someone else you were examining. Repent of your failure. Resolve, by the grace of Christ, not to fail in the same way tomorrow. On the morrow "set a watch at the door of your lips."

—From *Discipline and Discovery* by Albert Edward Day

As a young man, John Wesley calculated that twenty-eight pounds a year (about $65) would care for his own needs. Since prices remained basically the same, he was able to keep at that level of expenditure throughout his lifetime. When Wesley first made that decision, his income was thirty pounds a year. In later years sales from his books would often earn him fourteen hundred pounds a year, but he still lived on twenty-eight pounds and gave the rest away. Wesley, of course, was single much of his life and never had children, so he did not deal with the financial problems engendered by a family; but the idea is a sound one. We can do the same thing. Obviously we have to make adjustments for growing children, savings for college, and inflation, but the principle remains firm.

Here is another wineskin. If both the wife and the husband desire to work, discipline yourselves to live on one salary and give the other away. In this way, one couple could potentially support an entire missionary family. Why not? What better investment opportunity could there be than that? Think what would happen to the worldwide missionary enterprise if each Christian couple would determine to give every second salary to missions.

Try still another model. Take a careful look at your income. Are there ways to so simplify your lifestyle that you can live on half of what you make? If so, rather than quit your job so that your earnings drop to half, plan to give away half of your earnings.

Here is still another approach. Rather than just giving the money away, invest it for the Kingdom of God. It is usually best to set up a separate checking or savings account. Money put into this account is to be used entirely for Kingdom causes.

—From *Freedom of Simplicity* by Richard J. Foster

We begin, sometimes without realizing it, to worship things, to relate to them as persons. And in the process, we inevitably relate to other persons as if they were things.

No wonder Jesus spoke five times as often about money and earthly possessions as about prayer. And everywhere in scripture we hear the warnings; money has power; wealth is addictive. Be careful, be on your guard. . . .

When God breaks in on a sufficiently prepared people, a new generosity emerges, one that is outgoing, joyous, spontaneous and free. Growth in Christian discipleship manifests itself by compassion for the poor. A new stewardship unfolds, a stewardship that cares deeply for all of God's created order, including the earth and its fullness—people, animals and things.

—From *Gathering the Fragments* by Edward J. Farrell

❦ Power is a genuine paradox to believers. We love it and we hate it. We despise its evil and appreciate its good. We would like to do without it, but we know it is part and parcel of human life.

Our ambivalence about power is resolved in the vow of service. Jesus picked up a basin and a towel and, in doing so, redefined the meaning and function of power. "If I then, your Lord and Teacher, have washed your feet, you also ought to wash one another's feet. For I have given you an example, that you also should do as I have done to you" (John 13:14-15). In the everlasting kingdom of Christ, low is high, down is up, weak is strong, service is power. Do you sincerely want to engage in the ministry of power? Do you want to be a leader who is a blessing to people? Do you honestly want to be used of God to heal human hurts? Then learn to become a servant to all. "If anyone would be first, he must be last of all and servant of all" (Mark 9:35). The ministry of power functions through the ministry of the towel.

—From *Money, Sex, and Power* by Richard J. Foster

❦ Simplicity, then, is the gift to live a holy life. It is the gift to live in the deeper awareness of connectedness to others and to all creation. It is the gift to travel lightly because accumulation of things, people, and experiences are unnecessary for our joy. In Christ all things are ours, and we belong to them. When St. Francis called the sun and moon, water and fire his sisters and brothers, he was being not so much a romantic as he was witnessing to the wholeness of life. Since we do not have to accumulate things for our survival, we are able to care for all of life rather than use it up. We are able to live freely with compassion because we do not have to be minding our possessions.

—From *Living Simply* edited by David Crean and Eric and Helen Ebbeson

❧ Three Old Testament themes point to the fullness and the richness of *shalom* as the possibility for which we were created. The first is the theme of creation in the image of God. The Bible affirms the unique and precious quality of every person as a child of God. It also affirms the responsibility of each person. To be created in the image of God is a gift that brings with it the responsibility to care for God's creation (Genesis 1:28).

The commission to have dominion over the earth is a trusteeship of divine right; a trusteeship of God's own care for the creation and an entrusting to our stewardship of that care.

A second important theme from creation theology is the goodness of creation. At the end of the sixth day, God looked at all that had been made and saw that it was *very* good (Genesis 1:31). The intention of creation was for *shalom* to be experienced by all, for all to know the goodness of creation. We in this affluent culture of ours have come to define "fullness of life" in terms of more than beyond our basic needs. We have turned the tables on the biblical understanding. The desire of many for excess begins to deny enough for others, and the possibility of *shalom* is limited for some.

A third theme of shalom is this: in creation we are all related. Human beings are not self-sufficient. We need relationship to God, to others, and to nature. Jesus, when asked to sum up the Law, sums it up not simply in terms of love of God but love of neighbor as well. Genesis 2:18 tells us that God saw it was not good for [the] human creature to be alone. The story then goes on to express relationship to nature (garden, animals) as well as with other humans. *Shalom* is the possibility of harmonious relationship with every person and with nature. We are not only created as stewards of God to experience the goodness of creation, but we are created to be in community with all creation. Shalom only finds its fulfillment when we find that interrelatedness.

—From *Living Simply* edited by David Crean and Eric and Helen Ebbeson

Hymn: How Shall They Hear the Word of God

How shall they hear the word of God
Unless the truth is told?
How shall the sinful be set free,
The sorrowful consoled?
To all who speak the truth today,
Impart your Spirit, Lord, we pray.

How shall they call to God for help
Unless they have believed?
How shall the poor be given hope,
The prisoner reprieved?
To those who help the blind to see,
Give light and love and clarity.

How shall the gospel be proclaimed
That sinners may repent?
How shall the world find peace at last
If heralds are not sent?
So send us, Lord, for we rejoice
To speak of Christ with life and voice.
—Michael Perry

48: Who Enters God's Kingdom?

I. Invocation
    O God, whose kingdom is truth and love, help me in this hour to see more clearly and to journey more consistently along the narrow way that leads to life eternal. Equip me for the tests and rigors of this day. In the name of Jesus, I pray. Amen.

II. Psalm 33

III. Reading and Reflection

IV. Daily Scripture Readings
Monday	Matthew 10:40-42
Tuesday	Matthew 12:22-37
Wednesday	Matthew 12:46-50
Thursday	Luke 18:1-8
Friday	Luke 18:9-14
Saturday	Romans 8:31-39
Sunday	A. Exodus 33:12-23; Philippians 2: 1-13; Psalm 99; Matthew 21: 28-32
	B. Job 42:1-6; James 4:13-17; 5:7-11; Psalm 27:7-14; Mark 9:38-50
	C. Joel 2:23-30; 1 Timothy 6:6-19; Psalm 107:1, 33-43; Luke 16:19-31

V. Reflection: Silent and Written

VI. Prayers: For the Church, for Others, for Myself

VII. Hymn: "For All the Saints"

VIII. Benediction
    Thank you, my Lord, for this time of rest and nourishment. Now send me to my station; help me that I neither slip nor wander from the road you have marked out for me. Amen.

Readings for Reflection

ᔎ For sin begets death, and hell is its home.

We need not ask ourselves: Does hell exist?

We need only ask: Where does sin have its home?, and we will see and taste hell.

The [one] who is in sin is already in hell. Your hell is conditional as long as you can drag yourself out of it; it is permanent when you are helpless to emerge.

Come out, while you are still able!

But be afraid indeed of the awful possibility that lurks for us of "not being able any longer to come forth."

The prodigal son dragged himself out in time (cf. Luke 15:11-32); the rich man at his feast was no longer able (cf. Luke 16:19-30).

—From *The God Who Comes* by Carlo Carretto

ᔎ All life is an exodus and I think (again, this is only my personal opinion) that this exodus does not end with a car accident or a sudden heart attack or a bullet from some nasty little thug.

No way! Our exodus is much longer than the time spent under the sun here on earth—much longer.

Our exodus embraces vaster universes.

On earth an individual barely has time to be born, like a grass seed producing a shoot, say a centimeter long. Then comes physical death interrupting our earthly experience, while the shoot keeps growing, say to the height of a meter. Then there is the ear which to me represents the fullness of the kingdom, the harvest to be gathered into the barn, as the Gospel says.

If harvest came when the seed was sprouting where should we be?

Which of us would reach the maturity of Christ?

To be gathered into the Father's barn do we not need the "fullness of Christ" (cf. Eph. 4:13)?

To sit down at table with him, must we not have the same desires as him?

His state was divine,
yet he did not cling
to his equality with God
but emptied himself
to assume the condition of a slave,
and became as [we] are;
and being as [we] are,
he was humbler yet,
even to accepting death,
death on a cross. (Phil.2:6-8)

No, we shall not enter the kingdom until we have accepted the demands of love to the hilt, until we have desired to die for love of all our [brothers and sisters], until we have mounted the cross and ideally shed our last drop of blood!

And you want to enter the kingdom with your thoughts greedily revolving round the money left in your cashbox, on your check-book still on the table, with your clothes still smelling of tobacco, with your envelope of cocaine in your pocket?

Or, worse, with hatred for your landlord or dislike of your husband in your heart?

Before long the kingdom would grow ugly and the eternal banquet repulsive.

No, my sisters, no, brothers, believe me: the exodus begins when you receive baptism, normally baptism with water; and ends when you are baptized with your own blood—every last drop of it.

As happened to Jesus.

—From *Why, O Lord?* by Carlo Carretto

ᨠ If you are preoccupied with people who are talking about the poor, you scarcely have time to talk to the poor. Some people talk about hunger, but they don't come and say, "Mother, here is five rupees. Buy food for these people." But they can give a most beautiful lecture on hunger.

—From *Words to Love By* by Mother Teresa

🍂 When we come out of Egypt we are called by God to freedom, total freedom, true freedom, eternal freedom.

But in order to become free—what a task, what a struggle, what a purging!

Liberation from the clutches of the senses is no small thing for sensual creatures like us.

To reach the "night of the senses"—the time when we become rulers of our passions and are able to resist the extravagances of taste and physical pleasure—that takes some fasting!

But this is nothing yet. This is only the beginning—baby stuff, you might say.

There's more to come!

There is another darker, much more painful night.

It is the "night of the soul," the night in which we chatterboxes have to learn to keep still.

We who are so ready to ask for things—now we shall not dare to ask.

We fall silent, thunderstruck with the grandeur that confronts us: God.

The night of the spirit is the mature ability of the human being to love God in the dark, to accept the design even without seeing it, to bear the distance without complaining, even when love thrusts us towards him until we writhe with longing.

—From *Why, O Lord?* by Carlo Carretto

🍂 The amazing truth of the kingdom is its availability. The kingdom is not for buying. It is not exclusive. It can't be hoarded. It succumbs, not to power, not to birthright, not even to the magnitude and sparkle of one's achievements. It is available to those born of the Spirit, those imbued with a simple faith. It requires one possession, freedom. The freedom to recognize kingdom-events and to follow a kingdom-course.

—From *Every Bush Is Burning* by Joan Puls

🍂 True freedom, as true love, rids us of fear. In the economics of the kingdom, faith is sufficient. Faith the size of a mustard seed. The faith that is "confident assurance concerning things we hope for and conviction about things we do not see" (Heb.11:1). The faith that recognized the nobility of the poor and the beauty of the arthritic. In the spirit of such faith, one comes to a certain self-possession. And it is security and currency enough for life's transactions. If we possess ourselves, in truth and in humility, we need not fear what might be taken from us. For all else is bonus and non-essential. Anyone who has been given the kingdom need not fear the loss of lesser goods and more tangible riches.

—From *Every Bush Is Burning* by Joan Puls

Hymn: For All the Saints

For all the saints, who from their labors rest,
Who thee by faith before the world confessed,
Thy name, O Jesus, be forever blest.
Alleluia! Alleluia!

Thou wast their rock, their fortress, and their might;
Thou, Lord, their captain in the well-fought fight;
Thou, in the darkness drear, their one true light.
Alleluia! Alleluia!

O may thy soldiers, faithful, true, and bold,
Fight as the saints who nobly fought of old,
And win with them the victor's crown of gold.
Alleluia! Alleluia!

O blest communion, fellowship divine!
We feebly struggle, they in glory shine;
Yet all are one in thee, for all are thine.
Alleluia! Alleluia!

And when the strife is fierce, the warfare long,
Steals on the ear the distant triumph song,
Hearts are brave again, and arms are strong.
Alleluia! Alleluia!

From earth's wide bounds, from ocean's farthest coast,
Through gates of pearl streams in the countless host,
Singing to Father, Son, and Holy Ghost:
Alleluia! Alleluia!

—William W. How

Sunday between October 2 and 8
49: Faithful and Obedient

I. Invocation
    My God, I put myself before you to receive instructions for the course you assign me today. Give me strength according to my burdens and finish your good work in me so that I may grow to be your faithful and obedient child. Amen.

II. Psalm 92

III. Reading and Reflection

IV. Daily Scripture Readings
    Monday   Hebrews 11:1-16
    Tuesday   Acts 8:1-8
    Wednesday   Acts 11:19-26
    Thursday   Matthew 21:28-32
    Friday   Luke 12:35-40
    Saturday   Luke 12:41-48
    Sunday   A. Numbers 27:12-23; Philippians 3:12-21; Psalm 81:1-10; Matthew 21:33-43
                B. Genesis 2:18-24; Hebrews 1:1-4; 2:9-11; Psalm 128; Mark 10:2-16
                C. Amos 5:6-7, 10-15; 2 Timothy 1:1-14; Psalm 101; Luke 17:5-10

V. Reflection: Silent and Written

VI. Prayers: For the Church, for Others, for Myself

VII. Hymn: "God, Whose Love Is Reigning o'er Us"

VIII. Benediction
    Help me, my God, to manage the affairs of my life this day as though it were my last. Hold constantly before me the brevity of my fleeting days and the joy of hearing your "well done . . . enter into the joy of your Lord." I pray to be worthy of these words, today and always. Amen.

Readings for Reflection

❧ O merciful Father, who dost look down upon the weaknesses of Thy human children more in pity than in anger, and more in love than in pity, let me now in thy holy presence inquire into the secrets of my heart.

Have I to-day done anything to fulfil the purpose for which Thou didst cause me to be born?

Have I accepted such opportunities of service as Thou in Thy wisdom hast set before my feet?

Have I performed without omission the plain duties of the day?

> Give me grace to answer honestly, O God.

Have I to-day done anything to tarnish my Christian ideal of manhood?

Have I been lazy in body or languid in spirit?

Have I wrongfully indulged my bodily appetites?

Have I kept my imagination pure and healthy?

Have I been scrupulously honorable in all my business dealings?

Have I been transparently sincere in all I have professed to be, to feel, or to do?

> Give me grace to answer honestly, O God.

Have I tried to-day to see myself as others see me?

Have I made more excuses for myself than I have been willing to make for others?

Have I, in my own home, been a peace-maker or have I stirred up strife?

Have I, while professing noble sentiments for great causes and distant objects, failed even in common charity and courtesy towards those nearest to me?

> Give me grace to answer honestly, O God.

O Thou whose infinite love, made manifest in Jesus Christ, alone has power to destroy the empire of evil in my soul, grant that with each day that passes I may more and more be delivered from my besetting sins. Amen.

—From *A Diary of Private Prayer* by John Baillie

&. Our relationship or dialogue with God, our discovery of God, takes place in faith and only in faith.
—From *Love Is for Living* by Carlo Carretto

&. As soon as we make a serious attempt to pray in spirit and in truth, at once we become acutely conscious of our interior disintegration, of our lack of unity and wholeness. In spite of all our efforts to stand before God, thoughts continue to move restlessly and aimlessly through our head, like the buzzing of flies (Bishop Theophan) or the capricious leaping of monkeys from branch to branch (Ramakrishna). To contemplate means, first of all, to be present where one is—to be *here* and *now*. But usually we find ourselves unable to restrain our mind from wandering at random over time and space. We recall the past, we anticipate the future, we plan what to do next; people and places come before us in unending succession. We lack the power to gather ourselves into the one place where we should be—*here*, in the presence of God; we are unable to live fully in the only moment of time that truly exists—*now*, the immediate present. This interior disintegration is one of the most tragic consequences of the Fall. The people who get things done, it has been justly observed, are the people who do one thing at a time. But to do one thing at a time is no mean achievement. While difficult enough in external work, it is harder still in the work of inner prayer.
—From *The Power of the Name* by Kallistos Ware

&. All too readily we say: Why the suffering of the world, why the pain of the innocent, why hunger, why war?

We should do better to say: We rich nations have sucked the blood of the poor, and now we wonder why there are starving babies in Brazil.

You, mighty nation bent on extending your influence, sell guns and tanks to poor nations and then say: Poor nations have no idea how to live and let live.

What would the world be like if the mighty and the

weak began respecting one another, began respecting human beings, and above all began helping one another? What would happen if we became, or tried to become, brothers?

Earth would be a paradise, suffering would be immeasurably reduced.

I am certain that the mighty mountain of universal suffering afflicting us on earth is due first and foremost to human sin, to our violence, pride, lust, selfishness and greed.

Let me be plain: the immense catastrophes of war, social struggle, tribal clashes, famine, ecological imbalance, and so on are due to our disobeying the clear and simple laws of God, nature and life.

And that is no small thing.

—From *Why, O Lord?* by Carlo Carretto

❧ At the end of life we will not be judged by
    how many diplomas we have received
    how much money we have made
    how many great things we have done.

We will be judged by
    "I was hungry and you gave me to eat
    I was naked and you clothed me
    I was homeless and you took me in."
—From *Words to Love By* by Mother Teresa

❧ The call to a holy life is extended to everyone whose life has been touched by the reality of God. Holiness is not the fruit of specialness, but of faithfulness. For to be faithful in a relationship is to honor it by the way we live. The call to holiness in our day, as it has always been, is a call to live in the world as a sign of the Kingdom. It is a call to participate in those things that contribute to human solidarity, forgiveness and compassion, righteousness and justice, and ultimately, global peace (shalom!).
—From *Invitation to Holiness* by James C. Fenhagen

ᴥ The vows of simplicity, fidelity, and service are for all Christians at all times. They are categorical imperatives for obedient followers of the obedient Christ. They are the beginning point from which we explore the depths of the spiritual life and discover our mission in the world.

The vows prod us into seeking a deeper spiritual life. We turn our backs on the superficiality of modern culture and plunge into the depths by making use of the classical disciplines of meditation, prayer, fasting, study, simplicity, solitude, submission, service, confession, worship, guidance, and celebration. We help each other move forward in the spiritual life by encouraging those who advance and by comforting those who stumble.

The vows call us to a vigorous social witness. We stand in contradiction to the dominant culture, which has given its soul to the vows of greed, permissiveness, and selfishness. We critique the empty values of contemporary society, and call it to joyful discipleship to Christ.

The vows call us to evangelism and mission-mindedness. They are not ideals that we keep to ourselves and retreat into our cloistered homes to enjoy; they are to be freely shared with all who confess Christ as Lord and King. We have an obligation to win the nations and all peoples of the earth in anticipation of that day when "every knee should bow . . . and every tongue confess that Jesus Christ is Lord, to the glory of God, the Father" (Phil. 2:10-11).

—From *Money, Sex and Power* by Richard J. Foster

ᴥ The ability to let go, to abandon oneself in faith and obedience, creates a heart that is docile and humble. Both notions are fairly foreign to our independent, stubborn, self-reliant spirits. Both virtures are fairly absent in our assertive, self-confident, self-indulgent circles. But uncovering their meaning and their message to us twentieth century Christians is crucial for a spirituality of our times.

—From *Every Bush Is Burning* by Joan Puls

Hymn: God, Whose Love Is Reigning o'er Us

God, whose love is reigning o'er us,
Source of all, the ending true;
Hear the universal chorus
Raised in joyful praise to you:
Alleluia, Alleluia,
Worship ancient, worship new.

Word of God from nature bringing
Springtime green and autumn gold;
Mountain streams like children singing,
Ocean waves like thunder bold:
Alleluia, Alleluia,
As creation's tale is told.

Holy God of ancient glory,
Choosing man and woman, too;
Abram's faith and Sarah's story
Formed a people bound to you;
Alleluia, Alleluia,
To your convenant keep us true.

Covenant, new again in Jesus,
Star-child born to set us free;
Sent to heal us, sent to teach us
How love's children we might be:
Alleluia, Alleluia,
Risen Christ, our Savior he!

Lift we then our human voices
In the songs that faith would bring;
Live we then in human choices
Lives that, like our music, sing:
Alleluia, Alleluia,
Joined in love our praises ring!
—William Boyd Grove

50: *All Things Are Possible*

I. Invocation
Almighty God, for whom nothing is impossible, help us in the midst of our unbelief to live and work as people for whom nothing is impossible because you are with us. In the name of Jesus who is a miracle—and who yet performs miracles. Amen.

II. Psalm 103

III. Reading and Reflection

IV. Daily Scripture Readings
Monday   Exodus 3:7-22
Tuesday   Jeremiah 32:16-24
Wednesday   Isaiah 40:18-31
Thursday   Romans 4:13-25
Friday   Acts 12:1-17
Saturday   Hebrews 1:1-14
Sunday   A. Deuteronomy 34:1-12; Philippians 4:1-9; Psalm 135:1-14; Matthew 22:1-14
              B. Genesis 3:8-19; Hebrews 4:1-3, 9-13; Psalm 90:1-12; Mark 10: 17-30
              C. Micah 1:2; 2:1-10; 2 Timothy 2: 8-15; Psalm 26; Luke 17:11-19

V. Reflection: Silent and Written

VI. Prayers: For the Church, for Others, for Myself

VII. Hymn: "God, Who Stretched the Spangled Heavens"

VIII. Benediction
Send me now, my God, into the world to accomplish all you have assigned to me. Let me live and work without fear or timidity. Amen.

Readings for Reflection

&. When we stop to think about it, recognizing ourselves as disciples of Jesus puts everything in our lives into focus. It gives us a measuring stick for making decisions about what we will or will not do. We need to realize that Jesus, too, was a disciple. A disciple is one who learns through association with a master teacher, learns by sharing in the teacher's life as well as listening to his [or her] words. Jesus was a disciple of Our Father, and his deepest longing for his own disciples was to bring them into the communion he enjoyed with the God he trusted and in whose love he rejoiced. The Gospel of John reflects this longing:

> I pray not only for these,
> but for those also
> who through their words will believe in me.
> May they all be one.
> Father, may they be one in us,
> as you are in me and I am in you,
> so that the world may believe it was you
> who sent me.
> (John 17:20-21)

—From *How You Can Be a Peacemaker* by Mary Evelyn Jegen, SND

&. The disposition of hope is rooted in the fundamental biblical truth that all possibilities for life and its future are under the care and goodness of God. Reconciliation is a possibility for us because it begins with, and remains rooted in, God's love for us. The good news of Christian faith is that God's love is constant and undefeatable. This is most clearly evident in Jesus' being raised from the dead. The resurrection of Jesus (the best of all possible futures) is our ultimate warrant for hope. We cannot engage in or experience it, if we do not believe in God's love for us as a constant, undefeatable love—that is to say, unless we believe in "amazing grace." To accept God's unconditional love

for us is fundamental to the process of reconciliation in life and in sacrament.
—From *To Walk Together Again* by Richard M. Gula

❧ The only time that is fully real is the present. Yesterday is old news and tomorrow is full of maybes. This is obvious enough, when one reflects on it, but it takes most of us many years to realize its full implications. So most of us spend a great deal of our time daydreaming about the past or worrying about the future. Not realizing the value of the real bird we have in hand, we leave the present to go rooting in past or future bushes. As a result, the personal business that should stand highest on our agenda often never gets done. What is this personal business? Finding peace of mind, and so happiness, right here and now. Learning to live so that we savor each day, waste none of the precious moments God has given us.
—From *How to Make It Through the Day* by John Carmody

❧ Love, according to the Christian gospel, is what God is about. Therefore, according to the same gospel, love is what we are to be about. Love completes the dimensions of commitment and freedom. By commitment we take charge of our commitment intimations from God that the world is not random chaos, but an arena for purposeful activity to bring all things to God. As we mature in our commitments and participation in God's mission in the world, we come to moments of freedom when the creation becomes transparent, and the bright epiphany of God's direct and immediate presence shines through phenomenal reality. Then we see that God is all in all, in all things arising and passing away. In those moments of meditation we realize that reality is infinitely more marvelously magical than any supernatural expectations we could have manufactured. We are truly surprised by God and know that in the ultimate sense there are no limits—all things are possible for those who love God, who are called according to God's promise.
—From *Healing of Purpose* by John E. Biersdorf

❧ For in faithful prayer, we may be literally in touch with the universe of information far beyond our sensory capabilities. If that is so, then prayer is not self-manipulation, but participating in God's evolving universe.

—From *Healing of Purpose* by John E. Biersdorf

❧ We can do anything by prayer. If our prayers are not answered it is either because we are wanting in faith, or because we have not prayed enough, or else that it would be bad for us if our request were granted, or perhaps God gives us something better than what we ask. But never do we not get what we ask because it is too difficult to get. We need never hesitate to ask God for the most difficult things, such as the conversion of great sinners or of whole nations. The more difficult things are to grant the more we must ask for them, believing that God loves us passionately. But we must ask with Faith, constantly, instantly, willingly, and with great love. We may be sure that if we ask thus and with enough persistence we shall be answered and be given the grace we ask or something even better.

Let us then ask bravely from God things that seem impossibilities, if they are for [God's] glory.

—From *Meditations of a Hermit* by Charles de Foucauld

❧ The source of all our freedom is the freedom of Jesus Christ. By our association with him we are invited into the kingdom of liberation and love. We pledge our faith, "green as a leaf." We receive the spirit that disentangles us from sin, from the narrow perspectives of the law, and from the fetters of fear. We join all of creation in struggling to reject what is evil, in submitting to the greater law of love, and in sharing in the glorious freedom of those who belong to God.

—From *Every Bush Is Burning* by Joan Puls

Hymn: God, Who Stretched the Spangled Heavens

God, who stretched the spangled heavens,
Infinite in time and place,
Flung the suns in burning radiance
Through the silent fields of space,
We your children, in your likeness,
Share inventive powers with you.
Great Creator, still creating,
Show us what we yet may do.

Proudly rise our modern cities,
Stately buildings, row on row;
Yet their windows, blank, unfeeling,
Stare on canyoned streets below,
Where the lonely drift unnoticed
In the city's ebb and flow,
Lost to purpose and to meaning,
Scarcely caring where they go.

We have ventured worlds undreamed of
Since the childhood of our race;
Known the ecstasy of winging
Through untraveled realms of space;
Probed the secrets of the atom,
Yielding unimagined power,
Facing us with life's destruction
Or our most triumphant hour.

As each far horizon beckons
May it challenge us anew.
Children of creative purpose,
Serving others, honoring you.
May our dreams prove rich with promise,
Each endeavor well begun.
Great Creator, give us guidance
Till our goals and yours are one.
—Catherine Cameron

51: *Servanthood*

I. Invocation
Our God, sovereign Lord and master of all creation, in this hour let us hear again your call, always inviting us to serve by your side in your kingdom work. Equip us, Lord, to serve you well, in the spirit and power of Christ. Amen.

II. Psalm 71

III. Reading and Reflection

IV. Daily Scripture Readings
Monday	John 13:1-11
Tuesday	Romans 15:1-13
Wednesday	2 Corinthians 6:1-10
Thursday	2 Corinthians 4:1-13
Friday	2 Corinthians 7:1-13
Saturday	Matthew 10:24-39

Sunday   A. Ruth 1:1-19a; 1 Thessalonians 1:1-10; Psalm 146; Matthew 22:15-22
B. Isaiah 53:7-12; Hebrews 4:14-16; Psalm 35:17-28; Mark 10:35-45
C. Habakkuk 1:1-3; 2:1-4; 2 Timothy 3:14–4:5; Psalm 119:137-144; Luke 18:1-8

V. Reflection: Silent and Written

VI. Prayers: For the Church, for Others, for Myself

VII. Hymn: "O Master, Let Me Walk with Thee"

VIII. Benediction
Thank you, my Lord, for choosing me to serve as one of your kingdom workers. I am your willing servant. Let your life flow through me according to your will. Amen.

Readings for Reflection

❧ If there is one task that life sets us, one charge we must fulfill before we end our days, it is to love the whole world and labor for the whole world's prospering, despite the finitude, evil, and death afflicting each of the world's parts. Should we come to our end with such love, saying yes to all that (from the perspective of the finish) somehow "had" to be, we would be round successes. Should we not be able to muster such love, finish our time hateful or unsurrendering, our success would hang in brackets. Thus, the most practical wisdom any of us can grow, and the perennial reason for religion, is the strength to love life in the face of death, to respond "amen" to our history.

—From *How to Make It Through the Day* by John Carmody

❧ Hunger for the desperate poor, many of them small children, is an agonizing experience, an unsatisfied craving that will lead to illness and, for many, to death. For these hundreds of millions of our brothers and sisters, each of whom is Jesus in his most distressing disguise, hunger takes cruel and destructive forms. It is the shriveled limbs and swollen bellies of starving children. Each day on this beautiful planet of ours over forty thousand children, age five years and under, die of malnutrition-related illnesses. That adds up to over fourteen million lives a year. We need to come to terms with the fact that these children are not killed by a disease for which science has found no cure. No, these children are the victims of moral and political failure to see that every person has the basic necessities of life. The poverty-induced hunger rampant in our world today is, to use the words of Pope Paul VI, "an insult flung in the very face of God."

—From *How You Can Be a Peacemaker* by Mary Evelyn Jegen, SND

❧ There is perhaps no passage in the Gospels which stirs us more deeply than Saint Matthew's account of the Last Judgment. In the mysterious story of the king who will gather all the nations before him, separating good from bad as a shepherd separates sheep from goats, Jesus gave us his own vision of the meaning of human life. What matters in the end is love expressed in action for those in need. Jesus accepts as done to himself whatever we do to our neighbor.

> Come, you whom my Father has blessed. . . . For I was hungry and you gave me food. . . . Go away from me. . . . For I was hungry and you never gave me food. (Matthew 25:34,35,41,42)

With good reason we cannot be indifferent to anyone who lacks the necessities of life. As our knowledge and love of God grow, so does our concern to respond as fully as we can to Jesus in what Mother Teresa of Calcutta calls "his most distressing disguise."
—From *How You Can Be a Peacemaker* by Mary Evelyn Jegen, SND

❧ Yesterday, coming home on a crowded airline flight, my attention was captured by a young mother and her baby boy. How fragile, how absolutely dependent for survival he was, and how marvelous. Studying him, thinking about his promise and his hope for the future, I could not escape the fact that God became just like him. As always, I was uncomfortable with the thought, as I am uncomfortable with all the other truths of my faith that hang on this central mystery of God's love saving us from inside our own flesh and bone, nerve and muscle, mind and heart.

How can I comprehend such grace? Yet, if we are to be saved from the consequences of permitting the nuclear competition that is driving us to destruction, it will be as a consequence of grace, the gift to accept ourselves as we truly are: fragile, weak, disordered— yet loved and loving, a little less than the angels, entrusted with each other's lives. How delicate is the balance on which our survival depends!
—From *How You Can Be a Peacemaker* by Mary Evelyn Jegen, SND

☙ How can one pity anyone who is doing the will of Our Lord? Is there anything sweeter on earth than to do the will of him one loves? And if it gives one some trouble to carry it out, the sweetness is all the greater.
—From *Meditations of a Hermit* by Charles de Foucauld

☙ St. Anthony, the "father of monks," is the best guide in our attempt to understand the role of solitude in ministry. Born around 251, Anthony was the son of Egyptian peasants. When he was about eighteen years old he heard in church the Gospel words, "Go and sell what you own and give the money to the poor...then come and follow me" (Matthew 19:21). Anthony realized that these words were meant for him personally. After a period of living as a poor laborer at the edge of his village, he withdrew into the desert, where for twenty years he lived in complete solitude. During these years Anthony experienced a terrible trial. The shell of his superficial securities was cracked and the abyss of iniquity was opened to him. But he came out of this trial victoriously—not because of his own will-power or ascetic exploits, but because of his unconditional surrender to the Lordship of Jesus Christ. When he emerged from his solitude, people recognized in him the qualities of an authentic "healthy" man, whole in body, mind, and soul. They flocked to him for healing, comfort and direction. In his old age, Anthony retired to an even deeper solitude to be totally absorbed in direct communion with God. He died in the year 356, when he was about one hundred and six years old.
—From *The Way of the Heart* by Henri J. M. Nouwen

☙ Whenever I find myself becoming harsh, rigid, full of complaints, and uncharitable, I know I am harboring a negative spirit. Nothing is more harmful...than this spirit of negativity. It attracts to itself ill spirits, like hardness of heart, that may be etched into harsh facial lines; pettiness spilling over into cheap gossip; resentment that crops up in envy of another's creativity; lack of forgiveness that harbors feelings of displeasure toward another, to say nothing of maladies like pervasive fatigue, sickly self-pity, and depressive moods. . . . This unloving spirit is always divisive. It thrives on gossip and gripes. . . . Our gracious God has the power to dispel this spirit of negativity, to soften the mark of harshness, to give us the grace we need to prevail over evil and the darkness it breeds.

Instead of ignoring others or stepping over or on them, with the Lord's help, we may be able to open our hearts to all in charity, compassion, and commitment.

—From Karen Greenwaldt in *For Everything There Is a Season*

&. If you are really praying, you can't help but have critical questions about the great problems the world is grappling with, and you can't get rid of the idea that a conversion is not only necessary for yourself and your neighbor, but for the entire human community. This conversion of the world means a "turning-around," a revolution, which can lead to renewal.

—From *With Open Hands* by Henri J. M. Nouwen

&. Grant Thy servants, O God, to be set on fire with Thy Spirit, strengthened by Thy power, illuminated by Thy splendour, filled with Thy grace, and to go forward by Thine aid. Give them, O Lord, a right faith, perfect love, true humility. Grant, O Lord, that there may be in us simple affection, brave patience, persevering obedience, perpetual peace, a pure mind, a right and honest heart, a good will, a holy conscience, spiritual strength, a life unspotted and unblamable; and after having . . . finished our course, may we be enabled happily to enter into Thy kingdom; through Jesus Christ our Lord. Amen.

—Old Gallican Sacramentary

Hymn: O Master, Let Me Walk with Thee

O Master, let me walk with thee
In lowly paths of service free.
Tell me thy secret; help me bear
The strain of toil, the fret of care.

Help me the slow of heart to move
By some clear, winning word of love;
Teach me the wayward feet to stay,
And guide them in the homeward way.

Teach me thy patience; still with thee
In closer, dearer company,
In work that keeps faith sweet and strong,
In trust that triumphs over wrong;

In hope that sends a shining ray
Far down the future's broadening way,
In peace that only thou canst give,
With thee, O Master, let me live.
—Washington Gladden

52: *When Jesus Calls*

I. Invocation
    Lord, Jesus, I come to this place with ears tuned
    to your voice alone. How much I need you, how
    good to hear you speak my name. Come to me,
    my Lord, and tell me of your love—even as I
    long to tell you of my own. Amen.

II. Psalm 139

III. Reading and Reflection

IV. Daily Scripture Readings
     Monday   Luke 7:36-50
     Tuesday   Mark 5:1-20
     Wednesday   Matthew 9:1-12
     Thursday   Acts 9:10-18
     Friday   Luke 6:27-36
     Saturday   John 9:1-12, 35-41
     Sunday   A. Ruth 2:1-13; 1 Thessalonians 2:
                   1-8; Psalm 128; Matthew 22:34-46
                B. Jeremiah 31:7-9; Hebrews 5:1-6;
                   Psalm 126; Mark 10:46-52
                C. Zephaniah 3:1-9; 2 Timothy 4:6-
                   8, 16-18; Psalm 3; Luke 18:9-14

V. Reflection: Silent and Written

VI. Prayers: For the Church, for Others, for Myself

VII. Hymn: "Faith, While Trees Are Still in Blossom"

VIII. Benediction
       How good it is, my Lord, how blessed to be
       with you in this quiet place of prayer. Here your
       words are clear and my desires unconfused.
       Come with me from this humble oratory, Lord
       Jesus, and walk with me all the day through.
       Amen.

Readings for Reflection

❧ An impressive example of the value of the discipline of starting the day with a period of listening for God's guidance, and of asking instructions for the day, is that provided by the Iona Community of Scotland. This is the major discipline that holds all members of the Iona Fellowship together, wherever they may be. To a remarkable degree, their practice meets the test of social verification, since the way in which this small minority of disciplined men have penetrated the economic, educational, and religious life of their country is striking indeed. They are changing society because they have *been* changed.

Powerful and productive as individual silence may be, group silence may be even more productive. Many are able to report that a genuine entering into a group silence, when it is dynamic and not merely sleepy, can bring, in the briefest conceivable time, an entire flood of ideas not previously recognized. More than three hundred years ago, Robert Barclay, one of the acknowledged masters of the interior life, had such an experience that radically altered his succeeding career. "When I came into the silent assemblies of God's people," he reported, "I felt a secret power among them, which touched my heart, and as I gave way unto it, I found the evil weakening in me, and the good raised up, and so I became thus knit and united unto them, hungering more and more after the increase of this power and life, whereby I might feel myself perfectly redeemed."
—From *The New Man for Our Time* by Elton Trueblood

❧ Anyone who imitates Jesus to the full
must also share in his passion.

We must have the courage
to pray to have the courage to accept.
Because we do not pray enough, we see only the
human part.
We don't see the divine.
And we resent it.

I think that much of the misunderstanding
   of suffering today
      comes from that
      from resentment and bitterness.
Bitterness is an infectious disease
      a cancer
      an anger hidden inside.
Suffering is meant to purify
      to sanctify
      to make us Christlike.
—From *Words to Love By* by Mother Teresa

❧ It has never been either practical or useful to leave all things and follow Christ. And yet it is spiritually prudent.
—From *The Monastic Journey* by Thomas Merton

❧ Somewhat in contrast to John the Baptist, who preached a stern call to repentance almost as an end in itself, Jesus' call to repentance and conversion spotlighted a further dimension. One was to *turn around* in order to face a new, much more hopeful direction. One was to hear the word of judgment on one's sins, since that was the preliminary to hearing the glad tidings of salvation, of the Kingdom come. The Kingdom, as we have indicated, was Jesus' central preoccupation, and as the angels are imagined to have sung joyously at Jesus' birth, so "joy to the world" is a good epitome of Jesus' message. The world was to hear the surpassingly joyous news that God's reign was breaking forth, that all humanity's longings were on the verge of fulfillment. Moreover, those who then suffered from the world's injustices could count themselves especially blessed: The kingdom of God was theirs in a particular way.
—From *The Heart of the Christian Matter* by John Carmody

❧ What I am looking for is some sort of balance in my life—a balance "so delicate, so risky, so creative", as Maria Boulding puts it, that she likens it to a bird in flight, a dancer in motion. One of the favorite words in the Rule is "run". St. Benedict tells me to run to Christ. If I stop for a moment and consider what is being asked of me here, and what is involved in the act of running, I think of how when I run I place first one foot and then the other on the ground, that I let go of my balance for a second and then immediately recover it again. It is risky, this matter of running. By daring to lose my balance I keep it.

—From *Living with Contradiction* by Esther de Waal

❧ Nor yet do thou say, "I must do something more before I come to Christ." I grant, supposing thy Lord should delay his coming, it were meet and right to wait for his appearing, in doing, so far as thou hast power, whatsoever he hath commanded thee. But there is no necessity for making such a supposition. How knowest thou that he will delay? Perhaps he will appear, as the day—spring from on high, before the morning light. Oh do not set him a time! Expect him every hour. Now he is nigh! Even at the door!

—John Wesley

❧ But true religion, or a heart right towards God and [humanity], implies happiness, as well as holiness. For it is not only righteousness, but also "peace and joy in the Holy Ghost." What peace? The peace of God, which God only can give, and the world cannot take away, the peace which "passeth all understanding," all (barely) rational conception, being a supernatural sensation, a divine taste of "the powers of the world to come," such as the natural man [or woman] knoweth not, how wise soever in the things of this world, nor, indeed, can . . . know it, in his [or her] present state, "because it is spiritually discerned." It is a peace that banishes all doubt, all painful uncertainty, the Spirit of God bearing witness with the spirit of a Christian, that he [or she] is a child of God.

—John Wesley

Hymn: Faith, While Trees Are Still in Blossom

Faith, while trees are still in blossom,
Plans the picking of the fruit;
Faith can feel the thrill of harvest
When the buds begin to sprout.

Long before the dawn is breaking,
Faith anticipates the sun.
Faith is eager for the daylight,
For the work that must be done.

Long before the rains were coming,
Noah went and built an ark.
Abraham, the lonely migrant,
Saw the light beyond the dark.

Faith, uplifted, tamed the water
Of the undivided sea,
And the people of the Hebrews
Found the path that made them free.

Faith believes that God is faithful:
God will be what God will be!
Faith accepts the call, responding,
"I am willing, Lord, send me."
—Anders Frostenson, trans. by Fred Kaan

Sunday between October 30 and November 5
53: True Humanity

I. Invocation
Our God, you dressed yourself in the tattered
garments of our human nature, that we might
dress ourselves with your divine ways. Help us,
therefore, to wear our human frailties with the
dignity and resolve of those who are the earthly
cradles of the nature of God. Amen.

II. Psalm 4

III. Reading and Reflection

IV. Daily Scripture Readings
Monday	Romans 8:1-17
Tuesday	2 Timothy 1:1-14
Wednesday	1 Peter 2:21-25
Thursday	Romans 14:1-21
Friday	Matthew 6:25-34
Saturday	Matthew 19:16-29
Sunday	A. Ruth 4:7-17; 1 Thessalonians 2: 9-13, 17-20; Psalm 127; Matthew 23:1-12
	B. Deuteronomy 6:1-9; Hebrews 7: 23-28; Psalm 119:33-48; Mark 12: 28-34
	C. Haggai 2:1-9; 2 Thessalonians 1:5-12; Psalm 65:1-8; Luke 19:1-10

V. Reflection: Silent and Written

VI. Prayers: For the Church, for Others, for Myself

VII. Hymn: "When Our Confidence Is Shaken"

VIII. Benediction
Thank you, Lord Jesus, for this time together. I
have rejoiced to feel again your life and spirit
over-laying and changing my own. Hold me to
yourself today, as the groom holds his willing
bride. Amen.

Readings for Reflection

  Things tyrannize over us, too. Money, clothes, houses, furniture, food, automobiles—all the material paraphernalia of existence—captivate our interests and dominate our thoughts. "To have" concerns us a great deal more than "to be." Few of us have attained the freedom from things which can truthfully sing,

> *A tent or a cottage,*
> *Why should I care?*

The proof of our thing-mindedness is, again, very easy. Try for five minutes to give God the "loving attention," which is the essence of true prayer. You will find your mind reverting over and over to things—to what you are wearing or what you would like to wear, to what you had for breakfast or what you want for lunch, to the salary you receive or the increase you are seeking, to the house you live in or the house you are trying to find, to the condition of your car or the prospect of a new one! With amazing frequency, things in some fashion will insert themselves into your brief effort to keep your mind fixed on God.

—From *Discipline and Discovery* by Albert Edward Day

  I urge you to still every motion that is not rooted in the Kingdom. Become quiet, hushed, motionless until you are finally centered. Strip away all excess baggage and nonessential trappings until you have come into the stark reality of the Kingdom of God. Let go of all distractions until you are driven into the Core.

—From *Freedom of Simplicity* by Richard J. Foster

  There is no description of sin anywhere to compare with the powerful narrative out of the actual life of the Apostle Paul, found in Romans VII: 9-25. The thing which moves us as we read it is the picture here drawn of our own state. A lower nature dominates us and spoils our life. "What I would I do not; what I would not that I do."

The most solemn fact of sin is its accumulation of consequences in the life of the person. Each sin tends to produce a *set* of the nature. It weaves a mesh of habit. It makes toward a dominion, or as Paul calls it, a *law of sin* in the [person] who sees a shining possible life, but stays below, chained to a body of sin.
—From *The Double Search* by Rufus M. Jones

   ⁂ Everyone has [a] particular road which leads . . . to liberation—one the road of virtue, another the road of evil.

If the road leading you to your liberation is that of disease, of lies, of dishonor, it is then your duty to plunge into disease, into lies, into dishonor, that you may conquer them. You may not otherwise be saved.

If the road which leads you to your liberation is the road of virtue, of joy, of truth, it is then your duty to plunge into virtue, into joy, into truth, that you may conquer them and leave them behind you. You may not otherwise be saved.
—From *The Saviors of God* by Nikos Kazantzakis

   ⁂ When I think of wholeness in my own life, I think of a finely tuned orchestra in which each instrument, guided by the conductor, contributes its part toward a magnificent symphony of sound. There are times—and in recent years, increasing times—when I have heard this sound that I know that I am in tune with the Spirit of God who moves within me. Sometimes the sound is discordant, even harsh, but it is nonetheless one sound. This is wholeness. It can include themes of joy and themes of pain, but there is still one sound. This is very different from what happens when the instruments that represent the many-faceted aspects of my personality are playing in opposition to each other. When this happens, I experience inner chaos and confusion—the very opposite of wholeness. The answer is not to play louder, not to pretend we do not hear, but rather to take time to listen to the many sounds so that the message they contain can be brought to light. The inner

freedom the Gospel promises is experienced when our identity in Christ is honored and trusted and nourished. It is experienced when our inner lives are in tune, not in the sense of having arrived, but rather in the sense of being able to hear and respond to the themes and rhythms that the Spirit offers in calling us out of ourselves. The journey in Christ is a journey shaped by the biblical story of salvation in which is embodied a will to holiness.

Wholeness, when open to the Spirit of God, is a seedbed for holiness. When our center has been reformed in Christ, an environment is created that opens us to the promptings of the Kingdom. In biblical terms, like Bartimaeus we begin to see.

—From *Invitation to Holiness* by James C. Fenhagen

❧ Francis of Assisi described his own formation in terms of a single radical act. His initial contact with Lady Poverty was a transforming event. Francis had a horror of lepers. But one day he couldn't escape, or chose not to. He met one face to face. And he submitted himself to that forming encounter. Francis embraced the leper and kissed him. Fear died and conviction was born. Poverty was to be henceforth his school and his rule of life.

—From *Every Bush Is Burning* by Joan Puls

❧ The atheist is not always the enemy. Atheists can be among a Christian's best friends. Atheists, for instance, whose atheism develops out of protest: angry about what is wrong with the world, they are roused to passionate defiance. That a good God permits the birth of crippled children, that a loving God allows rape and torture, that a sovereign God stands aside while the murderous regime of a Genghis Khan or an Adolf Hitler runs its course—such outrageous paradoxes simply cannot be countenanced. So God is eliminated. The removal of God does not reduce the suffering, but it does wipe out the paradox. Such atheism is not the result of logical (or illogical) thought: it is sheer protest.

Anger over the suffering and unfairness in the world becomes anger against the God who permits it. Defiance is expressed by denial. Such atheism is commonly full of compassion. It suffers and rages. It is deeply spiritual, in touch with the human condition and eternal values.

—From *Earth and Altar* by Eugene H. Peterson

&. The passionately protesting atheist, sensitive to suffering, can be welcomed as a partner in a spiritual and moral struggle against evil. [That person's] companionship is a defense against smugness. The intellectually discriminating atheist can be accepted as an ally in skeptically rejecting all the popular, half-baked stupidities named "god" that abound in our time and invited into conversations that explore what the best minds thought, and think, about God.

But there is one form of atheism that cannot be treated so charitably. Psalm 14 energetically attacks the one kind of atheism that the world is most tolerant of but of which is has most to fear—the people who say in their hearts, "There is no God." This is a quiet, unobtrusive atheism that never calls attention to itself. These people do not say with their mouths, "There is no God." To the contrary, with their mouths they say what everyone else says about God. They recite the Apostles' Creed and the Lord's Prayer along with the best of them. With their mouths they articulate impressive arguments for God's existence. With their mouths they denounce the godless. With their mouths they demand public prayers and official religion.

But in their hearts they say, "There is no God." Their atheism is never voiced and may not even be conscious, but it is lived—with a vengeance. When asked what they believe these athesists either subscribe to one of the religious fads of the day or assent to whatever the churches say should be believed about God.

—From *Earth and Altar* by Eugene H. Peterson

Hymn: When Our Confidence Is Shaken

When our confidence is shaken
In beliefs we thought secure,
When the spirit in its sickness
Seeks but cannot find a cure,
God is active in the tensions
Of a faith not yet mature.

Solar systems, void of meaning,
Freeze the spirit into stone;
Always our researches lead us
To the ultimate unknown.
Faith must die, or come full circle
To its source in God alone.

In the discipline of praying,
When it's hardest to believe;
In the drudgery of caring,
When it's not enough to grieve;
Faith, maturing, learns acceptance
Of the insights we receive.

God is love, and thus redeems us
In the Christ we crucify;
This is God's eternal answer
To the world's eternal why.
May we in this faith maturing
Be content to live and die!
—Fred Pratt Green

Sunday between November 6 and 12
54: A Resurrection People

I. Invocation
    Lord Jesus, you alone are the resurrection and
    the life; those who believe in you will never die.
    Come to us, and speak new life upon all our
    dyings. Look upon us as we stand at the thresh-
    olds of our entombing experiences, unable to see
    or move because of the grave clothes which bind
    us. Set us free. In your name we pray. Amen.

II. Psalm 90

III. Reading and Reflection

IV. Daily Scripture Readings
    | Monday | John 11:1-16 |
    | Tuesday | John 11:17-27 |
    | Wednesday | John 11:28-37 |
    | Thursday | John 11:38-44 |
    | Friday | Acts 17:22-23 |
    | Saturday | Romans 6:1-11 |

    Sunday   A. Amos 5:18-24; 1 Thessalonians
                4:13-18; Psalm 50:7-15; Matthew
                25:1-13
             B. 1 Kings 17:8-16; Hebrews 9:24-
                28; Psalm 146; Mark 12:38-44
             C. Zechariah 7:1-10; 2 Thessalonians
                2:13–3:5; Psalm 9:11-20; Luke 20:
                27-38

V. Reflection: Silent and Written

VI. Prayers: For the Church, for Others, for Myself

VII. Hymn: "The Day of Resurrection"

VIII. Benediction
    Thank you for these moments together, my Lord.
    Thank you for the deep inner presence of your
    spirit. Stay with me all the day long, I pray.
    Amen.

Readings for Reflection

❧ Where in all the scriptures does God comfort [us] with a hereafter? The *earth* shall be filled with the glory of God. According to the Bible, that is the meaning of all the promises. Jesus, come in the flesh, what is his will? Of course, nothing other than the honor of his Father on earth. In his own person, through his advent, he put a seed *into the earth.* He would be the light of [humankind]; and those who were his he called "the light of the world" and "the salt of the earth." His purpose is the raising up of the earth and the generations of [humanity] out of the curse of sin and death toward the revelation of eternal life and glory.

Why else did he heal the sick and wake the dead? Why did he exalt the poor and hungry? Surely not in order to tell them that they would be blessed after death, but because the kingdom of God was near. Of course, God has a way out for those who, unfortunately, must suffer death; [God] gives them a refuge in the beyond. But shall this necessary comfort now be made the main thing? Shall the kingdom of God be denied for earth and perpetuated only in the kingdom of death, simply because God wants also to dry the tears of the dead? It is to discard the whole meaning of the Bible if one argues, "We have nothing to expect on earth; it must be abandoned . . ."

Truly, within the human structures of sin, we have no lasting home; we must seek what is coming. But what is it, then, that is coming? The revealing of an earth cleansed of sin and death. This is the homeland we seek. There is no other to be sought, because we do not have, and there cannot come to be, anything other than what God intended for us in the creation.

—From *Thy Kingdom Come: A Blumhardt Reader* edited by Vernard Eller

❧ Once upon a time I had a young friend named Philip. Philip lived in a nearby city, and Philip was born a mongoloid. He was a pleasant child—happy, it seemed—

but increasingly aware of the difference between himself and other children.

Philip went to Sunday School. And his teacher, also, was a friend of mine. My Sunday School teacher friend taught the third grade at a Methodist church. Philip was in his class, as well as nine other 8-year-old boys and girls.

My Sunday School teacher friend is a very creative teacher. Most of you know 8-year-olds. And Philip, with his differences, was not readily accepted as a member of this third-grade Sunday School class. But my teacher friend was a good teacher, and he had helped facilitate a good group of 8-year-old children. They learned and they laughed and they played together. And they really cared about each other—even though, as you know, 8-year-olds don't say that they care about each other out loud very often. But my teacher friend could see it. He knew it. He also knew that Philip was not really a part of that group of children. Philip, of course, did not choose nor did he want to be different. He just was. And that was just the way things were.

My Sunday School teacher friend had a marvelous design for his class on the Sunday after Easter last year. You know those things that panty hose come in—the containers look like great big eggs. My friend had collected ten of these to use on that Sunday. The children loved it when he brought them into the room. Each child was to get a great big egg. It was a beautiful spring day, and the assigned task was for each child to go outside on the church grounds and to find a symbol of new life, put it in the egg (the old panty hose containers), and bring it back to the classroom. They would then mix them all up, and then all open and share their new life symbols and surprises together one by one.

Well, they did this, and it was glorious. And it was confusing. And it was wild. They ran all around, gathered their symbols, and returned to the classroom. They put all the big eggs on a table, and then my teacher friend began to open them. All the children were standing around the table.

He opened one, and there was a flower, and they ooh-ed and aah-ed.

He opened another, and there was a little butterfly. "Beautiful," the girls all said, since it is very hard for 8-year-old boys to say "beautiful."

He opened another, and there was a rock. And as third graders will, some laughed, and some said, "That's crazy! How's a rock supposed to be like new life?" But the smart little boy whose egg they were speaking of spoke up. he said,"That's mine. And I knew all of you would get flowers, and buds, and leaves, and butterflies, and stuff like that. So I got a rock because I wanted to be different. And for me, that's new life." . . .

He (the teacher) opened the next one, and there was nothing there. The other children, as 8-year-olds will, said, "That's not fair—that's stupid!—somebody didn't do right."

About that time my teacher friend felt a tug on his shirt, and he looked down and Philip was standing beside him.

"It's mine," Philip said. "It's mine." And the children said, "You don't ever do things right, Philip. There's nothing there!"

"I did so do it," Philip said. "I did do it. It's empty—*the tomb is empty!*"

The class was silent, a very full silence. And for you people who don't believe in miracles, I want to tell you that one happened that day last spring. From that time on, it was different. Philip suddenly became a part of that group of 8-year-old children. They took him in. He entered. He was set free from the tomb of his differentness.

Philip died last summer. His family had known since the time that he was born that he wouldn't live out a full life span. Many other things had been wrong with his tiny, little body. And so, late last July, with an infection that most normal children could have quickly shrugged off, Philip died. The mystery simply enveloped him completely.

He was buried from that church. And on that day at that funeral nine 8-year-olds, with their Sunday

School teacher, marched right up to that altar and laid on it an empty egg—an empty, old discarded holder of panty hose.

—From "The Story of Philip" by Harry Pritchett Jr. in *St. Luke's Journal of Theology* (June 1976)

ᐞ One of the most outstanding features of the Gospels' treatment of women characters is the universal presence of women at the empty tomb, and their being the first to proclaim the resurrection. It is found in all four Gospels (Mark 15:40-16:8; Matthew 27:55-28:10; Luke 23:49-24:11; John 20:1-2, 11-18).

—From *Woman: First Among the Faithful* by Francis J. Moloney

ᐞ It is women whose faith and loyalty to Jesus sees them through the trauma of his death and burial, and eventually leads them to proclaim: "The Lord has been raised". There is a *primacy* in both the quality of the women's faith, and in their being the first to come to faith in the risen Lord.

This takes place within the context of a group of disciples who have fled in fear (see especially Mark 14:50, and the parabolic comment upon their flight in vv. 51-52: the young man who "followed" but, when threatened, ran away *naked in his nothingness*). The same disciples are universally presented as refusing to accept the Easter proclamation of the women. The faith of women stands out in strong contrast to the lack of faith among the male disciples, including the "pillars" of the discipleship group.

—From *Woman: First Among the Faithful* by Francis J. Moloney

Hymn: The Day of Resurrection

The day of resurrection!
Earth, tell it out abroad;
The passover of gladness,
The passover of God.
From death to life eternal,
From earth unto the sky,
Our Christ hath brought us over,
With hymns of victory.

Our hearts be pure from evil,
That we may see aright
The Lord in rays eternal
Of resurrected light;
And listening to his accents,
May hear, so calm and plain,
His own "All hail!" and, hearing,
May raise the victor strain.

Now let the heavens be joyful!
Let earth the song begin!
Let the round world keep triumph,
And all that is therein!
Let all things seen and unseen
Their notes in gladness blend,
For Christ the Lord hath risen,
Our joy that hath no end.
—John of Damascus, trans. by John M. Neal

Sunday between November 13 and 19

55: Faithful Witness

I. Invocation
    Our Lord, you prove that your witness is faithful and true. Help us discover in your example the determination we need so that our witness, in public and in secret, will also be faithful and true—a clear word spoken and lived without compromise. In your faithful name. Amen.

II. Psalm 16

III. Reading and Reflection

IV. Daily Scripture Readings
    Monday   Philippians 1:12-18
    Tuesday   Luke 12:1-12
    Wednesday   Colossians 4:1-6
    Thursday   Matthew 20:1-16
    Friday   John 5:30-47
    Saturday   Acts 10:34-38
    Sunday   A. Zephaniah 1:7, 12-18; 1 Thessalonians 5:1-11; Psalm 76; Matthew 25:14-30
              B. Daniel 7:9-14; Hebrews 10:11-18; Psalm 145:8-13; Mark 13:24-32
              C. Malachi 4:1-6; 2 Thessalonians 3:6-13; Psalm 82; Luke 21:5-19

V. Reflection: Silent and Written

VI. Prayers: For the Church, for Others, for Myself

VII. Hymn: "Jesus, Lord, We Look to Thee"

VIII. Benediction
    My Lord, thank you for this time together. Thank you for being my faithful companion and for your word of love spoken to my deepest need. I love you, my God, and pledge my allegiance to your kingdom, for today and forever. Amen.

Readings for Reflection

❧ I once had an opportunity to ask Mother Teresa a question that had been nagging at me. How could I, who am going through life well-fed and well-clothed, come to a genuine heartfelt identification with the poor and suffering? How could I come to her kind of generous and joyful sharing?

She looked at me as though I had asked for a self-evident answer. She explained that it was very easy. I simply had to go to our Lord in the Blessed Sacrament. There I should discover that Jesus becomes bread for us. She said it with great relish, as though she were tasting the most exquisite dish. I, too, should become bread for the poor.

For the past ten years I have pondered that mysterious answer. Mother Teresa's words continue to reveal treasures of wisdom from the heart of Jesus. Mother Teresa helped me, as she has helped so many others, to know the joy of life as Jesus knows it and to know it within the concrete circumstances of my own situation.

Did I know anyone who had become bread for others? Anyone who was there every day, ready to be "eaten up," giving time, energy, service day after day for love, and enjoying it? I thought immediately of my own parents, of my father's long hours of work, especially during the hard times of the Depression in the 1930s, and of my mother's attention to the details of homemaking, day after day, year after year, for five children and my father. Surely my parents had become bread for us, even as they lovingly provided it.

—From *How You Can Be a Peacemaker* by Mary Evelyn Jegen, SND

❧ Take up the challenge! Become a maker of peace! Work and pray for reconciliation wherever misunderstanding, suspicion, and enmity prevail. Engage others in your church and community in study, dialogue, and action to prevent a resort to arms. Put yourself to the hard task of making up your mind about specific issues of nuclear policy. Then use your influence to change public opinion and to influence governmental decisions. Dare to set your course toward the wholeness of the human family at peace and be bold enough to chart that course with faithful witness to Christ's way of love, justice and peace. For that way is *shalom*.

—From *Seeking God's Peace in a Nuclear Age: A Call to Disciples of Christ*

❧ The heart of Christianity is a cross, the sign of a love unto death, and beyond into resurrection. I am beginning to understand that there is no way of following Jesus except by undergoing what he underwent. Unless I die, I can never bear fruit.

No one in this world can escape suffering, but not all suffering is the cross. Suffering cannot be avoided, but one can escape the cross. The cross must be a choice, a free decision, or it is not the sign of Jesus' love. The cross is an invitation; each person must say yes. No one becomes a disciple without saying yes to Jesus taking us, blessing us, breaking us open, and passing us around.

—From *Gathering the Fragments* by Edward J. Farrell

❧ There are two ways in which education can be Christian. First, the object of study may be the Christian faith. The subject matter is then Christian, although perhaps only in a very objective sense. Buddhists and Moslems can make the Christian faith an object of their study. Second, the teacher can teach out of a deep belief in the Christian faith. Put otherwise, when teaching and learning take place in a community of those for whom the Christian faith is a matter of deep loyalty and ultimate concern, then teaching and learning will be shaped by the Christian understanding of truth. Education becomes Christian in the fullest sense when both criteria are followed: the teaching occurs within a community deeply committed to the Christian faith and the subject matter is the Christian faith.

—From *Story and Context* by Donald E. Miller

❧ Reverence has something to do with holiness and wholeness. It is a word ordinarily ascribed to God alone. When we speak about reverence in regard to ourselves we speak of the holiness of our relationship with God. This wholeness, this holiness, is given to us not because we are without sin, but in spite of our sin. We have to believe that God loves us so much that even though we are sinners we are holy. And we are holy in a way that we give holiness to others. We have been loved so much that there is enough left over to give to others. Love enables us to see into the depths of other people's lives. This inner stream of God's love, like running water, always refreshes us so that we might offer a cup to others.

—From *Gathering the Fragments* by Edward J. Farrell

❧ You are God's field, God's building. Everything you have and are should be concentrated on discovering this treasure. Truly, the kingdom of heaven is within you. Seek first, seek only the kingdom of God hidden in the depths of your heart, and all the rest will be given you over and above. Because they have grasped this, the monk and nun are people for whom God is enough.

—From *The Jerusalem Community Rule of Life*
  by Pierre-Marie Delfieux

❧ Today, almost two thousand years after the birth of Christ, Christianity still does not live in our so-called Christian hearts. Why is that? Why is the world not turning to Christ? It is not doing so because Christians are not living the gospel. We Christians have not followed Christ. Somewhere along the road of life we have compromised, and we continue to compromise. Had we really followed Christ, there would be no communism. There would be no wars.

—From *Soul of My Soul* by Catherine de Hueck Doherty

Hymn: Jesus, Lord, We Look to Thee

Jesus, Lord, we look to thee;
Let us in thy name agree;
Show thyself the Prince of Peace,
Bid our strife forever cease.

By thy reconciling love
Every stumbling block remove;
Each to each unite, endear;
Come, and spread thy banner here.

Make us of one heart and mind,
Gentle, courteous, and kind,
Lowly, meek, in thought and word,
Altogether like our Lord.

Let us for each other care,
Each the other's burdens bear;
To thy church the pattern give,
Show how true believers live.

Free from anger and from pride,
Let us thus in God abide;
All the depths of love express,
All the heights of holiness.

Let us then with joy remove
To the family above;
On the wings of angels fly,
Show how true believers die.
—Charles Wesley

56: *Christ the King*

I. Invocation
My Lord, king of my life, I crown you now;
yours shall all glory be. Help me in this hour to
discover again my place and service in your
kingdom. Speak to me, my God, the things you
want me to know and do. Amen.

II. Psalm 47

III. Reading and Reflection

IV. Daily Scripture Readings
Monday	Matthew 16:21-28
Tuesday	John 6:15-21
Wednesday	John 1:43-51
Thursday	Acts 17:1-9
Friday	1 Corinthians 15:20-28
Saturday	Revelation 1:1-8

Sunday   A. Ezekiel 34:11-16, 20-24; 1 Corinthians 15:20-28; Psalm 23; Mat-
thew 25:31-46
B. Jeremiah 23:1-6; Revelation 1:4-
8; Psalm 93; John 18:33-37
C. 2 Samuel 5:1-5; Colossians 1:11-
20; Psalm 95; John 12:9-19

V. Reflection: Silent and Written

VI. Prayers: For the Church, for Others, for Myself

VII. Hymn: "All Hail the Power of Jesus' Name"

VIII. Benediction
Lead on, O King eternal; yours shall all glory
be. I am your willing servant, today and always.
Amen.

Readings for Reflection

❧ At the heart of our new vision and new venture on the course toward peace will be Jesus the Christ. His way of love is infinitely more powerful than the way of war and violence. "Returning violence for violence multiplies violence, adding deeper darkness to a night already devoid of stars. Darkness cannot drive out darkness; only light can do that. Hate cannot drive out hate; only love can do that." Yet humankind still clings to the ancient fallacy which claims that we can use force to rearrange the external political configurations and thus the wrongs of the world will be set right. Instead of tinkering with these surface externals, Jesus the Christ attacks evil in its breeding place—the heart of humanity: the hearts of nations, the hearts of institutions, and the hearts of persons. Here is supremely the place where the church must focus its vision. Weapons of war are set to their task by the human hand, but the hand is set to its task by the human heart. Thousands of years of human experience have proved over and over again that the heart of all transformation is the transformation of the heart.
—From *Seeking God's Peace in a Nuclear Age: A Call to Disciples of Christ*

❧ In the same way, the world as it is now will become new in Jesus Christ. Nothing else need take place except that the love of God penetrate into all things. The hatred which has entered into [us] must finally be eradicated. Believe in Jesus Christ, and do not hate! To believe in him means to love; and, in so doing, you are relatives and friends of the only begotten Son. When you are rooted in him, all melancholy is a thing of the past. All sin is removed, because through the love of God one has entered upon a new way, one has become a totally new person. What concern now is that dead past?
—From *Thy Kingdom Come: A Blumhardt Reader* edited by Vernard Eller

ᵛ One person we know through whom things moved as they should; he is called Jesus Christ. And thus it is that light has again been given to creation. Then why do you wonder at the fact that Jesus has bread for four or five thousand people? It amazes us; but he is simply a true man again, and that is why the powers of the world are subservient to him. Or why are you surprised that when he touches a sick person healing takes place? He is a true man. Things go as they should through him, under the oversight of God. He is the image of God, the Son of God. This makes him a blessing and constitutes a power which also makes others blessed if only they come within his reach. Even people who in themselves are perverted and godless, if only they press to him, are touched by something of his true spirit so that something comes true in them as well.

—From *Thy Kingdom Come: A Blumhardt Reader* edited by Vernard Eller

ᵛ Jesus, who is the glory of God on earth, wants to help us become the same thing. In this man, God again shines forth. It is for a purpose, then, that he is here; he acts as God in the creation. . . . This is his work; consequently, he has eternal life and does not perish even though nailed upon the cross. Nothing, no possible situation, even the most disadvantageous you could conceive, can overcome this man, because he is here to accomplish something.

—From *Thy Kingdom Come: A Blumhardt Reader* edited by Vernard Eller

ᵛ Christian faith must constantly grow. It cannot remain static. Either it will slowly wither and die, or it will mature and bear ever more fruit. And as the stem grows higher and the branches heavier, it needs to strike deeper roots. Without deeper roots, there is little hope for survival.

> Some of the seed fell on rocky ground, where there was little soil. The seeds sprouted, because the soil wasn't deep. Then, when the sun came up, it

burned the young plants; and because the roots had not grown deep enough, the plants soon dried up (Mk 4:5-6).

Perhaps we are under the impression that Jesus himself did not need to undergo this process of deepening. Such an idea would be wrong. It is contradicted by all the indications that we can glean from the gospels, no less than by the explicit statement that Jesus grew in wisdom and grace (Lk 2:52). Being truly human in every sense of the word, Jesus needed to reflect, to incorporate new experiences into his self-concept, to reinforce his ideals and nurture his heart and mind with new images. Jesus was the most vibrant, open, sensitive, keen, inquisitive religious leader that ever lived. If his humanity, as we believe, presented "the exact likeness of God's own being" (Heb 1:3), it reflected also the irrepressible vitality of God. At the same time, being one of us, Jesus needed to learn— "Even though he was God's Son, he learned through his sufferings to be obedient" (Heb 5:8). And the need to suffer was precisely a very upsetting discovery Jesus made.

—From *Inheriting the Master's Cloak* by John Wijngaards

&. Most of us come to this knowledge that we exist *in God*, not through any esoteric means, but through the ordinary events of family or community living, in the intimacy of *presence* to one another. Obviously, life together does not, *ipso facto*, assure transcendent consciousness. Intentional and attentive reflection in our common life is needed. "To have lived is not enough," says Samuel Beckett in *Waiting for Godot*. "We have to talk about it."

The classic spiritual disciplines can help us "to talk about it." The disciplines include prayer and worship, spiritual direction, confession, the works of mercy, Scripture study—all of these can and do soften the heart so that we may welcome and attend to the stirrings of God within ourselves and within the matrix of our familial relationships.

A second assumption is that authentic Christian spirituality, rooted as it is in the doctrine of the Incarnation, is an inclusive spirituality, one that addresses all aspects of the human person: body and intellect, emotion and spirit, solitude and society.

The third assumption is that the family settings that reveal the fullness of our graced humanity are unique and varied. We grow in the knowledge of God in one-parent as well as two-parent families, in families that live with sickness and brokenness and uncertainty as well as those that enjoy the gifts of health, security, and compatibility. The God of Christianity comes to men and women, not only in the light, but in the darkness as well. Why do I say this? Because of Jesus. Because in my groping to know who God is, who I am, what the meaning of the world is and my relationship to the world, I am reminded of the New Testament affirmation that I can make some sense of these questions by studying the man Jesus (Philippians 2, John 14, and elsewhere).

—From Dolores Leckey in *Living with Apocalypse* edited by Tilden H. Edwards

❧ As an act of love, prayer is a courageous act. It is a risk we take. It is a life-and-death risk, believing in the promises of the gospel, that God's love is indeed operative in the world. In prayer we have the courage, perhaps even the presumption and the arrogance or the audacity to claim that God's love can be operative in the very specific situations of human need that we encounter.

—From *Healing of Purpose* by John E. Biersdorf

❧ Suffering for the unity of love? "Suffering for a cause" —is that biblical? Indeed it is. In Holy Scripture, it is an established fact, as the Apostle Paul says, "I rejoice in my sufferings for your sake, and in my flesh I complete what is lacking in Christ's afflictions"; "I will most gladly spend and be spent for your souls"; "I endure everything for the sake of the elect"; "I, Paul, a prison-

er for Christ Jesus on behalf of you Gentiles"; "I ask you not to lose heart over what I am suffering for you." (Col. 1:24; 2 Cor. 12:15; 2 Tim. 2:10; Eph. 3:1; 3:13)
—From *I Found the Key to the Heart of God* by Basilea Schlink

Hymn: All Hail the Power of Jesus' Name

All hail the power of Jesus' name!
Let angels prostrate fall;
Bring forth the royal diadem,
And crown him Lord of all.

Ye chosen seed of Israel's race,
Ye ransomed from the fall,
Hail him who saves you by his grace,
And crown him Lord of all.

Sinners, whose love can ne'er forget
The wormwood and the gall,
Go spread your trophies at his feet,
And crown him Lord of all.

Let every kindred, every tribe
On this terrestrial ball,
To him all majesty ascribe,
And crown him Lord of all.

Crown him, ye martyrs of your God,
Who from his altar call;
Extol the Stem of Jesse's Rod,
And crown him Lord of all.

O that with yonder sacred throng
We at his feet may fall!
We'll join the everlasting song,
And crown him Lord of all.
—Edward Perronet

Monthly Retreat
Models

Retreat Model 1: Prayer and My Life

Arrive and Get Settled
> Our God, who always calls us to prayer, teach me in these hours to pray as I should and for what I should. In Jesus name. Amen.

Thirty Minutes of Silent Listening

Scripture Reading (Use one passage for each cycle.)
> Matthew 4:1-11; Psalm 63; Matthew 6:1-17; Romans 8:18-39

Response
> Journal
> Prayer
> Action

Reading and Reflection
> Anthology
> Other

Reflection and Response

Recreation/Rest*

(Love Feast and/or Wesleyan Covenant Service)

Covenant Prayer
> My Lord, how good it is, how blessed, to be with you in this place in prayer. Send me from this place in the power of your ever present Spirit. Amen.

*Repeat cycle above or conclude retreat with Covenant Prayer. Groups of two or more may wish to conclude with Love Feast and/or Wesleyan Covenant Service on pp. 387–90.

Readings for Reflection

&. If our thirst for cosmic confirmation and caring is secretly longing to be quenched, and if God's transforming love yearns to quench that thirst, what are the conditions under which this double search of human beings for God, and God for human beings, can best be carried out? Prayer is obviously a proven channel. But prayer that transforms seems to require certain optimum conditions that tilt us towards its authentic practice and that clear the way in spite of the dispersion and the web upon web of preoccupations which tend to usurp our earthly life. When I go in to have my chest x-rayed each year, I am required to strip off my ordinary bodily coverings and to expose my chest to the piercing rays of this light. Solitude, solitariness, seems to express a similar preparatory readying function in its stripping me and preparing me for exposure to the radiant beams of love that the x-ray focus of prayer accomplishes.
—From *Together in Solitude* by Douglas V. Steere

&. "I would like to pray again." What a beautiful grace to want to pray. Prayer is a gift, yet it is the work of a lifetime. Why do people stop praying? Why do they begin again? Prayer is always a lost and found phenomenon. Prayer, like each human life, has many stages of growth and development, decline and loss.

Prayer, like love, is not something one achieves once and for all. It is a special kind of consciousness, awareness, attention, presence.
—From *Gathering the Fragments* by Edward J. Farrell

&. Christian prayer is always a response to a presence already felt. The awareness of a desire to pray again is already prayer. As the desert fathers so often said, "If you want to pray, you are already praying."
—From *Gathering the Fragments* by Edward J. Farrell

≈ God knows how to make sense of these bits and pieces of revelation. Prayer turns them over and lets them go, returning to a few well-worn images, phrases, feelings, or corners of dark peace like the tongue to a sore tooth. Some days prayer is absolutely minimal: a resentful body taking its chair, a mind dry and rebellious. Other days prayer is easy and obvious: How is it going, my love? But in maturity all days are prayerful. For better or worse, richer or poorer, in sickness and health, God has us until death parts the last barrier and we consummate our long longing. Mature prayer thinks of itself as paying with an old and battered blank check. Even though each payment increases its debt, it keeps pushing its dog-eared mite forward. For it knows, dimly but adequately, that progress is deeper indebtedness. If everything is grace, any better perception means more laud of God, greater abasement of self. So the Baptist's formula: He must increase, I must decrease. So the constant liturgical refrain: Praise God!

—From *Maturing a Christian Conscience* by John Carmody

≈ We tend to turn to prayer in extreme moments: great joy, "O, how good God is!" When all human sources have failed, "O, God help me." Anguish, guilt, fear send us to God when no aid is near or, if near, would not understand. But prayer may be so much more: a way of life, a resource, a comfort, a continuing communion.

This continuing communion does not come about without effort. It is an exercise of the spirit that has a discipline of its own. I like to send myself to a dictionary for the actual definition of a word which I have been using rather freely. Webster enlarges my concept of the word discipline: "training which corrects, molds, strengthens, or perfects." There is nothing harsh about that, rather something encouraging. Through training a desired end can be achieved.

—From *A Book of Hours* by Elizabeth Yates

⊰ More things are wrought by prayer
Than this world dreams of.
Wherefore, let thy voice
Rise like a fountain for me night and day.
For what are men better than sheep and goats
That nourish a blind life within the brain,
If, knowing God, they lift not hands of prayer
Both for themselves and those who call them friend?
For so the whole round earth is every way
Bound by gold chains about the feet of God.
—Alfred Lord Tennyson

⊰ Most people think of prayer as an audible activity which calls for the cessation of all other activities. There can also be an inwardness of prayer which does not interfere with other activities and produces no outward, visible indications that it is taking place. There can be a continual prayer of the heart and mind which does not interrupt our daily routine. There can be such a profound prayerfulness at the center of our beings that our entire lives are saturated with prayer. We need to rediscover the inwardness of prayer and the miraculous potential for having a continual inner communion with our Lord.
—From *Praying the Name of Jesus* by Robert V. Dodd

⊰ Prayer is something more than that which we do with our minds. It also involves our hearts and spirits— that deeper part of our personalities to which only the Spirit of Jesus has access. Prayer in its highest form requires more than conscious effort. It also requires the surrender of our innermost selves to Jesus, giving him permission to make our lives a continually flowing fountain of unceasing prayer. When we have learned how to do that, we will have discovered the secret of the prayer of the heart.
—From *Praying the Name of Jesus* by Robert V. Dodd

Retreat Model 2: Faithful Living in a Nuclear Age

Arrive and Get Settled
My God, I come to this place to renew my fidelity and desire for your kingdom that I may not grow faint before the promises and perils of this modern age. Feed me with your word; stay by me here, O my God. Amen.

Thirty Minutes of Silent Listening

Scripture Reading (Use one passage for each cycle.)
1 Peter 2:1-10; Romans 12:1-21; Mark 10:35-45; Matthew 7:1-29

Response
Journal
Prayer
Action

Reading and Reflection
Anthology
Other

Reflection and Response

Recreation/Rest*

(Love Feast and/or Wesleyan Covenant Service)

Covenant Prayer
My Lord, I must return to my station in a rushed and worried world. Help me in the days ahead to know that this age, too, shall pass, but your kingdom is forever. Amen.

*Repeat cycle above or conclude retreat with Covenant Prayer. Groups of two or more may wish to conclude with Love Feast and/or Wesleyan Covenant Service on pp. 387–90.

Readings for Reflection

❧ Obedience is one of the evangelical counsels, the three traditional Gospel principles that were made popular in the monastic movement and other forms of the religious life in Christianity. They were derived from the story of the man from the ruling class, who comes to Jesus and asks him, "Good Master, what must I do to win eternal life?" After a preliminary inquiry, Jesus comes to the nub of the matter, "Sell everything you have and distribute to the poor, . . . and come, follow me." Peter reports that the apostles have done all this and Jesus enigmatically replies, "There is no one who has given up home, or wife, . . . for the sake of the kingdom of God, who will not be repaid many times over" (Luke 18:18-30). Out of this passage comes the call to live a life of poverty, chastity, and obedience.
—From *Spirituality for Ministry* by Urban T. Holmes III

❧ And when I am Pope—or Presiding Bishop—I will come out strong for unilateral disarmament for Christians, for Jesus' "one sword is enough" was sure NOT "parity" with Caesar's armaments—and nowhere does he say, that I can find, "one sword is enough when Caesar reduces his stockpile to one sword, boys, and not before that!"

And if one sword, which he refused to use, was enough for Jesus, despite the number of swords Caesar had—then one nuclear warhead, which will not be used either—for first-strike, retaliatory strike, or any strike at all—will be enough for Christians as far as I am concerned, when I am running the Church!
—From *The Gospel According to Abbie Jane Wells* by Abbie Jane Wells

❧ Ultimately, it is probably more important to try *to be welcome* than to *welcome*. Welcomed for what you are.

Be your genuine self. Then people will know you as you really are.

Be perfect like your heavenly Father and you will bear witness to the One who makes you holy.

Be blameless and pure, children of God without stain in the midst of a world where you will shine with your brothers as a source of light. Fearlessly and noiselessly, let your life point the way to the source, and God . . . will welcome and appease the weary. Saints do not need to be heard; their very existence is a call. And God's wisdom speaks through their lips.

Come, eat my bread and drink my wine prepared for you. In the end it is God . . . who welcomes, nourishes, serves and teaches all of us.

—From *The Jerusalem Community Rule of Life* by Pierre-Marie Delfieux

❧ To retreat is always a time of knowing ourselves that we may know Christ, and of knowing Christ that we may know ourselves. To retreat is to take times of reflection, to pray rather than to analyze, to open oneself more fully to the Spirit. We cannot learn this deeply enough. In some way, this is all one has to do: to remember and to realize who Jesus is in order to know who we are.

There is never a time when we can say we are over the peak, we are done. The most precious moments are surely ahead of us. We need to be sensitive to the great power that is in Jesus. He will be with us forever doing all he can in us. If we could imagine the whole world coming into blossom through one tree, we might have a way to think of each one of us drawing upon the Body of Christ.

—From *Gathering the Fragments* by Edward J. Farrell

Retreat Model 3: Discerning God's Will

Arrive and Get Settled

My God, in the quietness of the desert you spoke to Moses, and in the quiet cave Elijah heard your voice. Even so, speak to me in the quietness of this place, that I, too, may know the direction of your will in all the great and small decisions of life. Amen.

Thirty Minutes of Silent Listening

Scripture Reading (Use one passage for each cycle.)
Luke 4:1-14; Luke 12:35-40; Acts 6:1-15; Hebrews 12:1-17

Response
Journal
Prayer
Action

Reading and Reflection
Anthology
Other

Reflection and Response

Recreation/Rest*

(Love Feast and/or Wesleyan Covenant Service)

Covenant Prayer
My Lord, you have spoken through the silence of these hours and having heard, so I will do. Amen.

*Repeat cycle above or conclude retreat with Covenant Prayer. Groups of two or more may wish to conclude with Love Feast and/or Wesleyan Covenant Service on pp. 387–90.

Readings for Reflection

❧ The best school for prayer continues to be the Psalms. It also turns out to be an immersion in politics. The people in the Psalms who teach us to pray were remarkably well integrated in these matters. No people have valued and cultivated the sense of the person so well. At the same time no people have had a richer understanding of themselves as a "nation under God." Prayer was their characteristic society-shaping and soul-nurturing act. They prayed when they were together and they prayed when they were alone, and it was the same prayer in either setting. These prayers, the psalms, are terrifically personal; they are at the same time ardently political.
—From *Earth and Altar* by Eugene H. Peterson

❧ Holiness, in one strand of biblical understanding, is closely associated with Jesus' teaching about the Kingdom of God. It is not concerned so much with accumulating desirable attributes that we call holy, as it is with the way we perceive reality and the way we act on these perceptions. Holiness, therefore, is a political word. A holy person is a person who sees the world, if only momentarily, through the eyes of Christ and is drawn to act in response to this vision.
—From *Invitation to Holiness* by James C. Fenhagen

❧ When was the last time you spent a week with Jesus? Imagine a week—seven sunrises and seven sunsets—resting with Jesus, perhaps wrestling with him a bit, becoming reacquainted with him, with yourself. Like Eucharist, a retreat is a time of remembrance, a time to experience unity and continuity.
—From *Gathering the Fragments* by Edward J. Farrell

  ❧ Moreover we must not forget that the word of God issues its challenges. The scriptures are not a passive store of answers to our questions. We indeed read the Bible, but we can also say that the Bible "reads us." In many instances, our very questions will be reformulated. In the gospels this happens frequently to those who approach Jesus. For example, when Jesus is asked: "Who is my neighbor?" he reverses the terms of the questions and inquires in turn: "Which of these three . . . proved neighbor to the man?" (Luke 10:29-36).

    The word of the Lord is abidingly new; it is a challenge that can radically change our lives, a grace that shakes us from our inertia, an answer that cannot be shackled by our questions.

—From *We Drink from Our Own Wells* by Gustavo Gutiérrez

  ❧ Theological reflection is reflecting on the painful and joyful realities of every day with the mind of Jesus and thereby raising human consciousness to the knowledge of God's gentle guidance. This is a hard discipline, since God's presence is often a hidden presence, a presence that needs to be discovered. The loud, boisterous noises of the world make us deaf to the soft, gentle, and loving voice of God. A Christian leader is called to help people to hear that voice and so be comforted and consoled.

—From *In the Name of Jesus* by Henri J. M. Nouwen

  ❧ The requirements of a work to be done can be understood as the will of God. If I am supposed to hoe a garden or make a table, then I will be obeying God if I am true to the task I am performing. To do the work carefully and well, with love and respect for the nature of my task and with due attention to its purpose, is to unite myself to God's will in my work.

—From *New Seeds of Contemplation* by Thomas Merton

  ❧ I give this time to You alone. Please guide me in this prayer. I ask only for honesty and total sincerity. May I

pray from my heart alone. If there is anything I should experience now, or any words I should hear, I am ready to receive them. In stillness and quiet listening, I now open myself to You.
—From *The Quiet Answer* by Hugh Prather

❧ When our purpose is clear, there is no question what to do. Ultimately, we cannot make a mistake, for God has provided a Purpose to all we have done even though our motives may have been insincere at the time. Love uses all to bless all.

Our progress is seen not in what we do but in what we perceive our goal to be. Either we assign our ego's objective or God's purpose, and that is determined by what we choose to consult within us at the time each decision is made. It is impossible not to consult something. If we think that our experience is our guide, we will not believe that the still and present urgings of Love direct us.
—From *The Quiet Answer* by Hugh Prather

❧ The word *will* as in "God's will" comes from a Greek word that carries feeling and even passion. When we say "What is God's will?" we are asking, "What is God's deep, heartfelt desire for our lives and our world? What does this God who loves us want for us above all? What is God committed to accomplishing on our behalf no matter what the cost?...

God's passion is not to remove every hardship life brings our way but to remove every obstacle to our living a life in grace. Not that God wills hardship and suffering! But given the way life is, God working through our faith wants to turn those very hardships (and even wrongs) on their head. Instead of chambers of death in which we quietly suffer life's assault on us and die, those experiences become crucibles of new life through which we mature spiritually and grow in grace (Rom.5:1ff).
—From "Letter to a Friend" by Stephen D. Bryant in *Weavings* (May/June 1989)

Retreat Model 4: Healing

Arrive and Get Settled
I come to you, my God, seeking healing for my sicknesses and balm for my wounds. O Great Physician, examine me thoroughly through the powerful lens of your love, and heal all you see of brokenness or malice. Amen.

Thirty Minutes of Silent Listening

Scripture Reading (Use one passage for each cycle.)
James 5:13-18; 2 Corinthians 5:11-21; John 9:1-12; John 4:43-54

Response
Journal
Prayer
Action

Reading and Reflection
Anthology
Other

Reflection and Response

Recreation/Rest*

(Love Feast and/or Wesleyan Covenant Service)

Covenant Prayer
Thank you, my Lord, healer and friend, for restoring my passion and fueling my resolve to serve you always and in all things. Amen.

*Repeat cycle above or conclude retreat with Covenant Prayer. Groups of two or more may wish to conclude with Love Feast and/or Wesleyan Covenant Service on pp. 387–90.

Readings for Reflection

❧ Christianity is not a religion that sees the human journey primarily in terms of growth (which implies a natural unfolding), but in terms of transformation (which implies a radical restructuring of the center of our being). Christianity is not fundamentally about wholeness, but holiness.

—From *Invitation to Holiness* by James C. Fenhagen

❧ Scripture tells us "the prayer of faith will save the sick" (James 5:15). Yet all of us can doubtless recall times—many times—when we prayed for a healing and it did not occur... Does that mean that God is not listening? that your faith is too weak? or that your prayers have not been fervent enough? I think not, but I also think it is fruitless to try to find an answer to why some people are healed and some are not.

Much of what happens on our earthly journey will remain a mystery until we get to risen life. . . .

I do not think we can ever say prayer is wasted. Although prayer may not change a situation and give us the miracle we want, *prayer changes us*. Through prayer, we become more aware of God's presence. Through prayer, we find inner resources and strength we didn't know we had. Through prayer, we are no longer facing our fears and pain alone: God is beside us, renewing our spirit, restoring our soul, and helping us carry the burden when it becomes too heavy for us to bear alone.

—From *Near Life's End* by Ron DelBene with Mary and Herb Montgomery

❧ One thing we definitely know. God has not deliberately sent tragedy and suffering upon us. Though they are allowed, endured by God, they are not God's *intention* for us. Not once in the gospels does Jesus say that God sends tragedy and pain either to test us or to punish us. Though the blocks that prevent full healing are many and mysterious, the New Testament makes it clear that God is *always* on the side of healing, release, and reconciliation.

We know another thing. We are given the witness in scripture that the day will come when the whole creation will freely accept this love, healing, and reconciliation. There will be no aspect of creation left weeping and alone. There will be no more desire to choose lovelessness. The risk and choice will be there forever, but that risk (that grave gift of God's honor) will be transcended by a creation joyfully and freely united with God in the embrace of lovers.

This is not a bland victory. God has paid a great price for love within freedom.

—From *Prayer, Fear, and Our Powers* by Flora Slosson Wuellner

     In the Gospel of Mark there is a series of stories and sayings through which the reader comes to know about Jesus, the exalted and victorious Son, whom God anointed with his Holy Spirit and power. Jesus' authority is demonstrated in both his teaching and his healing miracles that are signs of the power of God to change lives for the better.

The surprising events that occur in Jesus' presence are not done as tricks to astound people. They result from his caring for people and his obedience to the will of God.

Persons in need are confronted by a person who *loves* them and is completely obedient to God's will. This presence of Jesus, and the TRUST or FAITH of those whom he confronts allow these acts of God's power to occur. This relationship is central. Where these elements are present—Jesus' obedience and love, and the willingness of a person to trust God—evil is overcome and God is glorified.

Do you want to be healed? That's a question Jesus asked the man at Bethesda. Do you want to be healed? is a question he asks today.

Do you want to be healed?

Jesus Christ is still in the business of making *you* well, if you will trust in him.

—From the journal of Richard Allen Ward

Retreat Model 5: Forgiveness

Arrive and Get Settled
I come to this place apart, my God, with forgiveness on my mind. I pray, forgive me; forgive my sins and help me to forgive those who have sinned against me. Amen.

Thirty Minutes of Silent Listening

Scripture Reading (Use one passage for each cycle.)
Matthew 18:21-35; Philemon 1-25; Acts 2:37-47; Acts 7:54—8:1

Response
Journal
Prayer
Action

Reading and Reflection
Anthology
Other

Reflection and Response

Recreation/Rest*

(Love Feast and/or Wesleyan Covenant Service)

Covenant Prayer
My Lord, it is good to be here with you, again aware of your limitless love and quick forgiveness. Now as I go from this place, go with me, prompting and checking desire and action, that I may grow toward sinning less and loving purity of conscience more. Amen.

*Repeat cycle above or conclude retreat with Covenant Prayer. Groups of two or more may wish to conclude with Love Feast and/or Wesleyan Covenant Service on pp. 387–90.

Readings for Reflection

    ❧ Three old men, of whom one had a bad reputation, came one day to Abba Achilles. The first asked him, "Father, make me a fishing-net." "I will not make you one," he replied. Then the second said, "Of your charity make one, so that we may have a souvenir of you in the monastery." But he said, "I do not have time." Then the third one, who had a bad reputation, said, "Make me a fishing-net, so that I may have something from your hands, Father." Abba Achilles answered him at once, "For you, I will make one." Then the two other old men asked him privately, "Why did you not want to do what we asked you, but you promised to do what he asked?" The old man gave them this answer, "I told you I would not make one, and you were not disappointed, since you thought that I had no time. But if I had not made one for him, he would have said, 'The old man has heard about my sin, and that is why he does not want to make me any-thing,' and so our relationship would have broken down. But now I have cheered his soul, so that he will not be overcome with grief."

—From *The Sayings of the Desert Fathers* translated by
   Benedicta Ward

    ❧ A brother. . . committed a fault. A council was called to which Abba Moses was invited, but he refused to go to it. Then the priest sent someone to say to him, "Come, for everyone is waiting for you." So he got up and went. He took a leaking jug, filled it with water, and carried it with him. The others came out to meet him and said to him, "What is this, Father?" The old man said to them, "My sins run out behind me, and I do not see them, and today I am coming to judge the errors of another." When they heard that they said no more to the brother but forgave him.

—From *The Sayings of the Desert Fathers* translated by
   Benedicta Ward

🕭 Never tire of *forgiving*, and so give the devil no hold. Be merciful and compassionate, spontaneously and wholeheartedly. The Lord forgives you all day long; in the silence of your heart, then, do the same, untiringly and sincerely.

—From *The Jerusalem Community Rule of Life* by Pierre-Marie Delfieux

🕭 Good people are drawn to the goodness manifested in the lives of other good people. We notice what it is about them that makes us want to be in their presence.

I believe that genuinely forgiving people have certain qualities that are born of suffering and for which they have paid a high price. We are not compassionate, forgiving people simply by reason of our birth. We learn to forgive as we learn to love, beginning with early role models, continuing through life experiences and with reflection on the ways in which we respond.

Compassion is not a gift. It is an attractive quality that we may wish to choose for our lives. Like courage, it is born of a series of choices we make to forgive or not forgive, to love or not to love. Courage, along with love and forgiveness, shows itself in adversity.

Forgiving people are attractive to other good people because they are aware of their need for forgiveness, of their difficulty in seeking it, and of their suffering when it has been refused or delayed.

There is a personal discipline involved in becoming a person who forgives. Learning to do the difficult, choosing to risk being hurt, seeking the vulnerable place we put ourselves in when we forgive is learned only with repetition. It necessarily precludes ever setting ourselves in the position of judging another.

—From *Growing Strong at Broken Places* by Paula Ripple

Retreat Model 6: New Beginnings

Arrive and Get Settled
> Lord Jesus Christ, I come to you yearning for a new beginning. Reveal yourself to me in this hour, restore and renew my life and bind me once again to yourself. Amen.

Thirty Minutes of Silent Listening

Scripture Reading (Use one passage for each cycle.)
> John 3:1-21; James 1:2-18; Titus 3:1-11; 1 John 3:1-24

Response
> Journal
> Prayer
> Action

Reading and Reflection
> Anthology
> Other

Reflection and Response

Recreation/Rest*

(Love Feast and/or Wesleyan Covenant Service)

Covenant Prayer
> By your hand, my Lord, my famished soul has been fed. I have been given a foretaste of the new heaven and new earth. I rest in you, my God, who has and does, and will make all things new. O glorious hope! Amen.

*Repeat cycle above or conclude retreat with Covenant Prayer. Groups of two or more may wish to conclude with Love Feast and/or Wesleyan Covenant Service on pp. 387–90.

Readings for Reflection

❧ I have a friend who grew up in the marshlands of southern Louisiana. He is a good man with whom to walk those swamps, because he can smell a snake before anyone sees it. It is an acquired skill. Hollow men and women do not even know evil when they see it, much less smell it. They have shunned the discipline to acquire the skill.
—From *Spirituality for Ministry* by Urban T. Holmes III

❧ The Incarnation in Mary—of Mary—being a physical and visible showing of the spiritual and invisible incarnation within each one who is willing, ready or not, men and women alike, for the Holy Spirit to plant the seed of God within them—making them pregnant with God, by God, on a full-time basis, as any physical pregnancy is a full-time thing, and is an experience of growth and enlargement within—so it is also with a spiritual pregnancy.
—From *The Gospel According to Abbie Jane Wells* by Abbie Jane Wells

❧ The Christian life involves more than growth and development. It involves conversion and transformation, a radical turning of the Self toward the God who made us and who continues to sustain us. Christian faith is about an inner transformation of consciousness resulting from our encounter with the living Christ. "I have been crucified with Christ," proclaimed the Apostle Paul, "it is no longer I who live, but Christ who lives in me" (Gal. 2:20). "When anyone is united to Christ, there is a new world: the old order has gone, and a new order has already begun" (2 Cor. 5:17). The Christian revelation promises a radical vision of what it means to be a human being. The life of Christ does not change the way we look, nor does it eliminate our peculiarities or the results of our own brokenness and estrangement. What it does do is open us to the Spirit

of God in ways that increase in us the capacity for love.
The fruit of conversion is a life that can be used by God
for the healing of the world.
—From *Invitation to Holiness* by James C. Fenhagen

     Thou Hast Beset Me Behind and Before
(*selected lines*)

Thou hast beset me behind and before
And laid thine hand upon me!

Muscle by muscle,
Bone by bone,
Adding to strength and height,
This the journey from infancy to youth;
Growing by day, by night;
Growth makes an end.
Some order calls a halt!
Beset behind, before,
Growth gives way.
But life does not stop,
The twins keep pace:
    Joy, sorrow—
    Sickness, health—
    Success, failure—
    Hope, despair—
    Courage, fear—
    Peace, turmoil.
The tempo quickens:
Dreams long cherished fall apart;
Slumbering desires awaken in vital strength;
The good seems no longer good;
The evil allures and engulfs;
The will is weak, the path grows dim,
Doubts gather, confusion is confounded,
Endurance languishes,
The spirit holds—
Till life begins anew.

Thou hast beset me behind and before
And laid Thine hand upon me!
—From *The Inward Journey* by Howard Thurman

❧ Every human being knows prayer from experience. Have we not all experienced moments in which our thirsting heart found itself with surprise drinking at a fountain of meaning? Much of our life may be a wandering in desert lands, but we do find springs of water. If what is called "God" means in the language of experience the ultimate Source of Meaning, then those moments that quench the thirst of the heart are moments of prayer. They are moments when we communicate with God, and that is, after all, the essence of prayer.

—From *Gratefulness, the Heart of Prayer* by David Steindl-Rast

❧ The initial encounter with the Lord is the starting point of a *following*, or discipleship. The journeying that ensues is what St. Paul calls "walking according to the Spirit" (Rom. 8:4). It is also what we today speak of as a spirituality.

The term "spirituality" is a relatively recent one in the history of the church. It came into use around the beginning of the seventeenth century in French religious circles at a time that saw a wealth of contributions and works on the subject. Everything that had to do with Christian perfection fell under the heading of *spiritual life*, whereas reflection of the subject yielded a *spiritual theology*.

—From *We Drink from Our Own Wells* by Gustavo Gutiérrez

❧ Every great spirituality is connected with the great historical movement of the age in which it was formulated. This linkage is not to be understood in the sense of mechanical dependence, but the following of Jesus is something that penetrates deeply into the course of human history.

—From *We Drink from Our Own Wells* by Gustavo Gutiérrez

Retreat Model 7: Rest and Renewal

Arrive and Get Settled
Here I am again, my Lord, responding to your invitation to come away with you to this lonely place—to rest awhile. Amen.

Thirty Minutes of Silent Listening

Scripture Reading (Use one passage for each cycle.)
Matthew 11:25-30; John 6:15-40; John 4:7-38; Mark 6:30-62

Response
Journal
Prayer
Action

Reading and Reflection
Anthology
Other

Reflection and Response

Recreation/Rest*

(Love Feast and/or Wesleyan Covenant Service)

Covenant Prayer
How good it is, my Lord, to rest and to be renewed; my tiredness for your energy, my weakness for your strength. Amen.

*Repeat cycle above or conclude retreat with Covenant Prayer. Groups of two or more may wish to conclude with Love Feast and/or Wesleyan Covenant Service on pp. 387–90.

Readings for Reflection

❧ I Want to Stop Running

Eternal God, you are a song amid silence,
  a voice out of quietness,
  a light out of darkness,
  a Presence in the emptiness,
  a coming out of the void.
You are all of these things and more.
You are mystery that encompasses meaning,
  meaning that penetrates mystery.
You are God,
  I am man.
I strut and brag.
I put down my fellows
  and bluster out assertions of my achievements.
And then something happens:
  I wonder who I am,
    and if I matter.
Night falls,
  I am alone in the dark and afraid.
Someone dies,
  I feel so powerless.
A child is born,
  I am touched by the miracle of new life.
At such moments I pause . . .
  to listen for a song amid silence,
  a voice out of stillness,
  to look for a light out of darkness.
I want to feel a Presence in the emptiness.
I find myself reaching for a hand.

Oftentimes, the feeling passes quickly,
  and I am on the run again:
    success to achieve,
    money to make.
O Lord, you have to catch me on the run
  most of the time.
I am too busy to stop,
  too important to pause for contemplation.

I hold up too big a section of the sky
    to sit down and meditate.
But even on the run,
    an occasional flicker of doubt assails me,
And I suspect I may not be as important
        to the world
    as I think I am.
Jesus said each of us is important to you.
It is as if every hair of our heads were numbered.
How can that be?
But in the hope that it is so,
I would stop running,
        stop shouting,
    and be myself.

Let me be still now.
Let me be calm.
Let me rest upon the faith that you are, God,
    and I need not be afraid. *Amen.*
—From *A Book of Uncommon Prayer* by Kenneth G.
    Phifer

ᴥ When Dante appeared at the Franciscan monastery
door, a monk opened the door and asked him what he
wanted. "Peace!" was Dante's one word answer. That
eventually became the Lord's gift to him when he
learned to wait, pray, and listen. Later, in *The Divine
Comedy,* he wrote his oft-quoted line, "In His will is our
peace." The refreshment of Christ is peace to replace
our impatience. Then we can pray with Richard of
Chichester, the thirteenth-century saint,

O most merciful Redeemer, Friend and Brother, may
we know Thee more clearly, love Thee more dearly,
and follow Thee more nearly; for Thine own sake.—
Amen.

Christ is peace. Christ is patience. We could never
produce these graces in our own strength in the quanti-
ties they are needed in our families and our world. But

we do have access to an unlimited stockpile of patience because the same Spirit that enabled Christ is in us.

—From *Radiance of the Inner Splendor* by Lloyd John Ogilvie

ॐ There is a pleasure in being in a ship beaten about by a storm, when we are sure that it will not founder. The persecutions which harass the Church are of this nature.

—Blaise Pascal

ॐ And suddenly there it was. If life is Christ, the abundant life must be more of him! To be in Christ as believer, disciple, and a loved and forgiven person is one thing. To have Christ in us as motivator, enabler, and transformer of personality is something more. Much more.

—From *Radiance of the Inner Splendor* by Lloyd John Ogilvie

ॐ Be present, O merciful God, and protect us through the silent hours of this night, so that we who are wearied by the work and the changes of this fleeting world may rest upon Thy eternal changelessness; through Jesus Christ our Lord. Amen.

—An Ancient Collect

Retreat Model 8: Justice and Mercy

Arrive and Get Settled
My God, I put myself before you for these hours.
Reach down and change the gears within me that
I may go forward with you. Amen.

Thirty Minutes of Silent Listening

Scripture Reading (Use one passage for each cycle.)
1 John 5:1-20; Romans 5:1-11; John 15:1-11; Romans
6:1-14

Response
Journal
Prayer
Action

Reading and Reflection
Anthology
Other

Reflection and Response

Recreation/Rest*

(Love Feast and/or Wesleyan Covenant Service)

Covenant Prayer
God of justice and mercy, your word has been my
abode for these hours, and by your word I have
been fed. As I go from this sacred place may
justice and mercy flow like a river through me to
those in need. Amen.

*Repeat cycle above or conclude retreat with Covenant
Prayer. Groups of two or more may wish to conclude with
Love Feast and/or Wesleyan Covenant Service on pp.
387–90.

Readings for Reflection

❧ The people who warn that "religion and politics don't mix" certainly know what they are talking about. The mix has resulted in no end of ills—crusades, inquisitions, witch hunts, exploitation. All the same, God says, "Mix them." But be very careful how you mix them. The only safe way is in prayer. It is both unbiblical and unreal to divide life into the activities of religion and politics, or into the realms of sacred and profane. But how do we get them together without putting one into the unscrupulous hands of the other, politics *using* religion or religion *using* politics, when what we want is a true mixture, politics *becoming* religious and religion *becoming* political? Prayer is the only means that is adequate for the great end of getting these polarities in dynamic relation. The psalms are our most extensive source documents showing prayer in action.
—From *Earth and Altar* by Eugene H. Peterson

❧ Prayer acts on the principle of the fulcrum, the small point where great leverage is exercised—awareness and intensification, expansion and deepening at the conjunction of heaven and earth, God and neighbor, self and society. Prayer is the action that integrates the inside and the outside of life, that correlates the personal and the public, and that addresses individual needs and national interest. No other thing that we do is as simultaneously beneficial to society and to the soul as the act of prayer.
—From *Earth and Altar* by Eugene H. Peterson

❧ Prayer is a repair and a healing of the interconnections. It drives to the source of the divisions between the holy and the world—the ungodded self—and pursues healing to its end, settling for nothing less than the promised new heaven and new earth. "Our citizenship is in heaven," say those who pray, and they are ardent in pursuing the prizes of that place. But this passion for the unseen in no way detracts from their involvement in daily affairs: working well and playing fair, signing petitions and paying taxes, rebuking the wicked and encouraging the righteous, getting wet in the rain and smelling the flowers. Theirs is a tremendous, kaleido-scopic assemblage of bits and pieces of touched, smelled, seen and tasted reality that is received and offered in acts of prayer. They obey the dominical command, "Render to Caesar the things that are Caesar's and to God the things that are God's."

—From *Earth and Altar* by Eugene H. Peterson

&. There is no Christian life without "songs" to the Lord, without thanksgiving for God's love, and without prayer. But the songs are sung by persons living in particular historical situations, and these provide the framework within which they perceive God's presence and also God's absence (in the biblical sense of this term; see Jer. 7:1-7; Matt. 7:15-21). In our Latin American context we may well ask ourselves: How can we thank God for the gift of life when the reality around us is one of premature and unjustly inflicted death? How can we express joy at knowing ourselves to be loved by the Father when we see the suffering of our brothers and sisters? How can we sing when the suffering of an entire people chokes the sound in our throats?

These questions are troublesome and far from su-perficial; they are not to be stilled by facile answers that underestimate the situation of injustice and mar-ginalization in which the vast majority of Latin Ameri-cans live. On the other hand, it is also evident that this reality does not silence the song or make inaudible the voice of the poor. This state of affairs amounts to a critical judgment on many aspects of the spirituality that is still accepted in some Christian circles. At the same time, however, it represents a "favorable time" (2 Cor. 6:2, JB), a *kairos*, a moment of heightened revela-tion both of God and of new paths on the journey of fidelity to the word of God.

—From *We Drink from Our Own Wells* by Gustavo Gutiérrez

❧ What we have experienced over the past few decades has been a gradual recognition and verbalizing of a simple fact: women were not made inferior, and therefore should not be treated as such. The Judeo-Christian tradition has been founded on such a belief. As far back as the ninth century BC the Jahwist had already indicated that there was to be a radical equality and mutuality between man and woman (Genesis 2:18-25). The inequality that is so much a part of our own scene was also part and parcel of the world of the Jahwist. However, he rightly saw that it could only be understood as the result of sin. The whole story of subordination and pain is told as a result of the sinful situation that has come into the lives of men and women because they have decided that they would prefer to do things their way, rather than God's way (Genesis 3:14-19). It is tragic that twenty-eight centuries later we are still quite happy to settle for such disorder in the relationships that exist between man and woman—and ridicule those who suggest that such a situation is wrong.

—From *Woman: First Among the Faithful* by Francis J. Moloney

Retreat Model 9: God's Love and Care

Arrive and Get Settled
 I am here again, my Lord, drawn by faith that
 nothing shall ever separate me from your love and
 care. Love me, my God, care for me in this place,
 and equip me for the duties which await my
 return. Amen.

Thirty Minutes of Silent Listening

Scripture Reading (Use one passage for each cycle.)
 Luke 15:1-32; Ephesians 1:3-14; Colossians 1:9-23;
 Mark 8:1-21

Response
 Journal
 Prayer
 Action

Reading and Reflection
 Anthology
 Other

Reflection and Response

Recreation/Rest*

(Love Feast and/or Wesleyan Covenant Service)

Covenant Prayer
 I go from this place with new hope, my God, that
 tomorrow, even as today, your love will be my
 delight and your care my hiding place. So let it be.
 Amen.

*Repeat cycle above or conclude retreat with Covenant
Prayer. Groups of two or more may wish to conclude with
Love Feast and/or Wesleyan Covenant Service on pp.
387–90.

Readings for Reflection

❧ It can therefore be said without any fear of exaggeration that we are experiencing today an exceptional time in the history of Latin America and the life of the church. Of this situation we may say with Paul: "Now is the favorable time; this is the day of salvation" (2 Cor. 6:2, JB). Such a vision of things does not make the journey of the poor less difficult nor does it gloss over the obstacles they encounter in their efforts to defend their most elementary rights. The demanding, cruel reality of wretchedness, exploitation, hostility, and death— our daily experience—will not allow us to forget it. There is question here, then, not of a facile optimism but rather of a deep trust in the historical power of the poor and, above all, a firm hope in the Lord.

These attitudes do not automatically ensure a better future; but as they draw nourishment from a present that is full of possibilities, they in turn nourish the present with promises. So true is this that if we do not respond to the demands of the present, because we do not know in advance whither we may be led, we are simply refusing to hear the call of Jesus Christ. We are refusing to open to him when he knocks on the door and invites us to sup with him.

—From *We Drink from Our Own Wells* by Gustavo Gutiérrez

❧ Asking for guidance from our deep core of peace will facilitate our recognition of the loving consequence of all we do. Asking, however, is not what establishes a beneficial result. Blessing is our inheritance from God and is therefore our right. It cannot be negated, but it can most certainly be overlooked. Turning every decision over to God protects our mind from a loveless view.

—From *The Quiet Answer* by Hugh Prather

ᐒ It is nearly impossible to give love to those who will not receive it. Love cannot be forced upon anyone. Love is a gift that has to be received. If my children think I am a monster, there is no way in which I can get close to them and give them love. Our very attitude toward God determines how much love and caring can be poured out upon us.

Some Christians emphasize the justice and judgment of God, and certainly there is justice behind the love of which Jesus speaks. My own experience over many years of listening to people is that most of them are already judging themselves too harshly and that further emphasis on judgment only drives people away from God rather than drawing them to Abba. Most of us do not believe that anyone could accept us as we are, and we do not even try to turn toward God and receive the incredible gift of his love. It is so difficult to believe in God's love when so few of us have received unconditional love from any human being. One purpose of the Church and those who would be spiritual friends is to provide a human atmosphere in which the love of God may seem more plausible, and to give people the courage to have fellowship with the Holy One. When we are truly loved, we are drawn by that love to its life and goals, and judgment is seldom necessary for us. Research shows that children raised in a loving environment develop the most sensitive sense of conscience.

—From *Companions on the Inner Way* by Morton T. Kelsey

ᐒ It is all to the good that my body has called a halt, oh God. For I must rest a while if I am to do what I have to do. Or perhaps that is just another conventional idea. Even if one's body aches, the spirit can continue to do its work, can it not? It can love and *"hineinhorchen"* —"hearken unto"—itself and unto others and unto what binds us to life. *"Hineinhorchen"*—I so wish I could find a Dutch equivalent for that German word. Truly, my life is one long hearkening unto my self and unto others, unto God. And if I say that I hearken, it is really God who hearkens inside me. The most essential and the deepest in me hearkening unto the most essential and the deepest in the other. God to God.

—From *An Interrupted Life: The Diaries of Etty Hillesum, 1941-1943,* translated from the Dutch by Arno Pomerans

&. And if I should ask you to tell (to sing) your dreams of love? What images would you offer to your traveling companions as bread and wine? Those memories and hopes that call forth a smile and that, if realized, would make the world a more friendly place. If, as in children's stories, you were promised the fulfillment of one wish, just one, the most intense, most ardent, the one on which your life and death depended. Do you know what you would say? Or have you lost the memory of paradise, its desires forgotten, buried in the daily routine, mediocre and inexorable?

—From *I Believe in the Resurrection of the Body* by Rubem Alves

Retreat Model 10: What Does the Lord Require?

Arrive and Get Settled
In these hours search me, my God; know the motives and secrets of my heart. Test me and know my anxious thoughts. See if there be any hurtful way in me, and lead me in your ways now and always. Amen.

Thirty Minutes of Silent Listening

Scripture Reading (Use one passage for each cycle.)
Mark 10:1-30; Acts 10:1-48; John 21:15-19; Ephesians 4:1-16

Response
Journal
Prayer
Action

Reading and Reflection
Anthology
Other

Reflection and Response

Recreation/Rest*

(Love Feast and/or Wesleyan Covenant Service)

Covenant Prayer
My God, do you not require of me, first and foremost, the sacrifice of a broken and teachable heart? Here is my heart, Lord, take and seal it for your purpose and pleasure. Amen.

*Repeat cycle above or conclude retreat with Covenant Prayer. Groups of two or more may wish to conclude with Love Feast and/or Wesleyan Covenant Service on pp. 387–90.

Readings for Reflection

• Today, humility is not a popular virtue; but only because it is misunderstood. Many think that humility is a pious lie committed by people who claim to be worse than they know themselves to be, so that they can secretly pride themselves in being so humble. In truth, however, to be humble means simply to be earthy. The word "humble" is related to "humus," the vegetable mold of top soil. It is also related to human and humor. If we accept and embrace the earthiness of our human condition (and a bit of humor helps) we shall find ourselves doing so with humble pride. In our best moments humility is simply pride that is too grateful to look down on anyone.

—From *Gratefulness, the Heart of Prayer* by David Steindl-Rast

• We are living in a favorable time, a *kairos*, in which the Lord says: "Behold, I stand at the door and knock; if any one hears my voice and opens the door, I will come in to him and eat with him, and he with me" (Rev. 3:20). Not a violent entrance but a quiet knock that calls for an attitude of welcome and active watchfulness, of confidence and courage. Indifference, the privileges they have gained, and fear of the new make many persons spiritually deaf; as a result, the Lord passes by without stopping at their houses. But there are also many in our countries and in these times who hear the Lord's call and try to open the doors of their lives. We are living in a special period of God's saving action, a time when a new route is being carved out for the following of Jesus.

—From *We Drink from Our Own Wells* by Gustavo Gutiérrez

• The deep-rooted, me-first distortions of our humanity have been institutionalized in our economics and sanctioned by our psychologies. Now we have gotten for ourselves religions in the same style, religions that will augment our human potential and make us feel good about ourselves. We want prayers that will bring us daily benefits in the form of a higher standard of living, with occasional miracles to relieve our boredom. We come to the Bible as consumers, rummaging through texts to find something at a bargain. We come to worship as gourmets of the emotional, thinking that the numinous might provide a nice supplement to sunsets and symphonies. We read "The LORD is my shepherd, I shall not want," and our hearts flutter. We read "You will not fear the terror of the night," and we are tranquilized. We read "He does not deal with us according to our sins" and decide we have probably been too hard on ourselves. But when we read "The LORD says . . . The LORD has sworn," our interest flags and we reach for the newspaper to find out how the stock market is doing.

—From *Earth and Altar* by Eugene H. Peterson

&. Our commitment to Jesus Christ and our faith journey, while always personal, is never private. The scripture accents individual theophanies when God is revealed to persons in ecstatic moments of awareness and communion, but at the same time, the scripture warns against narcissistic attention to spiritual devotion while the world is convulsed in agony and one's neighbor cries out for help. Remember how the prophet Micah underscored it: "What does the Lord require of you but to do justice, and to love kindness and to walk humbly with your God?" (Mic.6:8, RSV). Personal piety is commended, but only when it leads to concern for the stranger and to moral righteousness and justice in society. To be alive in the Spirit and to follow Jesus is to put faith to work; it is to translate our love for God into caring concern for the least and the lost. Did not Jesus do that himself? His own moments of prayer and spiritual preparation were often followed by gestures of healing and help (Mark 1:35–39; Mark 9:2ff).

—From *Forever Beginning* by Donald J. Shelby

Retreat Model 11: Apprehended by God

Arrive and Get Settled
> In this moment, O sovereign Lord, I am content to surrender my will, my intellect, and my energies to your control. Do with me, speak to me, as you will, to the end that I may reflect your image to all the world. Amen.

Thirty Minutes of Silent Listening

Scripture Reading (Use one passage for each cycle.)
> John 15:12-17; Luke 5:1-11; Romans 1:1-17; Ephesians 5:1-20

Response
> Journal
> Prayer
> Action

Reading and Reflection
> Anthology
> Other

Reflection and Response

Recreation/Rest*

(Love Feast and/or Wesleyan Covenant Service)

Covenant Prayer
> Grant me now, O sovereign Lord, a vision of all that I might be and do for your kingdom, and ennoble me to live out of that great possibility. Amen.

*Repeat cycle above or conclude retreat with Covenant Prayer. Groups of two or more may wish to conclude with Love Feast and/or Wesleyan Covenant Service on pp. 387–90.

Readings for Reflection

❧ The word of God can require something of me today that it did not require yesterday; this means that, if I am to hear this challenge, I must be fundamentally open and listening. It is true that no relationship is more intimate, more rooted in being than that between the recipient of grace and the grace-giving Lord, between the head and the body, the vine and the branches.
—From *Prayer* by Hans Urs von Balthasar

❧ In a real sense, I'm beginning to dare to identify with all of those reluctant prophets. I'm not running away like Jonah or complaining quite as much as Jeremiah but I'm feeling closer to them than ever before. The enormity of the claim that God's hand is on my life is, on the one hand, presumptuous and immodest and, on the other, the most important recognition one can have. I know it is the essence of the faith that God leads individuals but during the times when I am cognizant of what that *really* means to me personally, I am totally overwhelmed. The Creator of all that is leading *ME*?! What can I say—why me—I'm not worthy—and in the end the answer can only be—yes, yes, yes. Ah, grace!
—From a letter by Janet Stephenson

❧ The mystical experience can be thought of as an unusually vivid feeling of the intimate presence of God, which may be accompanied by a profoundly moving and unexpected insight. It is a high-intensity experience, such as may be associated with religious conversion, rather than a low-intensity experience, such as the more placid calm and assurance of ordinary public worship. It is adequately described not by comparatives but only by superlatives. It is a feeling of certainty that one is directly in touch with profound depths of reality which are usually hidden.
—From *Explorations in Meditation and Contemplation* by Harvey Seifert

&. The church is still comprised of very human mortals who are inconsistent, who make exaggerated claims and play their little games. But paradox of paradoxes: Christ summons us with those limitations—and more—to be agents of his resurrection power and hope. "You did not choose me, but I chose you and appointed you that you should go and bear fruit and that your fruit should abide" (John 15:16); "Greater works than these will . . . [you] do" (John 14:12); "Go therefore and make disciples of all nations" (Matt. 28:19); "Heal the sick, raise the dead, cleanse lepers, cast out demons" (Matt. 10:8). Or, in the words of Paul: "As God's chosen ones, put on compassion, kindness, lowliness, forbearing one another, forgiving one another. Above all, put on love . . . and let Christ's Word dwell richly in you" (Col. 3:12ff., my paraphrase). We are called to be saints, who in our humanness are always saints without halos. Christ asks us to be his Easter people, to do for others what we ourselves need. He summons us to be for others what we have not yet become and to give to others what we have not yet completely received ourselves.

We are asked to be what we are not. We who follow Christ are called to offer to others what is still unrealized in us. Lessons of love and life are to be taught by us who are still learning them. Self-understanding in others is to be encouraged by us who do not yet understand ourselves. We are to witness, nurture, and admonish others in their spirtual pilgrimage while still struggling with our own. We who are sick are asked to heal others. We who are fractious and cause conflict are called by Christ to be peacemakers. We who have dark corners in our soul still unredeemed are sent out to baptize. We who need the Word ourselves are commissioned to proclaim and to preach. We who are possessed by irrational urges and baser motives are sent out to cast out demons. We are called by Jesus to do what we need, to offer what we ourselves need.
—From *Meeting the Messiah* by Donald J. Shelby

Retreat Model 12: Journey toward Life

Arrive and Get Settled
I have come to this place, my Lord, to trim my
wick and clean my glass, that I may shine as your
lesser light in the world. Help me, I pray. Amen.

Thirty Minutes of Silent Listening

Scripture Reading (Use one passage for each cycle.)
Philippians 1:3-30; 2 Timothy 2:1-13; 1 Peter 1:3-9;
Luke 24:13-35

Response
Journal
Prayer
Action

Reading and Reflection
Anthology
Other

Reflection and Response

Recreation/Rest*

(Love Feast and/or Wesleyan Covenant Service)

Covenant Prayer
My loving God, as you have spoken to me, so may
I go now to speak to others—for you. Amen.

*Repeat cycle above or conclude retreat with Covenant
Prayer. Groups of two or more may wish to conclude with
Love Feast and/or Wesleyan Covenant Service on pp.
387–90.

Readings for Reflection

❧ Few pictures are more ancient, more archetypal, than the picture of the pilgrim. None better expresses inner restlessness and outer uncertainty, the sense of continual movement and the ache of fatigue. A pilgrim is incomplete without his packsack into which is stuffed whatever is most precious, most essential. In comparison with all one's possessions, the backpack is a pathetic pittance; but without it a person would be forlorn indeed. Each day, the pilgrim must ask again: what am I able to take along? what must I take? So whenever we think of ourselves as pilgrims, we begin instinctively to choose and to reject, to weigh and to measure, whatever is to go with us.

—From *To Die and To Live* by Paul S. Minear

❧ We have sinned in not fulfilling the second commandment, which tells us to love our neighbor as ourselves. We haven't loved ourselves and, thus, we haven't been capable of loving our neighbor. We present-day Christians have sinned by not showing the face of Christ to the world at large. The early Christians showed his face to such an extent that the pagans said of them, "See how they love one another."

Why, then, do I feel hopeful? I feel hopeful because the Lord has plowed a field, harrowed and seeded it. I feel hopeful because green shoots of prayer are rising from the hearts of people everywhere, not only in those dedicated to religious life, but in men and women of all vocations. People are praying in their hearts, and they are taking time to go to quiet places to reflect. They are being drawn inwardly toward him who poured himself out in the service of others.

—From *Soul of My Soul* by Catherine de Hueck Doherty

❧ As I explore the height and the depth and the breadth of life, each discovery I make about life is a discovery about God, each is a step with God, a step toward God.

—From *Time and Myth* by John S. Dunne

ᵃ⁸ There is a really deep well inside me. And in it dwells God. Sometimes I am there too. But more often stones and grit block the well, and God is buried beneath. Then God must be dug out again.

I imagine that there are people who pray with their eyes turned heavenwards. They seek God outside themselves. And there are those who bow their head and bury it in their hands. I think that these seek God inside.

—From *An Interrupted Life: The Diaries of Etty Hillesum, 1941-1943*, translated by Arno Pomerans

ᵃ⁸ The journey by which we discover God is also the journey by which we discover, or uncover, our true self hidden in God. It is a journey that we all have to make.

It is so easy to play the world's game which is the power game, the game which depends on setting myself apart from others, distinguishing myself, seeking the limelight and looking for applause. I find that it is only too easy to become compulsive in my continual need for affirmation, for more and more affirmation, as I anxiously ask Who am I? Am I the person who is liked, admired, praised, seen as successful? My whole attitude towards myself becomes determined by the way in which others see me. I compare myself with others, and I try to emphasize what is different and distinctive about me. Those three temptations which Christ faced in the wilderness are equally my own temptations:

to be relevant
to be spectacular
to be powerful.

Am I able, like Christ, to put them down?

Am I prepared to shed all these outer shells, of false ambition, of pride?

Am I ready to admit that the mask is a disguise put on to cover up the insecure self? and the armour a shield to protect the vulnerable self?

Am I ready to receive a new self, based not on what I can achieve, but on what I am willing to receive?

—From *Living with Contradiction* by Esther de Waal

Love Feast

(Traditionally, worshipers were seated in a circle or around a table. Bread was broken into small portions, or a common loaf was passed from hand to hand. A loving cup with two handles was provided for water, but later individual glasses were used.)

A Hymn of Praise

The Scripture

Voluntary Prayers and the Lord's Prayer

A Hymn of Christian Fellowship

The Passing of the Bread
(Here this blessing shall be said): Blessed are you, O Sovereign, God of the universe, who brings forth bread from the earth. Amen.

Offering for the Poor

The Passing of the Cup
(Here this promise shall be said): Jesus said, Whoever drinks of the water I give shall never thirst. Amen.

A Thanksgiving in Unison (To be said by all):
Blessed are you, O God, the author of all sustenance, who hast nourished us from our youth up. Fill our hearts with joyfulness, that in your bountiful providence we may serve you with every good work; through Jesus Christ our Lord. Amen.

Testimonies

A Hymn of Thanksgiving

Covenant Prayer
My loving God, as you have spoken to me, so may I go now to speak to others—for you. Amen.

A Blessing

A Wesleyan Covenant Service

The Invitation

Dear friends, the Christian life, to which we are called, is a life in Christ, redeemed from sin and consecrated to God. Upon this life we have entered, having been admitted into that new covenant of which our Lord Jesus Christ is mediator, and which he sealed with his own blood, that it might stand forever.

On one side the covenant is God's promise that all that was declared in Jesus Christ, who is the author and perfecter of our faith, will ultimately be fulfilled in and through us. That his promise still stands we are sure, for we have known God's goodness and experienced God's grace in our lives day by day.

On the other side of this covenant we stand pledged to live no more to ourselves but to live for Christ who loved us and gave himself for us and who even today calls us to serve faithfully in the reign already established.

From time to time we renew our vows of consecration, especially when we gather at the table of the Lord; but on this day we meet expressly, as other generations have met, that we may joyfully and solemnly renew the covenant which bound them and binds us to God.

Let us, then, remember the mercies of God and the hope of God's calling, examining ourselves by the light of the Spirit, that we may see where we have failed or fallen short in faith and practice and, considering all that this covenant means, may give ourselves anew to God.

A Time of Quiet Reflection

The Act of Adoration

Let us adore the God of love who created us; who every moment preserves and sustains us; who has loved us with everlasting love, and has given us light, truth and grace in Jesus Christ.

We praise you O God; we acknowledge you to be the Lord of all.

Let us glory in the grace of our Lord Jesus Christ; who, though he was rich, yet for our sakes became poor; who went about doing good and preaching the gospel of the kingdom; who was tempted in all points like as we are, yet without sin; who became obedient unto death, meeting death on the cross; who was dead and yet lives forever more; who opened the kingdom of heaven to all believers; and who today sits at the right hand of God.

You are the king of glory, O Christ.

Let us rejoice in the communion of the Holy Spirit, the Lord and giver of life, by whom we are born into the family of God, and made members of the body of Christ; whose witness confirms us; whose wisdom teaches us; whose power enables us; whose guidance directs us; who promises to do for us exceedingly abundantly above all that we may ask or think.

All praise to you, O Holy Spirit. Amen.

The Covenant

And now, let us bind ourselves with willing bonds to our covenant God, and take the yoke of Christ upon us. This taking of the yoke upon us means that we are heartily content that God appoint us our place in work, and that God alone be our reward.

Christ has many services to be done; some are easy, others are difficult; some bring honor, others bring reproach; some are suitable to our natural desires and temporal interests, others are contrary to both. In some we may please Christ and please ourselves; in others we cannot please Christ except by denying ourselves. Yet the power to do all of these things is assuredly given us in Jesus Christ, who strengthens us.

Therefore let us make the covenant of God our own. Let us bind our hearts to the Lord, and resolve in God's strength never to turn back.

Being thus prepared, let us now in sincere dependance upon God's grace and trusting in God's promises, yield ourselves anew to the Lord.

The Covenant Prayer

O Lord God, you have called us through Jesus Christ to be partakers in this gracious covenant; we take upon ourselves with joy the yoke of obedience, and engage ourselves, for love of you, to seek and do your perfect will. We are no longer our own, but yours.

Put us to what you will, rank us with whom you will; put us to doing, put us to suffering; let us be employed for you or laid aside for you, exalted for you or brought low for you; let us be full, let us be empty; let us have all things, let us have nothing; we freely and heartily yield all things to your pleasure and to your disposal.

And now, O glorious and blessed God, Father, Son, and Holy Spirit, you are ours, and we are yours. So be it. May the covenant which we have made this day on earth be sustained for all of our days in this world and may it be ratified in Heaven. Amen.

A Blessing

Acknowledgments

The publisher gratefully acknowledges permission to reproduce the following copyrighted material:

Rubem Alves: From *I Believe in the Resurrection of the Body.* Copyright © 1986 by Fortress Press. Used by permission of Augsburg Fortress Publishers.

Anthony of Sourozh: From *Meditations on a Theme,* published by Mowbray, a division of Cassell Publishers, PLC. Used by permission of the publisher.

Johann Arndt: From *Johann Arndt: True Christianity,* translated by Peter Erb. Copyright © 1979 by The Missionary Society of St. Paul the Apostle in the State of New York. Used by permission of Paulist Press.

John Baillie: From *A Diary of Private Prayer.* Copyright 1949 Charles Scribner's Sons; copyright renewed © 1977 Ian Fowler Baillie. Reprinted with permission of Charles Scribner's Sons, an imprint of Macmillan Publishing Company and Oxford University Press.

Hans Urs von Balthasar: From *Prayer.* Copyright 1986. Ignatius Press, San Francisco. All rights reserved.

Albert Frederick Bayley (1901-84) "Lord, Save Thy World" and "Lord, Whose Love Through Humble Service" © Oxford University Press; reprinted by permission of Oxford University Press.

John E. Biersdorf: From *Healing of Purpose.* Copyright © 1985 by John E. Biersdorf. Used by permission of Abingdon Press.

Dietrich Bonhoeffer: "By Gracious Powers." Trans. by Fred Pratt Green. Copyright © 1974 by Hope Publishing Company, Carol Stream, IL 60188. All rights reserved. Used by permission.

Maria Boulding: From *The Coming of God.* Published by The Liturgical Press. © 1982 Maria Boulding. Reprinted by permission of SPCK, London and the author.

Robert Brizee: From *Where in the World Is God?* Copyright © 1987 by The Upper Room. Used by permission of the publisher.

Christopher Bryant: From *The Heart in Pilgrimage.* Copyright © 1980 by Christopher Bryant. Reprinted by permission of Harper & Row, Publishers, Inc. and Darton, Longman & Todd, Ltd.; from *The River Within.* Copyright © 1978 by Darton, Longman & Todd, Ltd. Used by permission of the publisher.

Stephen D. Bryant: From "Letter to a Friend." Reprinted from *Weavings: A Journal of the Christian Spiritual Life* (May/June, 1989). Copyright © 1989 by The Upper Room. Used by permission of the author.

Frederick Buechner: From *The Hungering Dark.* Copyright © 1969 by Frederick Buechner. Reprinted by permission of Harper & Row, Publishers, Inc.

Mary E. Bryne, trans.: "Be Thou My Vision." Alt. © 1989 The United Methodist Publishing House. Used by permission of the publisher.

Catherine Cameron: "God, Who Stretched the Spangled Heavens." Copyright © 1967 by Hope Publishing Company, Carol Stream, IL 60188. All rights reserved. Used by permission.

Dennis M. Campbell: From *The Yoke of Obedience.* Copyright ©1988 by Abingdon Press. Used by permission of the publisher.

John Carmody: From *The Heart of the Christian Matter.* Copyright © 1983 by Abingdon Press. Used by permission of the publisher; from *How to Make It Through the Day.* Copyright © 1985 by The Upper Room. Used by permission of the publisher; from *Maturing a Christian Conscience.* Copyright © 1985 by The Upper Room. Used by permission of the publisher.

Carlo Carretto: From *The God Who Comes.* Published and copyright 1981 by Darton, Longman & Todd, Ltd. Used by permission of Darton, Longman & Todd, Ltd. and Orbis Books; from *I, Francis.* Used by permission of William Collins Sons & Co., Ltd. and Orbis Books; from *I Sought and I*

Tilden H. Edwards, ed.: From *Living with Apocalypse*. Copyright © 1984 by Shalem Institute for Spiritual Formation, Inc. Reprinted by permission of Harper & Row, Publishers, Inc.

Vernard Eller, ed.: From *Thy Kingdom Come: A Blumhardt Reader*. Copyright 1980 by William B. Eerdmans Publishing Co., Grand Rapids, MI. Used by permission of the publisher.

Edward J. Farrell: From *Gathering the Fragments*. Copyright © 1987, Ave Maria Press, Notre Dame, IN 46556. All rights reserved. Used with permission of the publisher.

James C. Fenhagen: From *Invitation to Holiness*. Copyright © 1985, by James C. Fenhagen. Reprinted by permission of Harper & Row, Publishers, Inc.; from *Mutual Ministry*. Copyright © 1977 by The Seabury Press, Inc. Reprinted by permission of Harper & Row, Publishers, Inc.

James Finley: From *The Awakening Call*. Copyright © 1984, Ave Maria Press, Notre Dame, IN 46556. All rights reserved. Used with permission of the publisher; from *Merton's Palace of Nowhere*. Copyright © 1978, Ave Maria Press, Notre Dame, IN 46556. All rights reserved. Used with permission of the publisher.

Richard J. Foster: From *Freedom of Simplicity*. Copyright © 1981 by Richard J. Foster. Reprinted by permission of Harper & Row, Publishers, Inc. and Triangle/SPCK; from *Money, Sex & Power: The Challenge of the Disciplined Life*. Copyright © 1985 by Richard J. Foster, © 1988 by Harper & Row, Publishers, Inc. Reprinted by permission of the publisher and the author.

Charles de Foucauld: From *Meditations of a Hermit*. Copyright © 1981 Burns & Oates, Ltd. Used by permission of Burns & Oates, Ltd. and Orbis Books.

Laurence Freeman: From *Light Within*. Copyright © 1986 by Laurence Freeman. Reprinted by permission of the Crossroad Publishing Company.

Anders Frostenson: "Faith, While Trees Are Still in Blossom," trans. by Fred Kaan. Copyright © 1976 by Hope Publishing Company, Carol Stream, IL 60188. All rights reserved. Used by permission.

Fred Pratt Green: "O Christ, the Healer." Words copyright © 1969 by Hope Publishing Company, Carol Stream, IL 60188. All rights reserved. Used by permission; "Seek the Lord." Words copyright © 1989 by Hope Publishing Company, Carol Stream, IL 60188. All rights reserved. Used by permission; "When Our Confidence Is Shaken." Words copyright © 1971 by Hope Publishing Company, Carol Stream, IL 60188. All rights reserved. Used by permission.

Karen Greenwaldt: From *For Everything There Is a Season*. Copyright © 1988 by The Upper Room. Used by permission of the publisher.

Gracia Grindal: "To a Maid Engaged to Joseph." Copyright © 1984 by Hope Publishing Company, Carol Stream, IL 60188. All rights reserved. Used by permission.

William Boyd Grove: "God, Whose Love is Reigning o'er Us." Copyright© 1980 William Boyd Grove. Used by permission.

Richard M. Gula: From *To Walk Together Again*. Copyright © 1984 by Richard M. Gula. Used by permission of Paulist Press.

Gustavo Gutiérrez: From *We Drink from Our Own Wells*. English translation copyright © 1984 by Orbis Books. Used by permission of Orbis Books, SCM Press, Claretian Publications (Philippines) and Collins/Dove (Australia).

Douglas John Hall: From *Imaging God*. Copyright © 1986. Commission on Stewardship. National Council of the Churches of Christ in the U.S.A. Used by permission.

Georgia Harkness: "Hope of the World." Words copyright © 1954, renewed 1982 by The Hymn Society, Texas Christian University, Fort Worth, TX 76129. All rights reserved. Used by permission.

James A. Harnish: From *Jesus Makes the Difference!* Copyright © 1987 by The Upper Room. Used by permission of the publisher.

Thomas Merton: From *Cistercian Life*. Used by permission of Cistercian Publications; from *Contemplative Prayer* (original title: *The Climate of Monastic Prayer*, Cistercian Publications, 1969). Used by permission of Cistercian Publications; from *New Seeds of Contemplation*. Copyright © 1961 The Abbey of Gethsemani, Inc. Reprinted by permission of New Directions Publishing Corporation; from *Opening the Bible*. First published by The Liturgical Press, Collegeville, MN, 1970. Copyright © 1970 by the trustees of The Merton Legacy Trust. All rights reserved. Reprinted with permission of The Merton Legacy Trust; from *Raids on the Unspeakable*. Copyright © 1965 by The Abbey of Gethsemani, Inc. Reprinted by permission of New Directions Publishing Corporation and Laurence Pollinger, Ltd.

Donald E. Miller: From *Story and Context*. Copyright © 1987 by Abingdon Press. Used by permission.

Samuel H. Miller: From *The Dilemma of Modern Belief*. Copyright © 1963 by Samuel H. Miller. Reprinted by permission of Harper & Row, Publishers, Inc.

John S. Mogabgab: From "Editor's Introduction." Reprinted from *Weavings: A Journal of the Christian Spiritual Life* (January/February 1990). Copyright © 1990 by The Upper Room. Used by permission of the author.

Francis J. Moloney: From *Woman: First Among the Faithful*. Copyright © 1984, 1986 by Francis J. Moloney. All rights reserved. Used by permission of Collins/Dove (Australia) and Ave Maria Press, Notre Dame, IN 46556.

Frederick B. Morley: "O Church of God, United." Words copyright © 1954, renewed 1982 by The Hymn Society, Texas Christian University, Fort Worth, TX 76129. All rights reserved. Used by permission.

Mother Teresa: From *Words to Love By*. Copyright © 1983 Ave Maria Press, Notre Dame, IN 46556. All rights reserved. Used with permission of the publisher.

Henri J.M. Nouwen: From *A Cry for Mercy*. Copyright © 1981 by Henri J.M. Nouwen. Used by permission of Doubleday, a division of Bantam, Doubleday, Dell Publishing Group, Inc. and Gill and Macmillan, Dublin; from *In the Name of Jesus*. Copyright © 1989 by Henri J.M. Nouwen. Reprinted by permission of Crossroad Publishing Company; from *Lifesigns*. Copyright © 1986 by Henri J.M. Nouwen. Used by permission of Doubleday, a division of Bantam, Doubleday, Dell Publishing Group, Inc.; from *The Way of the Heart*. Copyright © 1981 by Henri J.M. Nouwen. Reprinted by permission of Harper & Row, Publishers, Inc.; from *With Open Hands*. Copyright © 1972 by Ave Maria Press, Notre Dame, IN 46556. All rights reserved. Used with the permission of the publisher.

Lloyd John Ogilvie: From *Radiance of the Inner Splendor*. Copyright © 1980 by The Upper Room. Used by permission of the publisher.

Michael Perry: "Blessed Be the God of Israel." Words copyright © 1973 by Hope Publishing Company, Carol Stream, IL 60188. All rights reserved. Used by permission; "How Shall They Hear the Word of God." Words copyright © 1982 by Hope Publishing Company, Carol Stream, IL 60188. All rights reserved. Used by permission.

Eugene H. Peterson: From *Earth and Altar*. © 1985 by InterVarsity Christian Fellowship of the USA. Used by permission of InterVarsity Press., P.O. Box 1400, Downers Grove, IL 60515; from *Working the Angles: The Shape of Pastoral Integrity*. Copyright 1987 by William B. Eerdmans Publishing Co., Grand Rapids, MI. Used by permission of the publisher.

Kenneth G. Phifer: From *A Book of Uncommon Prayer*. Copyright © 1981 by Kenneth G. Phifer. Used by permission of The Upper Room.

Roger Pooley and Philip Seddon, eds.: From *The Lord of the Journey*. Copyright © 1986 by Roger Pooley and Philip Seddon. Used by permission of Collins Liturgical Publications.

Hugh Prather: From *The Quiet Answer.* Copyright © 1982 by Hugh Prather. Used by permission of Doubleday, a division of Bantam, Doubleday, Dell Publishing Group, Inc.

Harry Pritchett, Jr.: From "The Story of Philip," Reprinted from *St. Luke's Journal of Theology* (June 1976). Copyright 1976, The University of the South. Used by permission.

Joan Puls: From *Every Bush Is Burning.* © 1985 WCC Publications, World Council of Churches, P.O. Box 2100, 1211 Geneva 2, Switzerland. Used by permission of the World Council of Churches and Twenty-Third Publications.

Michel Quoist: From *With Open Heart.* Reprinted by permission of the Crossroad Publishing Company.

William W. Reid, Jr.: "O God of Every Nation." Words copyright © 1958, renewed 1986 by The Hymn Society, Texas Christian University, Fort Worth, TX 76129. All rights reserved. Used by permission; "O God Who Shaped Creation." Words © 1989 The United Methodist Publishing House. Used by permission.

Paula Ripple: From *Growing Strong at Broken Places.* Copyright © 1986, Ave Maria Press, Notre Dame, IN 46556. All rights reserved. Used with permission of the publisher.

Edward Robinson: From *The Original Vision.* Copyright © 1977 by The Religious Experience Research Unit, Manchester College, Oxford. Reprinted by permission of Harper & Row, Publishers, Inc.

Martha Graybeal Rowlett: From *In Spirit and in Truth.* Copyright © 1982 by Martha Graybeal Rowlett. Used by permission of The Upper Room.

Jeffery Rowthorn: "Creating God, Your Fingers Trace." Words copyright © 1979 by The Hymn Society, Texas Christian University, Fort Worth, TX 76129. All rights reserved. Used by permission; "Lord, You Give the Great Commission." Words copyright © 1978 by Hope Publishing Company, Carol Stream, IL 60188. All rights reserved. Used by permission.

Joyce Rupp: From *Praying Our Goodbyes.* Copyright © 1988, Ave Maria Press, Notre Dame, IN 46556. All rights reserved. Used with permission of the publisher.

Basilea Schlink: From *I Found the Key to the Heart of God.* Published and copyrighted 1975, Bethany House Publishers, Minneapolis, MN 55438. Used with permission of the publisher.

Albert Schweitzer: From *The Quest of the Historical Jesus.* Used by permission of Rhena Schweitzer Miller.

Seeking God's Peace in a Nuclear Age: A Call to Disciples of Christ. Used by permission of CBP Press, St. Louis, MO.

Harvey Seifert: From *Explorations in Meditation and Contemplation.* Copyright © 1981 by The Upper Room. Used by permission of the publisher.

John Shea: From *Stories of God.* Copyright © 1978 by the Thomas More Association. Used by permission of the publisher.

Donald J. Shelby: From *Forever Beginning.* Copyright © 1987 by The Upper Room. Used by permission of the publisher; from *Meeting the Messiah.* Copyright © 1980 by The Upper Room. Used by permission of the publisher; from *The Unsettling Season.* Copyright © 1989 by Donald J. Shelby. Used by permission of The Upper Room.

Aleksandr Solzhenitsyn: From *A World Split Apart.* Copyright © 1978 by the Russian Social Fund for Persecuted Persons and Their Families, English translation copyright © 1978 by Harper & Row, Publishers, Inc. Reprinted by permission of the publisher.

Douglas V. Steere: From *Gleanings.* Copyright © 1986 by The Upper Room. Used by permission of the publisher; from *Together in Solitude.* Copyright © 1982 by Douglas V. Steere. Reprinted by permission of the Crossroad Publishing Company.

David Steindl-Rast: From *Gratefulness, the Heart of Prayer.* Copyright © 1984 by David Steindl-Rast. Used by permission of Paulist Press.

Janet Stephenson: From a letter. Used by permission of the author.

James S. Stewart: From *A Man in Christ.* Used by permission of Hodder & Stoughton.

Howard Thurman: From *The Inward Journey.* Harper & Row, 1961, paperback ed., Friends United Press, 1971. Used by permission of the Howard Thurman Educational Trust.

Elton Trueblood: From *The New Man for Our Time.* Copyright © 1970 by Elton Trueblood. Reprinted by permission of Harper & Row, Publishers, Inc.

Ann Belford Ulanov: From *Picturing God.* Copyright © 1986 by Ann Belford Ulanov. Used by permission of Cowley Publications, 980 Memorial Dr., Cambridge, MA 02138.

Benedicta Ward, trans.: From *The Sayings of the Desert Fathers,* published by Mowbray, a division of Cassell Publishers, PLC. Used by permission of Cassell Publishers, PLC.

Richard Allen Ward: From his journal. Used by permission of the author.

Kallistos Ware: From *The Orthodox Way.* Copyright © 1979 by Kallistos Ware. Used by permission of St. Vladimir's Seminary Press, Crestwood, NY; from *the Power of the Name: The Jesus Prayer in Orthodox Spirituality,* Fairacres Publication 43, SLG Press 1974, new edition 1986. Used by permission of SLG Press.

Abbie Jane Wells: From *The Gospel According to Abbie Jane Wells.* Copyright © 1985 by Abbie Jane Wells. Used by permission of the Thomas More Association.

John Wesley: From *John and Charles Wesley.* Copyright © 1981 by The Missionary Society of St. Paul the Apostle in the State of New York. Used by permission of Paulist Press.

Macrina Wiederkehr: From *A Tree Full of Angels.* Copyright © 1988 by Macrina Wiederkehr. Reprinted by permission of Harper & Row, Publishers, Inc.

John Wijngaards: From *Inheriting the Master's Cloak.* Copyright © 1985, Ave Maria Press, Notre Dame, IN 46556. All rights reserved. Used with permission of the publisher.

Miriam Therese Winter: "My Soul Gives Glory To My God." Words copyright © 1978, 1987 Medical Mission Sisters. Reproduced with permission of Medical Mission Sisters.

Brian Wren: "Christ Is Alive." Words copyright © 1975 by Hope Publishing Company, Carol Stream, IL 60188. All rights reserved. Used by permission; "Christ upon the Mountain Peak." Words copyright © 1977 by Hope Publishing Company, Carol Stream, IL 60188. All rights reserved. Used by permission; "How Can We Name a Love." Words copyright © 1975 by Hope Publishing Company, Carol Stream, IL 60188. All rights reserved. Used by permission; "Lord God, Your Love Has Called Us Here." Words copyright © 1977 by Hope Publishing Company, Carol Stream, IL 60188. All rights reserved. Used by permission.

Flora Slosson Wuellner: From *Prayer, Fear, and Our Powers.* Copyright © 1989 by Flora Slosson Wuellner. Used by permission of The Upper Room.

Elizabeth Yates: From *A Book of Hours.* Copyright © 1976 by Elizabeth Yates. Used by permission of The Upper Room; from *Up the Golden Stair.* Copyright © 1990 by Elizabeth Yates McGreal. Used by permission of The Upper Room.

While every effort has been made to secure permission, we may have failed in a few cases to trace or contact the copyright holder. We apologize for any inadvertent oversight or error.

Index of Readings:

Index of Hymn Lyrics:

Many of these hymns can be found in The United Methodist Hymnal.

Index of Lectionary Readings

Sundays of 1990: **Dec. 2**—1; **Dec. 9**—2; **Dec. 16**—3; **Dec. 23**—4; **Dec. 30**—5.

Sundays of 1991: **Jan. 6**—6; **Jan. 13**—7; **Jan. 20**—8; **Jan. 27**—9; **Feb. 3**—10; **Feb. 10**—15; **Feb. 17**—16; **Feb. 24**—17; **Mar. 3**—18; **Mar. 10**—19; **Mar. 17**—20; **Mar. 24**—21; **Mar. 31**—22; **Apr. 7**—23; **Apr. 14**—24; **Apr. 21**—25; **Apr. 28**—26; **May 5**—27; **May 12**—28; **May 19**—29; **May 26**—30; **June 2**—31; **June 9**—32; **June 16**—33; **June 23**—34; **June 30**—35; **July 7**—36; **July 14**—37; **July 21**—38; **July 28**—39; **Aug. 4**—40; **Aug. 11**—41; **Aug. 18**—42; **Aug. 25**—43; **Sept. 1**—44; **Sept. 8**—45; **Sept. 15**—46; **Sept. 22**—47; **Sept. 29**—48; **Oct. 6**—49; **Oct. 13**—50; **Oct. 20**—51; **Oct. 27**—52; **Nov. 3**—53; **Nov. 10**—54; **Nov. 17**—55; **Nov. 24**—56; **Dec. 1**—1; **Dec. 8**—2; **Dec. 15**—3; **Dec. 22**—4; **Dec. 29**—5.

Sundays of 1992: **Jan. 5**—6; **Jan. 12**—7; **Jan. 19**—8; **Jan. 26**—9; **Feb. 2**—10; **Feb. 9**—11; **Feb. 16**—12; **Feb. 23**—13; **Mar. 1**—15; **Mar. 8**—16; **Mar. 15**—17; **Mar. 22**—18; **Mar. 29**—19; **Apr. 5**—20; **Apr. 12**—21; **Apr. 19**—22; **Apr. 26**—23; **May 3**—24; **May 10**—25; **May 17**—26; **May 24**—27; **May 31**—28; **June 7**—29; **June 14**—30; **June 21**—34; **June 28**—35; **July 5**—36; **July 12**—37; **July 19**—38; **July 26**—39; **Aug. 2**—40; **Aug. 9**—41; **Aug. 16**—42; **Aug. 23**—43; **Aug. 30**—44; **Sept. 6**—45; **Sept. 13**—46; **Sept. 20**—47; **Sept. 27**—48; **Oct. 4**—49; **Oct. 11**—50; **Oct. 18**—51; **Oct. 25**—52; **Nov. 1**—53; **Nov. 8**—54; **Nov. 15**—55; **Nov. 22**—56; **Nov. 29**—1; **Dec. 6**—2; **Dec. 13**—3; **Dec. 20**—4; **Dec. 27**—5.

Sundays of 1993: **Jan. 3**—6; **Jan. 10**—7; **Jan. 17**—8; **Jan. 24**—9; **Jan. 31**—10; **Feb. 7**—11; **Feb. 14**—12; **Feb. 21**—15; **Feb. 28**—16; **Mar. 7**—17; **Mar. 14**—18; **Mar. 21**—19; **Mar. 28**—20; **Apr. 4**—21; **Apr. 11**—22; **Apr. 18**—23; **Apr. 25**—24; **May 2**—25; **May 9**—26; **May 16**—27; **May 23**—28; **May 30**—29; **June 6**—30; **June 13**—33; **June 20**—34; **June 27**—35; **July 4**—36; **July 11**—37; **July 18**—38; **July 25**—39; **Aug. 1**—40; **Aug. 8**—41; **Aug. 15**—42; **Aug. 22**—43; **Aug. 29**—44; **Sept. 5**—45; **Sept. 12**—46; **Sept. 19**—47; **Sept. 26**—48; **Oct. 3**—49; **Oct. 10**—50; **Oct. 17**—51; **Oct. 24**—52; **Oct. 31**—53; **Nov. 7**—54; **Nov. 14**—55; **Nov. 21**—56; **Nov. 28**—1; **Dec. 5**—2; **Dec. 12**—3; **Dec. 19**—4; **Dec. 26**—5.

Sundays of 1994: **Jan. 2**—6; **Jan. 9**—7; **Jan. 16**—8; **Jan. 23**—9; **Jan. 30**—10; **Feb. 6**—11; **Feb. 13**—15; **Feb. 20**—16; **Feb. 27**—17; **Mar. 6**—18; **Mar. 13**—19; **Mar. 20**—20; **Mar. 27**—21; **Apr. 3**—22; **Apr. 10**—23; **Apr. 17**—24; **Apr. 24**—25; **May 1**—26; **May 8**—27; **May 15**—28; **May 22**—29; **May 29**—30; **June 5**—32; **June 12**—33; **June 19**—34; **June 26**—35; **July 3**—36; **July 10**—37; **July 17**—38; **July 24**—39; **July 31**—40; **Aug. 7**—41; **Aug. 14**—42; **Aug. 21**—43; **Aug. 28**—44; **Sept. 4**—45; **Sept. 11**—46; **Sept. 18**—47; **Sept. 25**—48; **Oct. 2**—49; **Oct. 9**—50; **Oct. 16**—51; **Oct. 23**—52; **Oct. 30**—53; **Nov. 6**—54; **Nov. 13**—55; **Nov. 20**—56; **Nov. 27**—1; **Dec. 4**—2; **Dec. 11**—3; **Dec. 18**—4; **Dec. 25**—5.